# BOUND TO BE FREE

# Bound to be Free

*with the
Suffering Church*

## Compiled by Jan Pit
## for Open Doors International

Sovereign World

Sovereign World Ltd
PO Box 777
Tonbridge
Kent TN11 9XT
England

Scripture quotations are taken from:
The Good News Bible. Copyright © American Bible Society, New York
1966, 1971, 1976.
The Living Bible. Copyright © Tyndale House Publishers, 1971.
King James Version. Crown copyright.
The Holy Bible, New International Version. Copyright © 1973, 1978,
1984, International Bible Society. Published by Hodder & Stoughton.

Compiler: Jan Pit.
Cover photo: Jan Jaring, Haarlem, Holland.
Original title: Elke dag geboeid (Dutch version).
First publication in Dutch by: Gideon, Hoornaar, Holland.

ISBN: 1 85240 174 5

Typeset by CRB Associates, Lenwade, Norwich.
Printed in England by Clays Ltd, St Ives plc.

# Foreword

I wish I could write something so short and powerful that nobody would ever forget it. That is what this book deserves.

Now, I believe I have found it. **Read** this book.

You will then listen to people who have touched my own life and influenced it deeply.

*Brother Andrew*
September 1995

# Introduction

This devotional book does not contain theoretical meditations, but practical reflections. These are based on the Word of God and the experiences of people who have suffered for their faith in Jesus Christ.

More than twenty-five spiritual leaders from all over the world have cooperated in the preparation of this book. All have personally experienced what it means to be a Christian in an anti-Christian environment.

Many of them were persecuted or imprisoned for their faith. A total of more than one hundred years.

Some meditations were written in secret, others from solitary confinement. Some contributors are no longer alive. They paid the highest price and gave their lives for their faith. But though dead, they continue to speak through this book, and all of them speak not about their suffering, but about their God and Savior.

What is their secret? How can they stand, despite the pain? How can they be victorious, despite the heavy battle? That is what this book is all about. They share their secrets with us.

These secrets touch us with their simplicity and depth, lived through their daily lives. We find no complaints, only praise to God who was always faithful, especially when they were in great danger.

I have tried to give voice to their reflections as far as possible in their own style of writing. To some I have given an explanation but for others this was not necessary. Their message is enough in itself.

Some writers had an academic education, others could

hardly read or write. But when you read their meditations, your response will be the same as the one from Acts 4:13 '... and they took note that these men had been with Jesus.'

Many of them still live in danger. As you read this book please remember to pray for them.

It is striking how often they quote the Psalms of David. For that reason I chose a number of David's Psalms to be the thread running through this book.

Each month I start with a devotional about a biblical person. The suffering of the modern day contributors to this book is nothing new, because in Bible times people like Noah, Abraham, Moses and many others, knew what it was to suffer for God's Kingdom. So we start with their example – the Bible example, and thereafter we can listen to people living in our own time.

My choice of biblical persons is not complete, I realize that. People like Jeremiah, John the Baptist and Stephen were not chosen. This is a pity, but I had to make a choice.

You will recognize some of the writer's names. Perhaps you have prayed for them or have read about them. Many names you will miss. Not everyone was able to help us with this book.

At the end of each month I have included a number of quotations. Outstanding remarks which give us food for thought.

Some quotes may have been used by many people. Sometimes it is hard to establish the source of the material. When the real source is not known I print 'unknown'. Often it does not matter who said it for it is the message that counts.

The contributors to the book are briefly introduced at the beginning of each month for you to get to know the writer. Some names have been changed for security reasons. For my own reflections I have simply used 'somebody'.

Many people contributed to this book including a number of Open Doors co-workers from all over the world. I am very grateful for their help. Often, under serious and dangerous circumstances, they have collected the material from the writers.

Because of the diverse cultural and linguistic backgrounds of the various contributors to this book, we have not always striven for a precise English language rendering. You may, therefore, notice some colloquial expressions and non-English idioms in some of the pieces. Hopefully, this adds to the colour and character of the contributions.

I am grateful to those who assisted me in translating this book into English: Kathleen Hall, Anneke Companjen and the staff at Open Doors, England. I would also like to thank the Open Doors team in Asia who translated the handwritten, Chinese devotions into English.

I also want to thank Elly Stegewans and Klaas Muurling for their help, support and encouragement. For three years we worked on this book. When I was overwhelmed by the project, their encouragement helped me to continue.

Without the great help and support of my wife, Lies, this book would never have been finished. Her advice and prayers were precious, very precious. I am indebted to her for the choice of the Psalms of David.

Above all, I thank Him who keeps and builds His Church, through all the ages.

Together with the Suffering Church we lift our eyes to Him and say:

*'Where does my help come from?'*

And we proclaim:

*'My help comes from the Lord,*
*the Maker of heaven and earth.*
*Who remains faithful unto eternity*
*and never abandons the work of his hands.'*

May He use this book to nourish you daily. May these reflections captivate and motivate you, to pray for those who are still bound in captivity.

*Jan Pit*

# January

## Writers for the month

*Irina Ratushinskaya* from Russia was imprisoned for seven years in a labor camp. She has written about her experiences in a moving book entitled *Grey is the Colour of Hope* published by Sceptre Books, 1989.

*Gerhard Hamm* from Russia spent many years in prisons and labor camps in Northern Siberia.

*Constantin Caraman* from Romania was in prison three times for his faith.

*By faith Noah, when warned about things not yet seen, in holy fear built an ark to save his family . . .*

(Hebrews 11:7)

*. . . and he walked with God.* (Genesis 6:9)

## Noah

An extraordinary aspect of Hebrews 11 is that it tells the story of people who all did something which no one else had ever done before. They stepped out into the unknown.

Noah built an ark though there was no precedent he could look to for assistance. Nobody had ever built an ark before, simply because there had never been a flood before. Noah must have been regarded as an eccentric and his sons as simple people who foolishly followed in their father's steps of faith.

In blind, unquestioning faith Noah acted on God's revelation. 'Noah did everything just as God commanded him' (Genesis 6:22). In doing so he showed his unwavering faith and absolute obedience.

His secret: he walked with God amidst adversity. Throughout this year we will face circumstances which may seem absurd but let us learn from Noah that those who walk with God will never walk in darkness but will have the light of life.

*. . . Well done, good and faithful servant! You have been faithful with a few things: I will put you in charge of many things. Come and share your master's happiness!*

(Matthew 25:21)

## Noah

The building of the ark is the longest test of faith recorded in the Word of God. For one hundred and twenty years Noah was a preacher of righteousness which included God's impending judgement. He persevered in his faith though all the circumstances were against him. He did not receive any confirmation that he was on the right track, neither did he get any outsider on his side. What faithfulness: to preach, to evangelise for a hundred and twenty years and not have one convert.

Faith does not look for signs or confirmation. It simply follows God's direction and instructions.

To those who walk by faith God says: 'Well done!' Not: good and successful servant, but 'good and faithful servant.' God does not look for success, but for faithfulness. Then those faithful ones may hear the most beautiful words, 'come and share your master's happiness!'

*Come, let us bow down in worship,*
*Let us kneel before the Lord our Maker;*
*for he is our God and we are the people of his*
*    pasture...*
*Today, if you hear his voice*
*do not harden your hearts...*                   (Psalm 95:6–8)

## Noah

For one hundred and twenty years Noah preached by word
and deed, against the corruption and violence of his time. He
warned of the forthcoming judgement, but not one man or
woman believed. For more than one hundred years the people
saw the ark of rescue, but all refused to heed or accept Noah's
warning, including even the workmen, who helped Noah build
the boat, who heard Noah's witness and observed his godly
life. Because of their unbelief they perished outside the boat
they themselves had worked on. What a tragedy – so near
and yet so far. Time has not changed man. God still warns
people of impending judgement. He still offers rescue through
the ark of salvation, Jesus Christ.

'As it was in the days of Noah, so it will be at the coming
of the Son of Man. For in the days before the flood, people
were eating and drinking, marrying and giving in marriage,
up to the day Noah entered the ark; and they knew nothing
about what would happen until the flood came and took them
all away. That is how it will be at the coming of the Son of
Man, two men will be in the field; one will be taken and the
other left. Therefore keep watch, because you do not know on
what day our Lord will come' (Matthew 24:37–40, 42).

'Come, let us bow down before the Lord our Maker; for he
is our God...' (Psalm 95:6, 7).

*I have set my rainbow in the clouds, and it will be the sign of the covenant between me and the earth.*

(Genesis 9:13)

*Look, he is coming with the clouds, and every eye will see him, . . .* (Revelation 1:7)

## Noah

Noah lived in one of the most difficult times of history. In a world without God, where people were egocentric and corrupt. 'The Lord saw how great man's wickedness on the earth had become and that every inclination of the thoughts of his heart was only evil all the time. The Lord was grieved that he had made man ... and his heart was filled with pain ... But Noah found favor in the eyes of the Lord!' (Genesis 6:5–8). After God's punishment Noah entered a new era in the history of the world: 'I have set my rainbow in the clouds ... the covenant between me and the earth' (Genesis 9:13).

The rainbow was a reminder of the past and an assurance for the future, a visible sign of God's promise. Though at the end of this age the earth will once again be destroyed (by fire) mankind lives in a time of grace and promise. Before God will destroy the earth something else will become visible in the clouds – not a rainbow – but the Son of Man. Between Noah's rainbow and Christ's return we can walk with God. That means walking in God's direction. It involves a break with those who walk in the opposite direction. We may belong to the few who walk in His direction, but we have a great crowd of witnesses surrounding us. Men and women who dared take a stand for Christ. Let us therefore run with perseverance with our eyes fixed on Jesus – until we see Him at His glorious return.

*. . . be strong in the Lord . . . put on the full armor of God so that you can take your stand against the devil's schemes.* (Ephesians 6:10–11)

## Noah

The Bible is an honest book. It not only speaks of Noah's faith in God, but also reveals his weaknesses. Two verses from Scripture show the difference:

'Noah built an altar to the Lord . . . ' (Genesis 8:20).

'Noah . . . proceeded to plant a vineyard' (Genesis 9:20).

In the first instance he was in the presence of God whereas in the vineyard he was tempted by the devil. Victory and defeat are at either extreme, but never far apart.

'. . . your enemy the devil prowls around like a roaring lion looking for someone to devour' (1 Peter 5:8).

The hour of victory can easily become the hour of defeat. We will never be out of reach of temptation. We should always have the shield of faith in our hands as part of our spiritual armor. To 'walk with God' does not come automatically. It requires a daily exercise of entering into His presence, listening to His instructions and following them without reservation.

Those who do so will have the experience of never walking alone.

*But Noah found favor in the eyes of the Lord.*

(Genesis 6:8)

## Noah

In a time of moral darkness and corruption, Noah walked with God. When God wanted to destroy the human race, Noah found favor in God's eyes.

When we complain about the world in which we live, let us learn these important lessons from Noah's life.

1 That it is possible to walk with God in spite of surrounding lawlessness and godlessness.

2 That Noah was obedient when God asked him to accomplish a strange and difficult task.

3 That Noah warned his neighbors of impending judgement, thus offering them a way of repentance.

4 That Noah was protected and saved by God, who honored his faith by an everlasting promise.

When the waters of judgement covered the earth, Noah was safe within the Ark. What a wonderful illustration the Ark affords of Jesus Christ who preserves us from the fire of judgement which will come to our world.

'Therefore, since we have been justified through faith, we have peace with God through our Lord Jesus Christ...' (Romans 5:1).

There is hope – for you and your family, whatever the circumstances may be.

David composed this psalm when he had to flee from Absalom. What a tragedy when you have to flee from your own child!

The people reacted in an inhumane manner 'God will not deliver him.' He had every reason to complain. But David did not do that. He declares that the Lord God is always near, especially in times of pain and suffering. For him it was not mere theory but a practical experience of God's nearness.

'I lie down and sleep; I wake again, because the Lord sustains me.'

---

### David

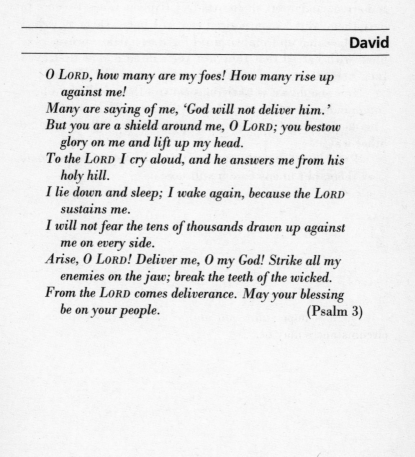

*O LORD, how many are my foes! How many rise up against me!*

*Many are saying of me, 'God will not deliver him.'*

*But you are a shield around me, O LORD; you bestow glory on me and lift up my head.*

*To the LORD I cry aloud, and he answers me from his holy hill.*

*I lie down and sleep; I wake again, because the LORD sustains me.*

*I will not fear the tens of thousands drawn up against me on every side.*

*Arise, O LORD! Deliver me, O my God! Strike all my enemies on the jaw; break the teeth of the wicked.*

*From the LORD comes deliverance. May your blessing be on your people.* (Psalm 3)

---

# January 8

*Bless those who curse you, pray for those who ill-treat you.* (Luke 6:28)

## Irina Ratushinskaya

Almost every demand from Christ seems impracticable. If we, however, want to follow the Lord, then there is no other way. More than once I experienced this from the KGB prisons.

The response of the world to the tormentors of the KGB is hatred, and every hour, the KGB gives more reasons to hate them. But I soon noticed that if I hated them as well, I would be eaten up from within. I have seen fellow prisoners so filled with hatred that they lost their mind and so destroyed their personality. And that's exactly what the KGB wants.

How should we as Christians control these feelings? Christ commanded us to cast out hatred by love. That is not easy. This demand by Christ seems impracticable. But there is no other way.

'Pray for those who mistreat you.' Such a prayer may save them, but in any case it will save us.

*For my yoke is easy and my burden is light.*

(Matthew 11:30)

## Irina Ratushinskaya

These words from Jesus seem strange. What is easy – and what is light?

Even the decision to start practising it is heavy. But once having decided, we notice that it is easy. I experienced this in a camp with political prisoners. The life that the prison guards arranged for us seemed one dark nightmare. But by the spiritual attitude of my friends and myself this nightmare changed completely.

Why? Because we had an amazing sense of protection around us. And a conviction that all the evil intentions of the guards ultimately would only lead us closer to the heavenly kingdom.

Knocked out by cold or hunger? Threatened with death?

But aren't we serving the Lord? The fear of suffering loses all its power when a person takes up that service.

The inevitable sadness only scratches the outer cover of the soul – but can never penetrate it. There, within, is only light and joy and peace. And from there comes new strength.

And every time you are astonished you remember: Christ did promise that it would be light!

# January 10

*Peter asked: 'Lord, why can't I follow you now? I will lay down my life for you.'* (John 13:37)

## Irina Ratushinskaya

Impatient Peter, who always longed to go beyond the limits of his possibilities. Who would not and could not accept those limits. He walked on water – but doubted and sank soon afterwards. Who defended Christ at his arrest – but who had fallen asleep a little earlier. He was prepared to give his life for the Lord – but a little later, he denied Him three times.

It's enough to make you despair, to start regarding yourself as a failure, an incorrigible sinner.

Yes, and that is what would have happened if he had been self-centered. But all the attention of his soul was focused on his Friend, on the One whom he was the first to recognize as the Christ, the Son of the Living God. It is the same Christ he calls out to when he sinks – and he is saved.

He loves his Christ too much to allow his problems to distract him from growing closer to Him. That is why Christ chose his testimony to be the basis for our growth: 'On this rock (Petra) I will build my church.'

We should always acknowledge failures, but never focus our attention on them.

'Let us fix our eyes on Jesus.' Not on our failures, but on His faithfulness.

*Be perfect, therefore, as your heavenly Father is perfect.*
(Matthew 5:48)

## Irina Ratushinskaya

It is the most shocking demand on Man: absolute perfection. No less than that. Is this really addressed to us? To people for whom it is already quite an achievement just to realize their own sinfulness?

Some people think that the acknowledgement of sinfulness is a pretty spiritual achievement. But does it help? It is not just the diagnosis, but medical treatment that is needed for the recovery of a sick person.

We often hear people say 'I am no saint', even with some kind of satisfaction, as if to say, 'I admit that I am no saint, so I have fulfilled my duty.' But that is only part of the duty.

Every demand made by Christ also contains a promise. He does not only command us to do things, He also offers us His help. If we would only believe it is possible! Perfection is an infinitely daring concept. It requires courage even to imagine it. Nevertheless the demand is addressed to you and to me.

How do our hearts respond to the demand ... and to the promise of this miracle?

# January 12

*I have much more to say to you, more than you can now bear.* (John 16:12)

## Irina Ratushinskaya

It is difficult for us to form an idea of the heavenly Kingdom. Our normal powers of imagination fall short, they are too limited.

But it is important to realize that it is real and awaiting us. Let us just try to imagine ourselves telling a human embryo what kind of world it will be born into. Let us assume that the embryo is really trying to understand us. How can we ever explain what sunlight is, or a family or a church?

If, however, on the basis of the fact that it isn't able to imagine the outside world, the unborn baby should decide not to be born ... it would die and never see the outside world. We are only the embryos of our future immortal souls. It is so difficult to picture the life that is to come, but it will come.

How wonderful it is that eternal life will be better than anything we could ever imagine now.

*Therefore I tell you, whatever you ask in prayer, believe that you have received it and it will be yours.*

(Mark 11:24)

## Irina Ratushinskaya

We usually add the following words to our prayer: 'Thy will be done, not mine.'

It sounds very devout, but is it? When a prayer is not granted, was it because it was against God's will or because we did not really believe it would be heard?

There is however one prayer that is always in harmony with God's will. You all know it. Its first words are, 'Our Father'.

Let us consider the prayer that Christ gave to us for a moment. The Kingdom of God will indeed come on earth, His will be done on earth as it is in heaven. We will be given our daily bread and our sins will be forgiven! And we will do no more sin. The attacks of the devil will not be successful, for God will protect us.

Isn't this miracle greater than the boldest of our own wishes?

Today, presently – we can do it with God's help.

Are we afraid it will not come true after all? So what? We can ask the Lord to strengthen our faith in Him. He can do it. Now.

# January 14

The people who surrounded David had no more fight left in them.

Did they lose a battle? Did their crops fail? We don't know.

They seem to have lost their faith in God and they criticize David who continues to trust in the Lord.

How does David react to this defeat and criticism? He prays.

## David

*Answer me when I call to you, O my righteous God.*
  *Give me relief from my distress; be merciful to me*
  *and hear my prayer.*
*How long, O men, will you turn my glory into shame?*
  *How long will you love delusions and seek false gods?*
*Know that the LORD has set apart the godly for himself;*
  *the LORD will hear when I call to him.*
*In your anger do not sin; when you are on your beds,*
  *search your hearts and be silent.*
*Offer right sacrifices and trust in the LORD.*
*Many are asking, 'Who can show us any good?'*
*Let the light of your face shine upon us, O LORD.*
*You have filled my heart with greater joy than when*
  *their grain and new wine abound.*
*I will lie down and sleep in peace, for you alone,*
  *O LORD, make me dwell in safety.*          (Psalm 4)

*Where is the wise man? Where is the scholar? Where is the philosopher of this age? Has not God made foolish the wisdom of the world?* (1 Corinthians 1:20)

## Gerhard Hamm

Paul describes here the main difference between human and divine wisdom. The world only acknowledges human wisdom and such was also the case in our country. We Christians were considered second-rate citizens. Oh how often children from Christian families had to suffer scorn and abuse! At school, they received lower marks and were labeled bad students.

Many things have changed in Russia since 1989. Never before has there been such openness for the Gospel as there is now. Once, during an open air meeting, a very learned woman came to me. She was a lecturer at the Atheistic University. She looked pale and confused. When I asked her what I could do for her, she answered: 'I have been fighting your God, your Bible, the Christians for twenty years now...' She hesitated for a moment and then continued: 'But I was wrong.' She fell silent again ... 'and now I want to know more of the truth. Help me.'

Her head bowed, this learned atheist stood before a Christian who had formerly been considered a second-rate citizen. I told her about the Gospel and prayed with her. Then she went home, walking in the light.

'The One enthroned in heaven laughs' (Psalm 2:4). For He is in command. Nothing is too difficult for Him. The Iron Curtain fell and God is building His Church.

Is anything too hard for the Lord?

# January 16

*Yet I am always with you; you hold me by my right hand. You guide me with your counsel, and afterward you will take me into glory.* (Psalm 73:23–24)

## Gerhard Hamm

It is not always easy to live close to the Lord, for the powers of evil are always attempting to disturb our relationship with God. But, thank God, Jesus is more powerful than Satan. People who know Christ may count on His protection when the devil is cunningly trying to tempt them.

I have often experienced this in Siberia. When I was still living in the polar region, where the temperature in winter was sometimes 56° below zero, the KGB one day offered to get me out of the cold, on condition that I help them out in 'a small matter'. I was offered a good job in a prison camp with a nice, heated room from which I was able to listen in to the conversations of other Christian prisoners. All I had to do was pass on the contents of those conversations to the KGB. 'We would only like to know what kind of things people talk about.' It was a very tempting offer: away from the cold, no more forced labor. But the Lord was there to help me. I saw the viciousness of the plan. 'Do you know what Judas did after his betrayal?' I asked. The man shook his head. 'Judas committed suicide . . . and I want to live.'

The conversation was over. I did not get the warm room and the attractive job. I had to get back into the cold. But my heart was warm.

Satan always offers us a compromise, so be watchful. Christians who enter into a compromise are of no value to God or Man. Only those who remain faithful to the Lord, anywhere and under any circumstance, are valuable.

*I tell you, open your eyes and look at the fields! They are
ripe for harvest.* (John 4:35)

## Gerhard Hamm

Although Christians in Russia were considered to be second-
rate citizens for many years, we are happy now to see that
many people show an interest in us. Many atheists and
communists are disappointed and are searching for a new
ideology. They ask Christians to tell them about the Gospel
of Jesus Christ. Yes, the fields are ripe for harvest in the
former Soviet Union.

After the downfall of communism, I spoke at an open air
meeting in Siberia. More than 4,000 people came to listen. I
knew this place in the woods very well because I had looked
after my father's cows there 50 years ago. Many, many people
were converted and accepted the Lord Jesus as their Lord and
Savior. Among them was a teacher. She came to us and said:
'Oh, Lord, forgive me, forgive me, forgive me please. For
years I have told the children that there is no God, but in my
heart I knew I was wrong. As from this day, I will tell the
children that there really is a God and that He forgives our
sins.'

Yes, the fields are ripe for harvest. If God can cause such
a breakthrough in this communist stronghold, we can only
say: 'Is anything too hard for the Lord?' (Genesis 18:14).

God makes all things new. In your life and in mine.
Today.

# January 18

*Then these men went as a group and found Daniel praying and asking God for help.* (Daniel 6:11)

## Gerhard Hamm

Daniel prayed in spite of the king's decree. He was aware that praying was dangerous, but he also realised that prayer was of vital importance. How odd that praying could cost him his life, while not praying would kill him spiritually. It was no difficult choice. To him, his relationship with God was more important than his position or his life.

In Russia, prayer also met with great opposition. The devil knows only too well that praying people are victorious people.

One day, I was arrested together with 30 other brothers in Moscow. We were taken to the police station and locked up in an ice-cold room. It was a few days before Christmas and we thought we would probably not be home by then. It was no use complaining, so one of the brothers said: 'Let's pray.' We all knelt down on the cold concrete floor and then there followed a miraculous hour of prayer. The policeman was dumbfounded, but afterwards he said: 'What kind of fanatics are you? How dare you pray in an atheist police station?' A long conversation followed.

Later on, an officer appeared and he said: 'We don't know what to do with you. If we imprison one of you, he will convert another prisoner. If we imprison two, another two will be converted. Go home, you won't bother us there.'

And he was right. Prayer gives strength and opens doors. If it doesn't open doors of prison cells, it opens the hearts of people inside prisons. What a powerful weapon! Use it.

*Lord, teach us to pray.* (Luke 11:1)

## Gerhard Hamm

I am so grateful to my parents for having taught us to pray. And above all, for having been praying people themselves.

We saw the value and the power of prayer in our parents. Father was shot and killed for it and mother deported to Siberia, where she died. We, their children, have never considered this a tragic loss, but a spiritual victory.

Their prayers were taken up to heaven by angels and put into golden censers (Revelation 8:3, 4). And their prayers were heard. They had twenty children, ten of whom are dead now, and many of them died in Siberia. We, the remaining ten children, suffered much in Siberia, but God has been good and merciful to us. All ten have become servants of the Lord. In times of severe persecution, we saw how our parents found strength in the Lord, through prayer and faith. We want to follow in their footsteps and go on. Do our children see the power of prayer in us?

'Lord, teach us to pray.'

*Those who sow in tears will reap with songs of joy.*
(Psalm 126:5)

## Gerhard Hamm

Crying is a natural human quality. You can cry out of grief, but also because of joy. You can cry out of anger, but also out of pity.

During a meeting in Siberia at which 11,000 people had gathered, I met a woman who was very depressed. She was crying about her own life as well as her daughter's, who she was very worried about. 'Oh, help me please, I am so worried about my child. She is an alcoholic and drinks all day. Her husband has beaten her up many times. Her life is hell on earth, is there still hope for her?'

I told her that God is able to make all things new. He can set people free from sin, from alcohol and bad habits, so that we become a new creation. I found out that the woman had not yet decided to give her life to Christ. So I asked: 'How can you expect God to do something for your child when you don't follow Him yourself?'

The next day, she came to the open air meeting again. She was beaming with joy through her tears. She cried: 'I have given my life to the Lord. His peace is in my heart now and I believe that He can forgive and cure my child too. I will pray for it every day.'

What a change! And the change will have its effect on her child. From tears to joy. 'Those who sow in tears will reap with songs of joy.' For God hears!

This psalm was probably written by David when Absalom was plotting to dethrone him. It seems that David was aware of this plan. What can he do to stop it? He turns to the Lord, his God.

## David

*Give ear to my words, O LORD, consider my sighing.*
*Listen to my cry for help, my King and my God, for to*
*    you I pray.*
*In the morning, O LORD, you hear my voice; in the*
*    morning I lay my requests before you and wait in*
*    expectation.*
*You are not a God who takes pleasure in evil; with you*
*    the wicked cannot dwell. . . .*
*Lead me, O LORD, in your righteousness because of my*
*    enemies – make straight your way before me.*
*Not a word from their mouth can be trusted; their heart*
*    is filled with destruction. Their throat is an open*
*    grave; with their tongue they speak deceit.*
*Declare them guilty, O God! Let their intrigues be their*
*    downfall. Banish them for their many sins, for they*
*    have rebelled against you.*
*But let all who take refuge in you be glad; let them ever*
*    sing for joy. Spread your protection over them, that*
*    those who love your name may rejoice in you.*
*For surely, O LORD, you bless the righteous; you*
*    surround them with your favor as with a shield.*
                                          (Psalm 5:1–4, 8–12)

*So Abram left, as the Lord had told him.*   (Genesis 12:4)

## Constantin Caraman

The next few meditations are about ordinary people who did extraordinary things.

People who blessed those who persecuted them.

People like Enoch who walked with God in a world of haste.

People like Job who trusted the Lord for better or for worse.

Is this not what God expects from us as well? If He does – He enables.

Abraham seems to have had a mission that was impossible. Emigrating at the age of 75, leaving his country without even knowing where to go.

Abraham heard and obeyed the Word of the Lord. No objections like: 'Lord, are You quite sure? Here in Ur are many more possibilities to serve You. This is the cultural, commercial and political centre of the world.' No, Abraham obeyed God unconditionally. And God changed his name: Abram (father of height) became Abraham (father of a multitude).

Abraham did an unusual thing which made him tower above all others (father of height) and as such he became a source of blessing (father of a multitude).

Abraham, God's friend.

What was his secret? Unconditional obedience to the Lord.

*Enoch walked with God.* (Genesis 5:24)

## Constantin Caraman

'Walking with God' ... Can it be done today?

Was it not much easier for Enoch to walk with God? Did he not live in the 'good old days'? No, those old days were not that good. They were times of change and apostasy.

In fact, people lived according to their own standards so much that it was not difficult to notice a man who had different standards, God's standards: he walked with God.

He did so in spite of the slander and temptation of the world around him.

No, it is not at all easy to walk with God. It is much easier to only believe in God in your hearts and live like the rest of the world. But that is not walking with God. That is a compromise which makes any walk with God impossible.

How then do we walk with God? By acknowledging Him in all things, in seeking Him and living for Him.

'In all your ways acknowledge him, and he will make your paths straight' (Proverbs 3:6).

How delightful it is to walk with God in those paths.

*I have sinned against the Lord.* (2 Samuel 12:13)

## Constantin Caraman

It takes courage to tell a king the truth, especially when the truth will result in punishment. Punishment for the king (by God) and punishment for yourself (by the king). John the Baptist did it and it cost him his head.

When David made some serious mistakes, God sent the prophet Nathan to point them out to him. It was a difficult task for Nathan. Which one of us would like to be a bearer of bad tidings? But Nathan went to tell the king what the consequences of his sin would be. How did David react? Did he have Nathan killed? No, David did something unusual – he accepted the criticism and admitted the guilt: 'I have sinned'.

He did not try to defend himself, but humbled himself before God. Is this not characteristic of a man after God's own heart?

*'Search me, O God, and know my heart;*
*test me and know my anxious thoughts.*
*See if there is any offensive way in me,*
*and lead me in the way everlasting.'*

(Psalm 139:23, 24)

*The Lord gave and the Lord has taken away; may the
name of the Lord be praised.* (Job 1:21)

## Constantin Caraman

When I was working as a doctor in the Romanian country-
side, I once met an old man. He was walking in the middle of
the road, crying. I stopped and asked if there was anything I
could do for him. He said, 'I had seven sons and all of them
have been killed.' I looked into the face of this man to whom
life had little meaning anymore. Automatically, the question
arises: 'O Lord, why so much suffering?'

'I can't go on any more and I don't want to either,' the
man said. In moments like these, it is better to be silent. Then
the only thing for a doctor to do is to entrust him to the care
of our Great Healer and pray for peace and strength. I was
thinking about Job. He would have understood and helped
this man much better. But Job was not there. But He, who
was tempted in every way, just as we are, He was there –
Jesus Christ. He is able to sympathize with our weaknesses.

Job knew grief like no other. His reaction to suffering was
not a fatalistic one. Fatalists say: 'It just happens to you and
there is nothing you can do about it.' But Job sought comfort
in the Lord in spite of his inner struggle and his questions. He
had the kind of submission that overcame the ordeal.

My life is in God's hand. It is safe there, whatever
happens.

# January 26

*But I tell you: Love your enemies and pray for those who persecute you.* (Matthew 5:44)

## Constantin Caraman

This is no easy assignment. We are inclined to dislike those who hurt us. The best thing we are able to do is to ignore them. But God requires something totally different. He wants us to bless those who hate us. To pray for those who persecute us. That seems impossible. Remember that blessing someone does not mean that we approve of his actions. In fact, we disapprove of their behaviour, but they need God. That's why we need to pray for them, and bless them with the love of the Lord.

In His sermon on the mount (Matthew 5:44–48), Jesus even tells us to love them. We ourselves could never find it in our hearts to love an enemy. It just goes against our nature. Where in the world will we find people who can? You will only find it in people who are no longer of this world, but now belong to the Kingdom of God.

In Christ, who forgave us first, we are able to do the unusual deed of embracing an enemy, of loving those who hate us, of praying for those who persecute us, of blessing those who curse us.

And so, through us, Christ can reach that hard heart, so that it may also discover Christ's forgiveness and have eternal life.

*Lord, do not hold this sin against them.*      (Acts 7:60)

## Constantin Caraman

I would like to end the list of ordinary people who did extraordinary things with Stephen. After he had proclaimed the Gospel in Jerusalem, he was in serious trouble. Some of the onlookers attacked him and dragged him out, intending to kill him. 'Away with him,' they shouted, 'we don't want to listen to this any longer.'

Stephen knew there could be a reaction like this. After all, the disciples had been picked up and punished several times already. Yet, none of them had been stoned and killed. Stephen would be the first martyr.

When they started throwing stones at him, he could have cried: 'Lord, help me, they are going too far. Lord, send down a fire from heaven to destroy these people. You don't want me to die, do you?'

While the stones came down and hit him, he knelt down and prayed. What did he pray for? Did he pray for strength to remain faithful? No, he prayed for those who cursed him: 'Lord, do not hold this sin against them.'

Until his last breath he had compassion on the sinners, and in doing so, he followed Christ's example.

Are we prepared to do this too?

*Jesus had compassion on them and touched their eyes.*
*Immediately they received their sight and followed him.*

(Matthew 20:34)

## Irina Ratushinskaya

Our attention is usually focused on the miracle instead of on the attitude of the one who is cured. And those who were cured reacted in different ways. Some of them followed Christ immediately – others did what Christ told them to do.

How about us? Christ has also touched us – physically or spiritually. How did we react? Did we follow Him? Or did we just live on as if nothing had ever happened?

Perhaps we steered the middle course and said: 'Lord, I am grateful and I intend to follow You, but I have to settle a few other things first. Furnish the house, paper the rooms, finish that new project,' and so on and so on.

The longer man makes plans to do something, the less chance there is that he will ever carry them out.

Significantly, the Gospel according to Luke mentions the fact that out of ten people who were cured of leprosy by Christ, only one returned to thank Him. And Jesus' question was: 'Were not all ten cleansed? Where are the other nine?' (Luke 17:17).

May the Lord never need to ask that question of you and me.

*Another angel, who had a golden censer, came and stood at the altar. He was given much incense to offer, with the prayers of all the saints, on the golden altar before the throne.* (Revelation 8:3)

## Open Doors Contact Person

He had been in prison in Siberia for many years.

Those were years of suffering, torture, brainwashing.

After his release we spoke to him and asked: 'What was the secret of your victory whilst you were in prison for so long?'

He pulled out a little notebook from his pocket. 'This is the secret' he said. 'These are the people who prayed for me while I was in prison. They sent me postcards and I kept their names. You have no idea how we depended on getting those postcards. They encouraged us and the other prisoners.'

God hears our prayers when we pray.

Prayers for those who suffer.

Prayers for our families.

Prayers for our own problems.

Never stop asking. One day all will be revealed.

The prayers of the saints are kept by God. Yours as well.

# January 30

What kind of suffering is David describing here? Is it sickness and other physical suffering? Or spiritual suffering and persecution? Whatever, in both cases enemies are lying in wait to take over his kingship when he dies. David's life is in danger and he cries out to God.

## David

*O LORD, do not rebuke me in your anger or discipline me in your wrath.*
*Be merciful to me, LORD, for I am faint; O LORD, heal me, for my bones are in agony.*
*My soul is in anguish. How long, O LORD, how long?*
*Turn, O LORD, and deliver me; save me because of your unfailing love.*
*No one remembers you when he is dead. Who praises you from the grave?*
*I am worn out from groaning; all night long I flood my bed with weeping and drench my couch with tears.*
*My eyes grow weak with sorrow; they fail because of all my foes.*
*Away from me, all you who do evil, for the LORD has heard my weeping.*
*The LORD has heard my cry for mercy; the LORD accepts my prayer.*
*All my enemies will be ashamed and dismayed; they will turn back in sudden disgrace.*          (Psalm 6)

## Remarkable Remarks
### *Victorious Under Pressure*

---

*Michael Khorev – formerly USSR:*

'Lord, if my bonds glorify you more than my freedom, why should I want freedom?'

*Chinese Evangelist* in a letter from prison to his wife:

'After you have drunk the cup of suffering, then comes a fountain of blessing.'

In another letter to his wife:

'Without fire, how can gold become pure?
Without chiseling, how can a rock become a statue?
Without pressing, how can grapes become wine?'

*Nepalese Christian* after years in prison:

'Persecution is only a sign of labour pains, giving birth to the Church.'

*Paul Claudel:*

'Jesus did not come to remove suffering, but to fill it with His presence.'

'. . . *unless a grain of wheat falls to the ground and dies, it remains only a single seed. But if it dies, it produces many seeds.'* (John 12:24)

'*Even though I walk through the valley of the shadow of death, I will fear no evil, for you are with me.'*
(Psalm 23:4)

# February

## Writers for the month

*Li An* from China. Because he is well-known in China, he requested that his real name was not published. We have used the pseudonym, Li An.

*Samuel Lamb* from China. This noted pastor was in prison for over 20 years. He is still under great pressure from the authorities. Hundreds attend his so-called House Church, especially young people. His story is available in a book *Bold as a Lamb* published by Zondervan, 1991.

*By faith Abraham, when called to go ... obeyed and went, even though he did not know where he was going.*
(Hebrews 11:8)

## Abraham

Abraham's story begins with God. The Lord called him to leave all that he loved and go to the country of God's choice. Nobody had ever done that before. He had no examples of how God had led others. He could not say: as the Lord led them, so He will lead me. Yet he went – by faith.

Obedience to God's call is a true expression of one's faith in God. Such obedience may involve hardship. It was not easy for Abraham to leave his home and relatives and go to a land he did not know. We must be prepared to take up our cross daily to follow Him. Each step may involve an altar on which some part of the self-life needs to be offered. Abraham stood at such altars again and again. Sometimes victoriously, at other times in failure and defeat.

Abraham did not know where to go. It was enough for him to know that he went with God.

As someone said: 'I would rather travel with God in the night, than travel alone in the day.'

Such people become God's friends.

# February 2

*Trust in the Lord with all your heart and lean not on your own understanding; in all your ways acknowledge him and he will make your paths straight.* (Proverbs 3:5, 6)

## Abraham

The man of faith was a man of failure also. This offers encouragement to all those who want to follow God but are aware of their own frailty. It gives assurance that God is willing to use ordinary men and women. This does not mean that failure is acceptable. We can learn from Abraham's failures – in order to be aware of the snares of the devil.

In Abraham's life these failures were incidental, not fundamental. When he fell, God drew him back and Abraham responded.

'There was a famine in the land.' A famine? A famine in the Land of Promise? Had Abraham made a wrong decision to come to Canaan? Abraham's faith did not waver, but his mind was not directed towards God. 'He went down to Egypt.' But Egypt was not the land God had shown him. Neither did God lead him to Egypt as God could have done in this time of despair. Abraham made the decision himself, without consulting God. Such disobedience always brings complications. In the end Abraham was willing to sacrifice his wife in the interest of his own safety. If we do not acknowledge God in all our ways we will soon be filled with panic instead of peace.

There was no altar in Egypt, no fellowship with God, no new promises. Only a desolate home and a time of great distress.

How thankful we should be that the Bible records the story of the sins of the saints. Not to condone their behaviour or mistakes, but to warn us that God requires implicit obedience.

Only then will we experience what Corrie ten Boom said: 'The safest place on earth is in the centre of the will of God; the most dangerous place is when you are outside that will.'

*Then Jesus told the disciples a parable to show them that they should always pray and not give up ... and will God not bring about justice for his chosen ones, who cry out to him day and night? Will he keep putting them off? I tell you, he will see that they get justice, and quickly.*

(Luke 18:1, 7, 8)

## Abraham

Nothing makes Satan so fearful as a Christian who understands the power of prayer.

Some time ago Brother Andrew wrote a book on prayer, entitled *And God changed His Mind because His people dared to ask*. Abraham dared to ask and in response God was willing to change His mind. 'For the sake of ten I will not destroy it' (Sodom and Gomorrah). Six times Abraham had prayed for the salvation of the people in those cities. What a pity he stopped at ten. Who knows what might have happened had Abraham gone on.

Ungodly men and women in sinful cities do not realise how much they owe to the presence of God's people in their midst. Godly people are too often unaware of their enormous responsibility to pray for a wicked world. Abraham was aware – and prayed. Let us plead with God for a break-through in countries where His presence is not allowed.

Let us also hold on to God when praying for those in our own families who live without Christ. Prayer changes situations – never give up.

# February 4

*You need to persevere so that when you have done the will of God, you will receive what he has promised.*

(Hebrews 10:36)

## Abraham

A right motive – a wrong method; that is what happened when Abraham took Hagar to secure a successor. Instead of waiting for God's timing, he tried to help God fulfill His promise.

It is always dangerous to take things into your own hands. Abraham adopted carnal means to achieve a spiritual end. The consequences were enormous and are still being felt today. God's chosen successor was Isaac – from which line came Jesus Christ. Abraham's chosen plan was Ishmael – from which line came Mohammed. Through faith Abraham was to become a blessing to all the nations. Through unbelief one of the greatest foes of Christ would be born – the founder of Islam which claims that God has no Son.

Abraham had to send Ishmael away. He did so, with only a water bottle, yet God took care of Ishmael. When the boy would have died of thirst God provided more than a water bottle – he provided a well.

He still does.

May all of Ishmael's offspring drink from that fountain of living water – provided by God, through Jesus Christ, His Son. May we be willing to be God's channels.

*By faith Abraham, when God tested him, offered Isaac as a sacrifice.* (Hebrews 11:17)

## Abraham

Temptation is Satan's way of getting us into his camp – away from God. A test is God's way of bringing us closer to Himself – away from Satan. Abraham knew the difference.

God must have had great confidence in Abraham, and Abraham in God. God's vote of confidence in Abraham not only concerned his obedience, but also his faith and love.

*Obedience* When the Lord commanded Abraham to offer his son, he responded immediately. He did not plead for time to consider the consequences. He did not argue with God. 'Early the next morning he got up . . . ' (Genesis 22:3).

Obedience without reservation.

*Faith* Isaac was the child of promise. How could God keep His promise and let Isaac die? Because Abraham knew: God is able. 'He reasoned that God could raise the dead' (Hebrews 11:19). What faith. Abraham had never heard of anyone having been raised from the dead yet he believed: God is able.

Faith without doubt.

*Love* Who comes first? Isaac was the answer to God's promise, the child of his old age, the laughter of his life. His dearest possession on earth. Yet, God came first.

Love without limits.

Abraham passed the test. Have you?

If Abraham was to have received an award it would have contained this inscription: 'Abraham, pioneer of faith – friend of God.'

# February 6

*Jehovah Jireh – The Lord will provide.* (Genesis 22:14)

## Abraham

True deliverance will come only when we have reached the mountain of sacrifice. As long as we hold on to what is precious to us, God cannot take over. As soon as we let go – we let God.

It reminds me of that young boy who wanted to get a precious gift out of a bottle. It was a painful exercise but at last he got hold of the precious gift. He tried to get it out of the bottle, but his hand clutching on to the gift was too big to get it back through the bottle neck. There was only one way to get his hand out of the bottle. He had to let go of the gift. It will always be like that in our spiritual lives.

Leave the miracle to God. Abraham experienced that. 'The Lord will provide.' His obedience to God resulted in blessing for all the nations.

'...and through your offspring all nations on the earth will be blessed because you have obeyed me' (Genesis 22:18).

A prayer for deliverance from the enemy.

David is accused and incriminated. He cries to God, the heavenly judge, who knows that David is honest and just. He puts his faith in his God. The God who is a righteous judge.

### David

*O LORD my God, I take refuge in you; save and deliver*
*me from all who pursue me,*
*or they will tear me like a lion and rip me to pieces with*
*no one to rescue me.*
*O LORD my God, if I have done this and there is guilt*
*on my hands —*
*if I have done evil to him who is at peace with me or*
*without cause have robbed my foe —*
*then let my enemy pursue and overtake me; let him*
*trample my life to the ground and make me sleep in*
*the dust.*
*Arise, O LORD, in your anger; rise up against the rage*
*of my enemies. Awake, my God; decree justice.*
*Let the assembled peoples gather around you. Rule over*
*them from on high;*
*let the LORD judge the peoples. Judge me, O LORD,*
*according to my righteousness, according to my*
*integrity, O Most High.*
*O righteous God, who searches minds and hearts, bring*
*to an end the violence of the wicked and make the*
*righteous secure.*                                       (Psalm 7:1–9)

*The Lord is my light and my salvation; whom shall I fear?* (Psalm 27:1)

## Li An

During the time I was persecuted because of the Gospel, I was once condemned to die. But the Lord protected me. Instead of taking my life they threw me into prison.

Some time afterwards, something strange happened. The judge who had sentenced me got into trouble himself. Because of his political activities he was himself sentenced to a long prison term. He was not only put into the same prison, but he was put into the same cell with me.

After he found out my name he started to cry: 'O God, I surrender. Oh Jesus I really surrender.'

He went on for four or five minutes and then turned to me. 'So it is you. Do you remember me? Your life was in my hands. I had already sentenced you to die and I did try to execute the sentence many times, but every time I tried to get you executed something happened which kept delaying the execution. But who would have thought I would be here, in prison, with you? I see that your God has preserved your life. You are in His hands. But I am in the hands of the Marxists. They will not let me live. Forgive me please. I need your Jesus.'

I looked at him. He had been my judge. Now I was his judge. And the Lord told me what kind of sentence I should pass on him.

'Are not two sparrows sold for a penny? Yet not one of them will fall to the ground apart from the will of your Father' (Matthew 10:29).

God forgives, and so should we.

*Christ, who is your life.*                    (Colossians 3:4)

## Li An

A brother was put into prison for his faith in Jesus Christ and was only tried after having spent a long time in jail.

The following 'conversation' was recorded during the trial: 'Do you still believe in Christianity?' the prosecutor asked scornfully.

The brother replied: 'I don't believe in Christianity.' The prosecutor laughed: 'Finally, we have reformed you.' But the brother responded: 'I never believed in Christianity, I believe in Christ.'

'Don't play with words,' the prosecutor yelled. 'Christianity and Christ are the same.'

'No there is a big difference.' 'What do you mean?' the judge asked. 'The difference is that Christianity is a religion. It has churches, sets of rules and regulations, ministers and other church workers. You can close down the church, dismantle the regulations, arrest the ministers, but Jesus Christ lives in my heart, He is my life. You can never take that away. He is with me, always, even today in this court room. How can I reject Him who saved me? I just cannot not believe in Him.'

If we put our trust in a religion, we may be restricted. But if we live in Christ we can never change, whatever the circumstances. Better in jail as a Christian, than outside jail as a 'religious person'.

And more than that, who can separate us from the love of Christ? He lives in us and that makes us victorious, wherever we may be.

*Faith by itself, if it is not accompanied by action, is dead.* (James 2:17)

## Li An

I have a brother-in-law who works for the government of China. He strongly believed in Marxism and rationalism. He tried to persuade me to give up my faith in God. And I tried to convince him of the truth of the Gospel. In the end nobody won the argument.

But then he made a very interesting statement: 'I do not believe in God, nor that Jesus ever existed. However, one thing I do confess, is that I admire your father's deeds. If there is a God, your father surely will be Jesus' image.'

A few years later, he and his whole family became Christians. It taught me a very, very important lesson. My faith must be accompanied by works and deeds. 'Faith by itself, if it is not accompanied by action, is dead.'

'Let your light shine before men, that they may see your good deeds and praise your Father in heaven' (Matthew 5:16).

*. . . a woman came with an alabaster jar of very expensive perfume, made of pure nard. She broke the jar and poured the perfume on his head.* (Mark 14:3)

**Li An**

To be broken and then poured out is the secret of spreading the fragrance of the Lord through our lives.

Many a time we can't be poured out because we are not willing to be broken.

We must be broken before we can be poured out. Each one of us has 'perfume' inside of us. But the jar of selfishness must be broken. When the selfishness and self-centredness is not broken, the sweet fragrance of perfume can never be poured out. The more we are broken the more fragrance will come out.

'The sacrifices of God are a broken spirit; a broken and contrite heart, O God, you will not despise' (Psalm 51:17).

This brokenness can be the result of repentance from sin, the acceptance of circumstances or the willingness to offer to the Lord that which is very dear to us. The result will be that a sweet aroma will flow into our own souls and through it to people around us.

# February 12

*Since they did not think it worthwhile to retain the knowledge of God, he gave them over to a depraved mind, to do what ought not to be done.* (Romans 1:28)

## Li An

A brother was on trial for his faith in the Lord. When the prosecutor interrogated him he asked the brother: 'You believe in God, tell us where your God is.'

The brother replied: 'He lives in my heart.'

'Prove it, we do not believe in spiritual things.'

So the brother gave his testimony.

'You are speaking rubbish,' the prosecutor said angrily. 'You are making things up; they are a pack of lies.'

'You can go and find out for yourself,' the brother replied.

Two years later the brother was brought to the court again. To his surprise the prosecutor said: 'We have carefully looked into the things you told us; 80% is true, but we still don't believe there is a God.'

'Then how do you explain the 80%?' our brother asked.

'We don't need to explain. We have enough evidence to conclude that you are a weird person.' So they sent this brother back to jail...

What can we learn from this?

- That we must never compromise. We must be willing to pay the price – any price – for our faith.
- That, because of their unwillingness to acknowledge God, people can fall into deeper darkness than ever before.

Have you seen God at work? Have you responded?

*I want to know Christ.* (Philippians 3:10)

**Li An**

Paul's greatest goal in life was: 'That I may know Him, His character, His works, His grace.'

But can that ever be achieved? God truly is a mystery. He has no beginning and no end. Who can comprehend this? How can we, simple, imperfect, foolish and insignificant human beings fully understand this sovereign and holy Lord?

Humanly speaking we can't. But praise God, He reveals Himself to us. He takes the initiative. It is His desire that we might know Him. That gives me confidence. We don't have to climb up to meet Him. No, He comes down to our level and communes with us.

That's where it starts. The closer our walk with Him, the better we get to know Him. Oh, for a closer walk with You – my Savior and my Lord.

# February 14

This psalm is a eulogy to God's greatness in creation. The great, almighty God, who created everything, is concerned about us insignificant human beings.

## David

*O LORD, our Lord, how majestic is your name in all the
    earth! You have set your glory above the heavens.*
*From the lips of children and infants you have ordained
    praise because of your enemies, to silence the foe and
    the avenger.*
*When I consider your heavens, the work of your fingers,
    the moon and the stars, which you have set in place,*
*what is man that you are mindful of him, the son of
    man that you care for him?*
*You made him a little lower than the heavenly beings
    and crowned him with glory and honor.*
*You made him ruler over the works of your hands; you
    put everything under his feet:*
*all flocks and herds, and the beasts of the field,*
*the birds of the air, and the fish of the sea, all that swim
    the paths of the seas.*
*O LORD, our Lord, how majestic is your name in all the
    earth!* (Psalm 8)

*The arrows of the Almighty are in me; my spirit drinks in their poison, God's terrors are marshaled against me.*

(Job 6:4)

## Pastor Samuel Lamb

When we suffer we should never grumble against God. Many people cannot endure suffering. They grumble all the time. Job had experienced a lot of suffering.

In the beginning he was spiritually strong. He even rebuked his own wife ' . . . shall we accept good from God, and not trouble?' (Job 2:10).

Unfortunately, after a while he cursed his own birthday. Yes, he even grumbled against God. Some people, when they suffer, do not dare to complain to God. They let it out on people around them.

This incident in Job's life meant a lot to me when I was in prison for my faith for 21 years. I can understand Job's victories and Job's defeats. It taught me that grumbling does not help. Not against God, not against those who persecuted me. My dear wife died while I was in prison. I was not allowed to attend her funeral. It was like an arrow of the Almighty, until I understood: God allows the pain, the loss, the torture, but we must grow through it.

'Bless those who persecute you. Bless and do not curse' (Romans 12:14). 'Blessed is the man who does not fall away on account of me' (Matthew 11:6). May God teach us to rejoice when things go wrong – knowing that in all things God works for the good of those who love him (Romans 8:28).

# February 16

*Therefore, since Christ suffered in his body, arm your-selves also with the same attitude, because he who has suffered in his body is done with sin.* (1 Peter 4:1)

## Pastor Samuel Lamb

Different people may have different reasons for suffering. Needless to say that there is no gain in suffering that is caused by sin.

As Christians we all experience different degrees of suffering. Therefore, we should arm ourselves with a right attitude – the attitude of accepting spiritual suffering as a mark of true discipleship.

Jesus said: 'You will indeed drink from my cup' (Matthew 20:23). We need to be willing to suffer daily, even though God did not call us to suffer daily. If we fall through the trials that come our way, then we do not have the right attitude towards suffering.

Suffering is limited – but the attitudes of accepting suffering should be limitless ... even unto death. Do we have the right attitude? When you grumble you lose your peace, when you curse suffering you have no victory.

We must make up our minds daily to be willing to suffer for Christ. Then, and only then, will we experience blessing, peace and victory.

*It was good for me to be afflicted so that I might learn your decrees.* (Psalm 119:71)

*. . . if you suffer as a Christian do not be ashamed, but praise God that you bear that name.* (1 Peter 4:16)

## Pastor Samuel Lamb

A suffering Christian should never boast in his suffering. Some people suffer as a result of their sins. Their suffering has no room for boasting, but actually it is 'good' for them to suffer because through their suffering God calls them back to Himself.

I have been in prison for my faith for more than twenty years. During those years I experienced a lot of suffering and persecution. I asked the Lord daily to help me to remain faithful to Him whatever the pain and sorrow might be that day. Praise the Lord, God answered my prayers. I am not boasting in this, because I did not do it by myself, but by the One who gave me strength.

If I would have relied on my own strength, I would have disowned Him thirty times, or even three hundred times. Let him who suffers because of sin repent and return to God. Let him who stands firm for Christ boast in the Lord.

# February 18

*Blessed are you when people insult you, persecute you and falsely say all kinds of evil against you because of me.* (Matthew 5:11)

## Pastor Samuel Lamb

Those who are persecuted because of righteousness are 'blessed'. When people insult you because you are a Christian, you are 'blessed'. Suffering for righteousness is participating in the sufferings of Christ. Every Christian should participate in this suffering; 'Blessed are you when people insult you ... great is your reward in heaven' (Matthew 5:12).

I want to look to the reward, not to the circumstances. The greatest help during these times of persecution is to keep looking to Jesus. He is always near. The greater the persecution, the nearer He is. The reward in heaven is only an extra bonus.

'Blessed are you.' Blessed is **He.**

*Consider it pure joy my brothers, whenever you face trials of many kinds.* (James 1:2)

## Pastor Samuel Lamb

In the Old Testament, people received joy *after* they suffered. But in the New Testament the disciples rejoiced *while* they suffered (1 Peter 4:14; Matthew 5:11, 12).

When we suffer for Christ, not only do we have to rejoice, but we have to rejoice greatly. 'In this you greatly rejoice...' (1 Peter 1:6).

'Blessed are you when men hate you ... because of the Son of Man. Rejoice in that day and leap for joy' (Luke 6:22, 23).

'The apostles left the Sanhedrin, rejoicing because they had been counted worthy of suffering disgrace for the Name' (Acts 5:41).

In Luke 6 the disciples are told to leap for joy because they will receive a great reward in heaven. In Acts 5:41 the apostles rejoiced because of their unity with Jesus. Because we love Him, the world will hate us.

We should not look at the hatred, the insults, the persecutions or hardships but at Jesus. He suffered – so will we. He was glorified – so shall we be. He lives forever – so will we.

'I consider that our present sufferings are not worth comparing with the glory that will be revealed in us.'

Twenty years in prison is long. Very long. But not worth comparing with the eternity which awaits us. What a future – what a joy!

*If we endure, we will also reign with him.*

(2 Timothy 2:12)

## Pastor Samuel Lamb

Endurance means suffering here. In English the word 'patient' is the same for a sick person and for a person who endures. A sick person cannot choose. He must be patient. As we suffer for Christ we have to be like the patient who must be patient.

Those who endure suffering for Christ's sake are patients who are very healthy. They secure blessing upon blessing and will reign with Him in glory.

When we share in His sufferings we will also share in His glory. Do not complain about your sufferings – but pray for endurance. 'Ask and you will receive, seek and you will find; knock and the door will be opened to you' (Matthew 7:7). Not just prison doors but also spiritual doors of darkness and defeat. So that we might walk in the light.

'I am the light of the world. Whoever follows me will never walk in darkness, but will have the light of life' (John 8:12).

David thanks the Lord for his help and salvation. We so often forget to do that. David recognises the help of the Lord and thanks him for it.

Not to him, the king, is honour due, but to Him, the heavenly King.

## David

*I will praise you, O LORD, with all my heart; I will tell*
*of all your wonders.*
*I will be glad and rejoice in you; I will sing praise to*
*your name, O Most High.*
*My enemies turn back; they stumble and perish before*
*you.*
*For you have upheld my right and my cause; you have*
*sat on your throne, judging righteously.*
*You have rebuked the nations and destroyed the wicked;*
*you have blotted out their name for ever and ever.*
*Endless ruin has overtaken the enemy, you have*
*uprooted their cities; even the memory of them has*
*perished.*
*The LORD reigns forever; he has established his throne*
*for judgement.*
*He will judge the world in righteousness; he will govern*
*the peoples with justice.*
*The LORD is a refuge for the oppressed, a stronghold in*
*times of trouble.*
*Those who know your name will trust in you, for you,*
*LORD, have never forsaken those who seek you.*

(Psalm 9:1–10)

*God is our refuge and strength, an ever-present help in
trouble.* (Psalm 46:1)

## Pastor Samuel Lamb

When we suffer for our faith in Jesus Christ we should never
complain to God or hate those who cause the suffering. The
Bible teaches us again and again that suffering is a mark of
true discipleship. Those who complain do so at their own cost,
they will only suffer more and thus lose their victory, and
when you lose your victory, you lose God's blessings. Therefore, hardships and trouble are times to experience the help of
God and is that not what we want: God's help?

'God is our refuge and strength, an ever-present help in
trouble.'

I have had the privilege to be punished by 21 years of
imprisonment. That's what my accusers named it: punishment. It turned out to be my privilege.

The troubles were many. Oh, how I longed for God's help.
It has taught me this spiritual truth: The greater the need,
the greater the help. What a blessing. I dare say – if a
preacher has never suffered he cannot fully comprehend God's
help. I have experienced plenty of trouble ... it opened the
way to see plenty of God's help. Available for me, available
for you.

*Jesus Christ is the same yesterday and today and forever.*
(Hebrews 13:8)

## Pastor Samuel Lamb

We too often think that God only performed miracles in the time that Jesus walked on earth. What a pity to think that way. Not only because it is not true, but also because it stops us from expecting God's miracles in our own life today.

When I was a child I became very sick one day. The doctor who examined me told my father that I only had a ten per cent chance to stay alive. I was taken to a hospital where the doctor confirmed that there was hardly any chance for me to survive. My father said: 'If my son has only a ten per cent chance of survival and is going to die I want to take him to die at home.' When we arrived home he asked all the Christians in the village to come to our house to pray. They prayed all through the night. The next day the doctor came to our house thinking I must be dead by now. When he saw me and examined me, he could only speak one word: 'miracle'. I was completely healed. You see, God not only knows about our spiritual suffering, but also about our physical problems. Jesus Christ is the same today. He still performs miracles, trust Him and seek His help. Too many people never ask – they only discuss: 'What if God does not help?' Discuss less, pray more, and you will experience the power of God – even when God answers in a way you did not expect Him to.

# February 24

*Therefore, my dear brothers, stand firm. Let nothing move you.* (1 Corinthians 15:58)

## Pastor Samuel Lamb

The Lord's blessings are different to different people. Some people suffer physically or through illness, the only important thing is: how do we react? Some people suffer spiritually, because of their faith in Jesus Christ. Again, the only importance is: how do we react?

There is no need for us to chase after miracles, but if we need a miracle: God specialises in miracles. The greatest miracle God can do in our lives is to give us peace, whatever the circumstances may be. A Chinese proverb says: 'A crisis reveals our character.' How do we react in terms of crisis? Do we get confused, angry, disappointed – in God and men? Or do we trust God – who is still in control? Our spiritual character must be built before we enter a crisis so that in the midst of the trouble we can draw from our spiritual knowledge and experience.

*Let the word of Christ dwell in you richly.*

(Colossians 3:16)

*I have hidden your word on my heart that I might not sin against you.* (Psalm 119:11)

## Pastor Samuel Lamb

I mentioned already that I had been in prison for more than 20 years – of course without a Bible. And yet I had a Bible . . . in my heart. It did not come there automatically or easily. It has cost me a lot of hard work and many, many hours of study.

It started when I was young. We lived in a little hut – not even a house, but my parents did not complain. The beauty was not in the house but in those who dwelt in it. My father called our residence the 'Hallelujah-hut'. A strange name maybe, but it was that word which was heard and spoken many times in that hut. Around the hut we hung all kinds of verses from the Bible – a very strange sight for other people, but very good for me because I started to memorize them. Throughout the years that I had a Bible, I started to memorize the Scriptures and by the time I was thrown into prison I had memorized the Bible from Romans to Hebrews, as well as many psalms and some other parts. Don't ask me why I memorized those Scriptures – only God knows, but when I was thrown into prison I had the Word of God in my heart – and nobody could steal it away from me. It took me a few years to learn it – it was a blessing for 20 years. And it still is.

# February 26

*Simon, Simon, Satan has asked to sift you as wheat. But I have prayed for you, Simon, that your faith may not fail.* (Luke 22:31, 32)

## Pastor Samuel Lamb

During the sixteenth year of my imprisonment something dramatic happened. All the prisoners – Christian and non-Christians – were called together to have a session of so-called self-criticism. Some Buddhists were asked to criticize Buddhism – others were asked to criticize Confucius. I was asked to criticize Christ. I quickly prayed to God. 'Sir, I cannot criticize or deny my God. He is the way, the truth and the life.' 'Criticize' the man shouted, 'it will benefit you.' I thought: Will I be released after sixteen years instead of after twenty years? It would save me four years of hard labor. But then I thought: If I criticize Christ to come out of jail four years early, the sixteen years in jail would all have been in vain. I was trembling. Freedom so near – temptation so real. Then the Scripture I mentioned came to my mind: 'Be alert, your enemy the devil prowls around like a roaring lion looking for someone to devour. Resist him, standing firm in the faith...' (1 Peter 5:8). I also thought of Peter, who boasted in himself ... and fell. 'O Lord, keep my faith' I cried. If Peter denied Him three times, I could easily deny Him thirty times, three hundred times. Thank God, He heard my prayer. In those twenty years in jail I have not denied the Lord once, not because I was so strong – but because the Lord protected me. Praise be to Him and to Him alone. 'I have prayed for you.' Thank you Jesus.

*He regarded disgrace for the sake of Christ as of greater value than the treasures of Egypt, because he was looking ahead to his reward.* (Hebrews 11:26)

## Open Doors Contact Person

She is living in China. A young woman of merely thirty years of age. Her family moved to Canada. They were allowed to emigrate because of the many problems they had encountered in China.

Ding-Ding, that is her name, chose not to go with them but to remain in China. A hard decision to make, for Ding-Ding too was suffering hardship in China. Yet she stayed. Her decision to remain was not taken overnight. She said: 'There is so much work to be done here. The fields are ripe for harvest. God has called me to take the Gospel to the Chinese. The future is uncertain, but the Lord is with me. And His return is imminent. That is why I cannot leave. My people need Christ.'

It is written about Moses that he regarded disgrace for the sake of Christ of greater value than the treasures of Egypt. The same can be said of Ding-Ding.

And about many, many others like her. Are you one of those?

This psalm is a lamentation, a lament to God.

The reason for it is not mentioned. Is it war, or perhaps suppression? Those who are innocent and weak are the ones first hit. The godless say: 'There is no God'.

The believer David, cries out to God to intercede.

Not just to save the innocent, but also for the honor of His Name and His Kingdom.

## David

*Why, O LORD, do you stand far off? Why do you hide*
    *yourself in times of trouble?*
*In his arrogance the wicked man hunts down the weak,*
    *who are caught in the schemes he devises.*
*He boasts of the cravings of his heart; he blesses the*
    *greedy and reviles the LORD.*
*In his pride the wicked does not seek him; in all his*
    *thoughts there is no room for God.*
*His ways are always prosperous; he is haughty and*
    *your laws are far from him; he sneers at all his*
    *enemies.*
*The LORD is King for ever and ever; the nations will*
    *perish from his land.*
*You hear, O LORD, the desire of the afflicted; you*
    *encourage them, and you listen to their cry,*
*defending the fatherless and the oppressed, in order that*
    *man, who is of the earth, may terrify no more.*
(Psalm 10:1–5, 16–18)

### Remarkable Remarks
*Trust and Confidence*

*Pakistani Christian:*

'I would rather travel with God in the night, than travel alone in the day.'

*Corrie ten Boom – Holland:*

'When I try, I fail,
when I trust, He succeeds.'

*Unknown:*

'Patience is: trusting God to solve your problem, without setting a deadline for Him to do it.'

*Ralph Waldo Emerson:*

'All I have seen teaches me to trust the Creator for all I have not seen.'

*Francis Ridley Havergal:*

'Let us be calmed by the thought that what is hidden from us, is not hidden from Him.'

*Earl Riney:*

'The stars are always shining, but often we do not see them until it is dark.'

*'Oh Lord, you have searched me and you know me.*
*You know when I sit and when I rise;*
*You perceive my thoughts from afar.*
*You discern my going out and my lying down,*
*You are familiar with all my ways.'*    (Psalm 139:1–3)

# March

## Writers for the month

*Lucien Accad* from Lebanon. He is the Director of the Bible Society in Beirut. His house was severely damaged many times during the war in Lebanon.

*Naji Abi-Hashem* from Lebanon. He now lives in the free West.

*You intended to harm me, but God intended it for good to accomplish what is now being done, the saving of many lives.* (Genesis 50:20)

## Joseph

The story of Joseph appeals to young and old alike. Joseph who went from pit to palace. Joseph who kept his conscience clean and his character pure. Who was faithful under the most difficult circumstances. The man who resisted temptation. Who was unspoiled by sudden prosperity. Joseph who proved that 'prison walls do not make a prison'. Who enjoyed the presence of God and waited for his deliverance from God.

The man who answered cruelty with love and hatred with goodwill. Joseph, the perfect type of Christ. An outstanding young man. While we learn from him in the coming days, we acknowledge that we may not have all his gifts, but realize that we can practise all his principles. We may never reach his greatness, but we can show forth his goodness. To friends and foes alike. Resulting in the saving of many lives. Quite a challenge.

*Joseph had a dream, and when he told it to his brothers, they hated him all the more.* (Genesis 37:5)

*Pharaoh said to Joseph: 'I had a dream, and no-one can interpret it. But I have heard it said of you that when you have a dream you can interpret it.' 'I cannot do it' Joseph replied to Pharaoh, 'but God will give Pharaoh the answer he desires.'* (Genesis 41: 15, 16)

## Joseph

Dreams are empty, the saying goes. That's how it seemed in Joseph's life. His brothers did not bow down before him, as he had dreamt; instead he had to bow deeply before them. No respect, but rejection. No throne but a prison. His dream world collapsed. Thirteen difficult years of imprisonment followed. From the age of seventeen until the age of thirty. What could have been the best years of his young life, became the most difficult ones.

He could have asked (and maybe he did!) 'what about my dreams?' In spite of all these 'broken dreams' he remained faithful to God. No regrets – only service. Instead of complaining he proclaimed the greatness of God. Instead of dreaming about his past, he explained the dreams of others regarding the future.

His many years of imprisonment excelled in faithfulness, purity and servitude. As a result he was victorious despite the circumstances.

'...the Lord was with Joseph and gave him success in whatever he did' (Genesis 39:23).

Victorious living will always be the reward for those who live up to God's standards.

Why should you not be that person?

*Turn from evil and do good; then you will dwell in the land forever. For the Lord loves the just and will not forsake his faithful ones.* (Psalm 37:27, 28)

## Joseph

Joseph was always motivated by principle, not by expediency. He would rather lose his freedom than his peace. He was stripped of his coat, but never of his character.

In his confrontation with Potiphar's wife he deliberately closed his eyes to sin and to worldly advantage. It was important for Joseph to stand in good stead with Potiphar's wife. To please her would secure his standing and reputation. To cross her would ruin his hopes of a better future. But he shut his eyes to worldly advantage and clung to moral principles. Joseph looked beyond the temporary. He saw eternal principles, timeless laws. He saw God. Had he given in to Potiphar's wife, he might have acquired temporary favors, but they would not have lasted, and he would not have become prime minister of Egypt. The secret: Joseph was walking in undisturbed fellowship with God. He was in touch with God – and consequently protected by God.

'Turn from evil and do good; then you will dwell in the land forever.'

> *Blessed is the man who does not walk in the counsel of the*
> *wicked ... he is like a tree planted by streams of water*
> *... whatever he does prospers.* (Psalm 1:1a, 3)

## Joseph

We might conclude that Joseph's magnificent moral victory would be rewarded by God. Instead, it was followed by more calamity.

He may well have asked: 'Does godliness really pay?' That is also the big question in Psalm 73. The poet Asaph was confused about the prosperity of the wicked, and the troubles of the believers.

'When I tried to understand all this, it was oppressive to me ... till I entered the sanctuary of God; then I understood their final destiny' (Psalm 73: 16, 17).

There is a price to be paid for godliness. Christians who suffer for their faith experience this almost daily. There certainly is a cost of discipleship: rejection, loss of friends, work, family, privilege. And yet ... throughout this book you will read the triumphant testimonies of those who experienced persecution. They testify of victory, blessings and close intimate fellowship with God.

They made a choice. The best choice – as Joseph did – which leads to life and life abundantly.

*But one thing I do: forgetting what is behind and straining towards what is ahead.* (Philippians 3:13)

## Joseph

Joseph had two sons, Manasseh and Ephraim. Manasseh means: God made me forget all my trouble. Ephraim means: God made me fruitful in the land of my sufferings.

Joseph wanted to forget the past. He wanted to be fruitful despite the circumstances. In giving names to his two sons he wanted to express that God brings good out of evil, privilege out of pain, triumph out of tragedy, hope out of despair.

In spite of any afflictions that may be yours today do you want to be fruitful in the place where you are?

*By faith Joseph . . .* (Hebrews 11:22)

*Where, O death is your victory? . . . thanks be to God! He gives us the victory through our Lord Jesus Christ.*
(1 Corinthians 15:55, 57)

*So Joseph died . . . he was placed in a coffin in Egypt.*
(Genesis 50:26)

## Joseph

What a strange ending to a marvellous book. Is God's work ending in a poor mummy? No, it is not. These may be the closing words of Genesis, the book of beginnings, but if you read on you will come to the great Exodus.

Joseph knew that it would come: deliverance from persecution and the entering of the promised land.

That is why these last words of the book of Genesis are not pessimistic but instead full of hope. Joseph's bones were a constant reminder to the persecuted Jews that the day of their deliverance would come. Joseph did not know how or when; he was only certain it would happen.

We have no unburied bones to encourage our faith in a great future. We have an empty grave! Jesus is risen. The empty grave tells us that resurrection is certain. He is alive. He will be with us in times of trouble . . . until He returns.

'For the Lord himself will rise first. After that we who are still alive and are left will be caught up together with them in the clouds to meet the Lord in the air. And so we will be with the Lord forever' (1 Thessalonians 4:16, 17).

What a glorious moment that will be. What a hope. What a future. What a God. The best is yet to come.

Even though it is difficult to determine the circumstances in which David wrote this psalm, its content speaks for itself. In the midst of danger, David takes refuge in the Lord. What can I do? he sighs. The opposition is enormous, but God is in control. That is why he takes refuge in Him.

## David

*In the LORD I take refuge. How then can you say to*
*me: 'Flee like a bird to your mountain.*
*For look, the wicked bend their bows; they set their*
*arrows against the strings to shoot from the shadows*
*at the upright in heart.*
*When the foundations are being destroyed, what can the*
*righteous do?'*
*The LORD is in his holy temple; the LORD is on his*
*heavenly throne. He observes the sons of men; his*
*eyes examine them.*
*For the LORD is righteous, he loves justice; upright men*
*will see his face.* (Psalm 11:1–4, 7)

# March 8

*I tell you the truth, anyone who will not receive the Kingdom of God like a child will never enter it.*

(Mark 10:15)

## Lucien Accad

It was early in June at the beginning of the war in our country. I had to attend to some business in town and took my five-year old son with me.

Suddenly shooting erupted. Bullets whistled all around us. People, panicking, were running for shelter.

I was trying to remain calm as I did not want my son to panic, and I prayed in my heart for God's protection.

When everything had calmed down 'after the storm' I wanted to make sure my son was okay and asked him: 'Yves, are you okay? Did you see what happened?' 'Yes, dad,' he said, 'people were trying to kill each other.' 'Were you afraid?' I asked. 'Of course not' was his answer. 'Daddy, I was holding your hand.'

What confidence. As if my hands could protect him from the bullets. Sixteen years later, the war is still raging. But I have never forgotten those simple words from my little son. It has always reminded me that if I have my hand in the Father's hand I don't need to panic.

*By faith Noah, when warned about things not yet seen, in holy fear built an ark to save his family. By his faith he condemned the world and became heir of the righteousness that comes by faith.* (Hebrews 11:7)

### Lucien Accad

As parents we like our children to be safe and to have the best training for a happy future. Too often, however, these wishes are according to human standards.

Noah knew that obedience to God is the standard by which we can face the future in a positive way. He was able to perceive that the real danger came from a sinful society which is only interested in material benefits and which is predominantly selfish.

The building of our boat has to become a family enterprise around the person of Jesus Christ. It is only in Him that we will find real safety.

Sometimes we, as a family, have been tempted to run away from Lebanon because of the war, assuming that other parts of the world would be safer for our family. But God's Word reminds us that our real security, happiness and future are in Christ and in obeying God's will.

The safest place on earth is still in the centre of His will. The most dangerous place is to be outside His will.

# March 10

*It will rejoice greatly and shout for joy. The glory of Lebanon will be given to it, the splendour of Carmel and Sharon; they will see the glory of the Lord, the splendour of our God.* (Isaiah 35:2)

## Lucien Accad

Nothing is impossible for God. We do not plant in a desert but our Lord grows all kind of plants in areas where nothing wants to live. Moreover, it is amazing to see some parts of the world which have been deserts for hundreds of years and which today have the attention of men who plant trees, grass, flowers and all sorts of shrubs.

It is true that some parts of the world are becoming deserts, but where money and attention are available, deserts are turned into green fields. This gives hope for areas of the world that have become spiritual deserts. They seem out of the reach of God and the rain of the Word of God. But suddenly miracles start to take place; especially where the focus of prayer is concentrated. Walls of darkness come down, and rain from heaven turns arid soil into gardens of trees and fruit.

*He will cover you with his feathers, and under his wings you will find refuge; his faithfulness will be your shield and rampart.* (Psalm 91:4)

## Lucien Accad

It was late at night. We woke up suddenly because of the noise of shelling and realized we were again in the midst of a battle. I heard a knock at our bedroom door. Two of our young children came in and said: 'Dad, Mom, it's frightening in our room. Can we stay in your bed? If we die, let's die together!' The youngest child did not wake up.

We started praying together and sang a few hymns, after which they fell asleep, but I could not. Many questions were coming to my mind. 'Can the Lord keep us another time? Should we go and take refuge in the nearby shelter?'

I put on my clothes and looked out of the window in the direction of the shelter. The electricity wires had been cut by shrapnel and we were in the dark. Cars were ablaze just in front of the shelter not far from our own car, but no one dared go to extinguish the fire because of the shelling. Dark smoke was being blown in the direction of the shelter, and I could hear screams coming from there.

I heard a knock at the door of our home. Some of our neighbours asked if they could stay with us and sat down. 'Please let us stay here,' they said. 'Why don't we all go to the shelter?' I asked. 'No' they answered, 'your home is safer because it is a place of prayer; please read to us from the Bible.'

Joy filled my heart. 'You are the light of the world ... let your light shine before men that they may see your good deeds and praise your Father in heaven' (Matthew 5:14, 16).

# March 12

*For he will command his angels concerning you to guard you in all your ways.* (Psalm 91:11)

## Lucien Accad

It was 4.00 pm. 'Don't go home tonight,' they told me at the office.

I had to cross from the side of town where our office was located to the other side where we lived. 'It is too dangerous; a group of young men are kidnapping people crossing between the two sides of town.'

I knew I had to go; there was no way I could telephone home. As I reached the last crossing point the soldier told me to wait. 'You can't cross now, there is a sniper, a man in a car has just been injured.'

I asked if they were going to reopen the road soon, and was told they were, and that I could wait where I was. In the meantime a long queue of cars had formed and was waiting behind me.

After 10 minutes the soldier said: 'You can go now.' 'How do you know things have changed?' I asked. 'I haven't heard anyone contact you.' 'Well, it has been like this every day lately; someone has to try ... !'

It was not easy to be the first to try. In a situation like this it is good to remember that God is on our side and the angels are in charge, but it remains a frightening experience. No one was following me. At the end of the road the young men I had been warned about stopped me, demanding to see my ID papers. When they discovered that I was a pastor, instead of kidnapping me, they asked for a copy of the Bible.

'Great is thy faithfulness, O God my Father.'

*He humbled you, causing you to hunger and then feeding
you with manna, which neither you nor your fathers had
known, to teach you that man does not live on bread alone
but on every word that comes from the mouth of the Lord.*
(Deuteronomy 8:3)

## Lucien Accad

Jesus' call is to forsake all and follow Him, and we willingly
do this, declaring there is nothing too precious for us to give
up for Him should He require it of us.

But then, just as our lives are settled, the Lord takes
away our precious things and we are left empty. Had we
given up these things voluntarily it would be different, but
this is out of our control. We see ourselves small, crying out
to God in our pain, truly humbled, there is nothing we can do.

We are left with a void – an emptiness, described in the
verse as hunger. The Lord does not replace what He took
away – no, He teaches us to do without, and His promise is
that He will feed us with manna from heaven – something we
had never thought of before or are able to imagine.

Though we hunger, we don't want the manna, it is not
real to us, can it really satisfy us? We want the solid flesh
pots of Egypt – the things we have known before. But then
we see and know: we submit to our Lord; we trust in His
causing us to hunger, and eagerly await His manna. We get a
taste of the heavenly blessings – not a replacement of what we
lost, but a completely new thing.

# March 14

In this psalm, it is evident how much power there is in the words: 'We will triumph with our tongues.'

Intimidation, bragging and blasphemy are used to bring God and David into discredit. To oppose these blasphemous words of the godless, David uses the sanctifying, cleansing Word of God.

## David

*Help, LORD, for the godly are no more; the faithful have
vanished from among men.*
*Everyone lies to his neighbor; their flattering lips speak
with deception.*
*Because of the oppression of the weak and the groaning
of the needy, I will now arise, says the LORD. I will
protect them from those who malign them.*
*And the words of the LORD are flawless, like silver
refined in a furnace of clay, purified seven times.*
*O LORD, you will keep us safe and protect us from such
people forever.*
*The wicked freely strut about when what is vile is
honored among men.* (Psalm 12:1–2, 5–8)

*Though an army besiege me, my heart will not fear; though war break out against me, even then will I be confident.* (Psalm 27:3)

## Naji Abi-Hashem

To experience tranquility in the midst of tribulation is indeed a divine gift. One evening, during the long years of troubles in Beirut, the shelling over our part of the city was very heavy. However, I felt an urgency to go out and check on a certain family from our congregation. So I asked a brother, who happened to be in the church building waiting for the shelling round to end, to accompany me.

At first he hesitated and said: 'If people see us running on the deserted streets they will think we have lost our senses.' But then, we briefly prayed and left. We took with us some bread, fresh water, and candles for the family, some basic needs which were not always available those days.

Bombs and shells were exploding right and left. We walked close to walls and took short cuts when possible. Finally, we arrived. The household was very surprised by our unexpected visit. Although they warmly received us, they looked afraid, frustrated, and very distressed. We visited with them, talked about the Lord, laughed and ate together, and soon forgot about the horror of the war around us. We carefully read Psalm 27 twice and we all prayed. Before we left, their faces looked cheerful, radiant, and relieved. They said they felt as if two angels had visited them during a dark hour.

On our way back, we marveled at the power of God's Word and Spirit. Although the shelling never stopped the whole evening, we learned that the climax of the Christian experience comes after we respond to and obey the Lord's calling in the time of danger and serious challenge.

# March 16

*But he knows the way that I take; when he has tested me,*
*I shall come forth as gold.* (Job 23:10)

## Naji Abi-Hashem

By nature we tend to escape suffering and avoid pain. We frequently complain about hardships and dream of a life without sorrow. But is that realistic? An old proverb in the Midrash Tehillim says: 'If you want life, expect pain.'

When we suffer, God often surprises us with a special blessing. Although we tend to blame Him, at times, for what we are going through, He is gracious enough to bestow on us a unique measure of grace. As a result, we surprise ourselves with the degree of strength we have acquired to bear the unbearable and endure the hard seasons of life.

He is willing to give our suffering a new meaning. Certainly, our character is best sharpened through pain. Hardships are not meant to defeat us but to develop us. Therefore, we become brighter and more refined, like the rays of the sun after the rain.

*Splendor and majesty are before him; strength and glory are in his sanctuary.* (Psalm 96:6)

## Naji Abi-Hashem

If we had walked through the streets of Beirut, Lebanon in 1985 or Vukovar, Croatia in Europe, in 1994, we would have seen severe destruction and death, experienced deep sorrow and sadness, and would have come in touch with the dark side of human nature. But if we enter the sanctuary of God, we will be greatly moved and impressed by His glorious personal attributes and divine presence.

The very thought of entering into the presence of the Almighty God causes us to feel a sense of awe and reverence, the emotion of delight, and an attitude of trust and faith. The result is often a deliberate act of worship and commitment on our part. We come to realize that our God is still in charge.

Thus our spirits will be filled with peace, despite the circumstances. Our bones will be charged with energy and our mouths will testify the mercy of God for a dying world.

*He is the image of the invisible God, the firstborn over all creation. For God was pleased to have all his fullness dwell in him.* (Colossians 1:15, 19)

## Naji Abi-Hashem

Jesus Christ is the full revelation of God. He is the absolute Word and God incarnate.

He is the person that overshadows all other persons and the name that surpasses all names. He is the powerful Son of God and loving Savior of mankind. His personality and works are so profound that a genius cannot comprehend them.

In addition, Jesus Christ is the ultimate standard for moral-ethical values and the supreme example of personal maturity.

He is our role model and comprehensive guide, gentle Master and wise mentor, empathetic Counselor and therapeutic Healer, reliable Savior and accomplished Redeemer, close Friend and faithful companion, our holy and yet merciful Lord.

This is the Christ whom we love and serve and in whom we believe and trust. May His magnificent person be glorified forever.

*In a very short time, will not Lebanon be turned into a fertile field and the fertile field seem like a forest?*

(Isaiah 29:17)

## Naji Abi-Hashem

How many times, while I was in the United States pursuing my doctorate, and when Beirut was under heavy shelling and bombing, I wished I could go home. I remembered the tragedies, fears, and endless agonies of my people. Oh, how many times I wished I could be with them, to go through the same suffering, bear the same pain, and experience the same horror. However that triggered me to intercede intensely on their behalf and raise prayer support.

In the States people would often ask: 'Aren't you glad you are here instead of there?' My immediate reply always was: 'No, I'd rather be with my people at this critical time.' For I have tasted the trouble of wars. City wars mean surviving on extremely scarce resources, staying in basements for weeks with no electricity, fresh water, heat, or telephone lines. It means seeing your house hit or your car burned, hearing that a neighbor, friend, or relative has been killed, and putting your life on the line each time you go out and try to buy some bread or vegetables, if any were available.

Many others like me, who love Lebanon and are genuinely interested in its future and potential for a productive ministry in the whole Middle East, are earnestly praying for its healing and recovery, are closely watching the unfolding of events, and are fervently claiming the precious promises of old: 'Is it not yet a very little while until Lebanon shall be turned into a fruitful field?'

Will you please pray with us that this promise will soon be fulfilled?

# March 20

*Love your enemies and pray for those who persecute you.*
(Matthew 5:44)

## Naji Abi-Hashem

I met Brother Jamil right after I committed my life to Christ in the mountain town of Bhamdoun. There, I saw him in action, inside the meeting place and on the street, witnessing, praying, distributing literature, and quoting Scriptures from his ever-present and well-used Bible.

Some believers labelled him an 'aggressive evangelist', for he constantly seized the moment to present Christ.

The years passed and I became a pastor amidst the unresolved political and military tensions. For the first nine months, I led the Wednesday night meetings by studying the Sermon on the Mount. Brother Jamil used to show up every week. We arrived at Matthew 5:44 and carefully examined our Lord's teaching here. Brother Jamil made his contribution as usual.

After a few days, we all were shocked to hear about Brother Jamil's death. It was not a normal death or an accident. He was persecuted, tormented, and murdered by a militant Shiite group. He died as a martyr. He was triumphant both in his life and death. He was a living example of boldly serving Christ regardless of the price. And finally, he was more evidence that martyrdom is still a vital part of church life today, as it has been through the ages.

I still hear Jamil echoing Stephen's words: 'Lord do not hold this sin against them! Lord Jesus, receive my spirit.' When they spoke death, hatred, and destruction, he spoke love, forgiveness, and peace. That is authentic Christianity under severe testing.

Although David feels like he has been deserted by God and men, he still knows that God will help him in times of need. 'But I trust in your unfailing love; my heart rejoices in your salvation.'

## David

*How long, O LORD? Will you forget me forever? How long will you hide your face from me?*
*How long must I wrestle with my thoughts and every day have sorrow in my heart? How long will my enemy triumph over me?*
*Look on me and answer, O LORD my God. Give light to my eyes, or I will sleep in death;*
*my enemy will say, 'I have overcome him,' and my foes will rejoice when I fall.*
*But I trust in your unfailing love; my heart rejoices in your salvation.*
*I will sing to the LORD, for he has been good to me.*

(Psalm 13)

*The righteous will flourish like a palm tree, they will grow like a cedar of Lebanon.* (Psalm 92:12)

## Naji Abi-Hashem

Lebanon is mentioned in the Bible over 300 times. It is a symbol of beauty, pride, and prosperity. The Scriptures often refer to the fragrance of the trees in Lebanon and to the gardens that cover the hills.

This psalm makes a beautiful analogy between the true believer and the cedar of Lebanon.

First, the cedar tree is evergreen. It is always fresh throughout the changing seasons. And so is the believer who has received the overflowing life of Christ. His faith and joy are fresh as the Lord nurtures and looks after him.

Second, the cedar tree grows on high altitudes and opens its branches to the skies. So does the believer who is called to live on higher ground and who keeps his thoughts and affections in the heavenlies. He opens up his soul to heaven in worship and supplication. He generously receives grace and power. In turn, he becomes a blessing to others.

Third, a cedar tree is deeply rooted and could live for thousands of years. So is the believer who is standing on the Rock of Ages and has received everlasting life from Christ.

Fourth, the cedar tree spreads an elegant fragrance and its wood is very expensive. Likewise is the Christian, who was bought with an extremely precious price and was graciously brought into the family of God. Consequently, he is commissioned to spread the fragrance of Christ and to be an open letter of love, faith, and hope to all the nations of this earth.

*By the rivers of Babylon we sat and wept, when we remembered Zion. There on the poplars we hung our harps.* (Psalm 137:1–2)

## Naji Abi-Hashem

When you face a loss, it is alright to feel the sadness and stay with that feeling for a while. Grief and bereavement, like any other God-given emotions, are legitimate feelings. We should allow ourselves to express them in a healthy way and never deny, escape from, or push them away.

However, it is equally important not to exaggerate the losses, painful memories, or sad events to the extent that we fall into deep sorrow, despair, or depression. Naturally, disappointments are part of life but we should never allow them to generate self-pity and hopelessness. Like failures, losses are not meant to defeat us but to develop us.

No matter what your experience or personal situation may be, God is still in control. Just be patient with yourself and press on! After a major crisis of loss, work through your frustration, anger, or pain with someone who knows how to listen and who understands your intense emotions. Do not give up, sit down, or lament for the rest of your life.

My beloved Christian friend, stand up and reach out to the willow. Bring down your harp and start playing your favorite music. Revive your old melody and sing again that beautiful song, for the Lord is still on His Throne. Again, let me stress, do not give up and you shall see the glory of God. For in Christ the best is yet to come.

# March 24

*I will exalt you, my God the King; I will praise your name for ever and ever.* (Psalm 145:1)

## Naji Abi-Hashem

The Book of Psalms is among the most read and admired books in the whole Bible. While most of the Scriptures speak *to* us, the psalms speak *for* us. They express our deepest feelings. We find in them music, truth, beauty, comfort, strength, and most of all praise.

Worship is an act of the will, employing the thoughts and emotions. Besides its theological significance, praise also has a true psychological significance.

On the conscious level, praise clarifies our thinking and purifies our mind. It heightens our awareness of God's presence and might. Praise helps us to dwell on the positive rather than the negative. It virtually facilitates our personal growth towards wholeness and inner balance.

On the unconscious level, praise helps us to get in touch with the unpleasant thoughts and painful memories stored within us, like anger, hurt, loss, fear, guilt, and grief. Praise brings healing to some of our damaged emotions. It slowly infiltrates our mind until it is saturated. Thus, the new sacred thoughts gradually replace the old, resulting in restoration, harmony, empowerment and growth.

*My frame was not hidden from you when I was made in the secret place.* (Psalm 139:15)

## Naji Abi-Hashem

This psalm accurately describes some precious moments and draws from three beautiful aspects of our life.

Firstly, *Formation*. 'For thou didst form my inward parts ... thy eyes beheld my unformed substance.' He saw our personality being formed. He wants to be part of our personal development and gently directs our growth towards His likeness.

Secondly, *Information*. 'Thou dost beset me behind and before, and layest thy hand upon me. Such knowledge is too wonderful for me; it is so high I cannot attain it.' God is perfectly aware of our strengths and bright sides and of our weaknesses and dark sides. One great comfort to me is that God knows me better than I know myself. Socrates once said: 'Know thyself!' In my journey of self-discovery, I realize that I will not totally comprehend myself nor begin to grasp God's immense knowledge. But someday, 'I shall understand fully even as I have been understood' (1 Corinthians 13:12b).

Thirdly, *Transformation*. 'Search me, O God, and know my heart; Try me and know my thoughts; and see if there be any wicked way in me, and lead me in the everlasting way.' This cry is a precious pearl in the crown of prayer. It is a marvelous call for an intimate soul-searching process. It springs from our honest and deepest need for transcendence. Only the Lord can touch our emotional and psychological roots and bring insight, healing, fulfillment and peace. To Him be the glory, for ever. Amen.

*Restore to me the joy of your salvation and grant me a willing spirit, to sustain me.*          (Psalm 51:12)

## Naji Abi-Hashem

Every time we violate our values or faith, we suffer from inner tension and guilt feelings. This principle is true, regardless of our religious commitment or ideological orientation. It is a function of conscience that God has designed, as part of His image within us. Each time we intentionally commit a sin or consciously fall into a temptation, we endure serious consequences. Some element dies inside of us, as if sin has a destructive power to kill healthy spiritual cells in our organism. To recover from that impact is, at times, like recovering from a major surgical operation.

On the other hand, our conscience will stop bothering us if we repeatedly violate the same value or standard. Gradually, we lose the intensity of the guilt, not because our conscience has become crippled but because our norms have been modified, softened, and therefore, compromised. Mercifully, God affirms us in that when failure occurs, restoration is needed and forgiveness is available. We are called to be a people of principles, to cultivate righteousness and to have clear moral and ethical values based on sound biblical standards. May the Lord grant us that virtue.

*My times are in your hands.*                  (Psalm 31:15)

## Naji Abi-Hashem

Have you ever wondered why God would not intervene in your most difficult situation only to find out afterwards that He did, but His timing was different from yours? How often we struggle to receive an immediate answer from the Lord only to thank Him later for not responding to our emergencies, according to our wishes.

This does not mean that God is removed from our particular situation, or does not care about our own despair. But he sees the needs differently, and therefore, plans special strategies to see us through. This does not necessarily mean resolving the critical situation immediately, but equipping us with confidence and power to endure it. R Niebuhr wrote once: 'Living one day at a time, enjoying one moment at a time, and accepting hardship as a pathway to peace.'

During the long years of turmoil and foreign wars on our beloved land, Lebanon, we diligently and earnestly longed for peace. We desperately wanted the severe troubles to end. A prominent Lebanese pastor later testified: 'For years we prayed for peace and for the end of war in our country and God did not seem to answer us. So we stopped praying for the troubles to end and instead we started praying for courage, endurance, and strength. And God immediately answered!'

Beloved friend, although at times you may not fully understand, even when you cannot see God's hand, trust in His heart. For God is too wise to be mistaken, and He is too good to be unfair. He is definitely too omnipotent to be unable to be with you and relieve your despair.

*To him who loves us and has freed us from our sins by his blood, and has made us to be a kingdom and priests to serve his God and Father – to him be the glory and the power for ever and ever! Amen.* (Revelation 1:5–6)

## Lucien Accad

Although I do not always understand the things my God does, nor see the reasons behind the way He does them, I am glad that this is how He works. It is truly wonderful. I love the ways of the Lord.

Even though I ask questions; 'Why Lord?' from deep in my heart, and while I wonder how I can carry on, I have no doubt in my soul that He knows and loves and cares. He is described as the one 'who loves us', Jesus who 'freed us from our sins', and at what a price. Jesus who has made us to be priests to serve His God and Father.

I don't expect answers to all my questions, just the peace that comes from knowing that He loves me, the peace of being free to love Him. If I am to serve my God I cannot claim as my right an easier life than that of Jesus. No, it will be hard at times. Answers are not necessary. All I need is to know how to live righteously before Him and, through the sadness and trials of this terrible world, praise and glorify His wonderful, mighty name.

*But God came to Abimelech in a dream one night.*

(Genesis 20:3)

*If you are pleased with me, teach me your ways so I may know you.* (Exodus 33:13)

## Open Doors Contact Person

Some believers in Sabah have begun a new prayer strategy. Since they are prevented by law from reaching out to the Muslims, they are asking the Lord to bring the Muslims to them, through signs and wonders. And the Lord is answering their prayers.

In one case, a man came into a Christian bookshop, requesting to buy a Bible. He told the following story.

'Some time ago he had a dream. In that dream, he was taken to several places to find peace. He could not find it anywhere. He heard a voice telling him to go to such and such a place and buy a Bible. The man believed his dream and came to that very book shop to get his Bible. He has since found peace with God through the reading of His Word.'

God certainly works in mysterious ways.

We may not have a dream today, but we have God's Word. A light to our path and a lamp for our feet. He who reads it and obeys it will never walk in darkness. Not even in the darkest night.

# March 30

David witnesses the backsliding and sin of his people. They claim not to need God any more. 'There is no God.' David calls such people 'fools'. He prays for his people and asks God for help and deliverance from this dangerous situation.

## David

The fool says in his heart, 'There is no God.' They are
   corrupt, their deeds are vile; there is no one who does
   good.
The LORD looks down from heaven on the sons of men
   to see if there are any who understand, any who seek
   God.
All have turned aside, they have together become
   corrupt; there is no one who does good, not even one.
Will evildoers never learn – those who devour my people
   as men eat bread and who do not call on the LORD?
There they are, overwhelmed with dread, for God is
   present in the company of the righteous.
You evildoers frustrate the plans of the poor, but the
   LORD is their refuge.                    (Psalm 14:1–6)

## Remarkable Remarks
### *Prayer*

*Pastor Ha – Vietnam:*

> 'My simple theology is:
> If you have problems: pray
> If you have many problems: pray more.'

*Unknown:*

> 'God does not lay a burden on our back to break our neck,
> but to get us on our knees.'

*John Bunyan* (from jail):

> 'Were it lawful, I could pray for greater trouble for
> greater comfort sake.'

*Phillip Brooks:*

> 'I do not pray for a lighter load,
> but for a stronger back.'

*Somebody:*

> 'If your problems are too small to pray for,
> they are also to small to worry about.'

*William Cowper:*

> 'Satan trembles when he sees,
> the weakest saint upon his knees.'

> *'Lord, teach us to pray. . . . '*     (Luke 11:1)

# April

## Writers for the month

*Horacio Herrera* from Cuba. Because of his leading role in the Cuban Church, he writes using a pseudonym.

*Andrés Noriega* from Cuba. This pastor and Bible distributor has a tremendous task in the spreading of the Gospel in Cuba. He also uses a pseudonym.

*Gustava Figueroa* from Cuba. An itinerant evangelist and writer also with a pseudonym.

*The Israelites groaned in their slavery and cried out, and their cry for help because of their slavery went up to God. God heard their groaning and he remembered his covenant with Abraham, with Isaac and with Jacob. So God looked on the Israelites and was concerned about them.*

(Exodus 2:23–25)

## Moses

God knows our needs. He is aware of our struggles, our hardships and our tears. He sees how His people are being persecuted. He sees your spiritual groaning: for your children, for your health, for your loneliness.

'And God remembered his covenant.' God's promises are 'yes' and 'amen'.

Despite all our circumstances He assures us; 'I am with you.' We may groan and cry – as long as we direct our cries towards Him who is our help and our salvation.

'He was concerned about them.' He still is. He is concerned about his children who suffer.

Whatever your situation may be: 'Your help comes from the Lord ... He will not let your foot slip ... the Lord watches over you ... the Lord will keep you from all harm ...' (Psalm 121).

'And God is faithful; He will not let you be tempted, he will also provide a way out so that you can stand up under it' (1 Corinthians 10:13).

# April 2

*By faith he left Egypt, not fearing the king's anger; he persevered because he saw him who is invisible.*

(Hebrews 11:27)

## Moses

Moses identified himself with his people in word and deed. His confrontation with the cruel Egyptian is one example of this. Even so Moses committed a cardinal fault. His motive (to help the Israeli slave) was good, but his method (killing the Egyptian slave) was wrong.

This incident became a turning point in his life. He fled from the palace to the desert. There he tended the sheep of his father-in-law Jethro, for forty years. Only after that was God able to use him to lead the 'sheep of Israel' out of Egypt. Moses had to learn that he was unable to save the people of Israel in his own strength, only in the strength of God.

What a change! The killer-prince became, 'a very humble man, more humble than anyone else on the face of the earth' (Numbers 12:3). 'By faith Moses ... refused to be known as the son of Pharaoh's daughter. He chose to be ill-treated along with the people of God rather than to enjoy the pleasures of sin which are for a short time' (Hebrews 11:24, 25).

'He persevered because he saw him who is invisible.'

Whoever sees the Invisible can do the impossible. To do this may require a return to the place where the problems began ... not to take revenge but to save.

*The one who calls you is faithful and he will do it.*

(1 Thessalonians 5:24)

## Moses

God had prepared Moses to lead his people out of Egypt, but was he willing to accept the task? No, he was not. Five times he argued with God. Five times God gave him a promise. Forty years before, Moses was so self-confident that he was convinced he could deliver Israel in his own strength. Now he felt inferior and unqualified. He told God that he lacked prestige. 'Who am I?' That he lacked a message; 'What shall I tell them?' He was convinced that the people would not believe him: 'The Lord did not appear to you.'

He presented God with a long list of disabilities. But instead of winning God's approval, God became angry with Moses. God always will, when His children limit Him, merely because they feel unqualified.

'Not that we are competent in ourselves ... but our competence comes from God' (2 Corinthians 3:5).

When He calls He enables. No reason to complain – every reason to trust.

When I try – I fail. When I trust – He succeeds.

*When they came to Marah, they could not drink its water
because it was bitter.*                    (Exodus 15:23)

*Then they came to Elim, where there were twelve springs
and seventy palm trees, and they camped there near the
water.*                                    (Exodus 15:27)

## Moses

If I were to sum up the situation of the Suffering Church I
would use the two above mentioned verses. Hardship, defeat,
persecution and bitterness on the one side, and provision,
victory, and springs of living water on the other side.

Is this not a picture of our walk with God as well?

Beside each bitter Marah pool there grows a tree. When
that tree is cast into the water, the bitterness changes into
sweetness.

A beautiful picture of the cross of Jesus, symbol of
redemption and salvation.

Praise God, there are more Elims in life than Marahs. No
desert march without palm trees and springs at last. We may
stay at Elim for a while. To be refreshed and strengthened
God permits disappointments (Marah) but also gives plenty
of surprises (Elim).

Where are you today? Remember, even at Marah there is
the tree of life.

And in between Marah and Elim we find these wonderful
words:

'...If you listen carefully to the voice of the Lord
your God and do what is right in his eyes, if you pay
attention to his commands and keep all his decrees, I
will not bring on you any of the diseases I brought on
the Egyptians, for I am the Lord, who heals you.'
                                    (Exodus 15:26)

*In the desert the whole community grumbled against Moses and Aaron. The Israelites said to them, 'If only we had died by the Lord's hand in Egypt. Then we sat round pots of meat and ate all the food we wanted, but you have brought us out into the desert to starve this entire assembly to death.'* (Exodus 16:2, 3)

## Moses

We may stay at Elim for a while, but we may not live there. We need to move on – to the promised land. 'The whole Isralite community set out from Elim and came to the Desert of Sin, which is between Elim and Sinai' (Exodus 16:1).

There are certain spiritual lessons which cannot easily be learned at Elim, they need to be learned in the desert of life: that God can supply all our needs whatever they may be, wherever we are.

When the Isralites had no more food to eat they grumbled against Moses and Aaron, yes, against God.

They said things they should never have said. Unfortunately, we often do likewise during times of grumbling.

Unbelief has a short memory. They remembered the food in Egypt, but forgot the lashes of the Egyptians. They forgot how they had cried to God for help. They forgot God's miracles, the great Exodus, the miraculous walk through the Red Sea, the refreshing stay at Elim, just a couple of days ago. Alas, unbelief has a short memory.

Praise God. **He** has endless patience. He provided miracle food: manna. Enough for every day. Whenever a grumbling fit threatens you, review the past and recount the Lord's deliverance in years gone by. Did He supply in the past? He will do so in the future. Because He is the 'I AM'.

# April 6

*So Moses went back to the Lord and said, 'Oh, what a great sin these people have committed! They have made themselves gods of gold. But now, please forgive their sin – but if not, then blot me out of the book you have written.'*

(Exodus 32:31–32)

## Moses

This is one of the most moving and pathetic verses of the Old Testament.

Moses' intercession on Israel's behalf is an overwhelming lesson in love and concern. He made it clear to God that he wanted to die with his people if they were not spared. He offered the greatest sacrifice he knew: his own relationship with God and his hope of eternal salvation. Of course Moses could not atone for the people; that is why Jesus had to come. But Moses was Christlike as he offered himself. We can never be the atonement for sin as Christ was, but we can play a Christlike sacrificial role. When we intercede for others – our children, our family, our country, our brothers and sisters who suffer – they will be protected. In doing so I am willing to get the blows.

There is a great difference between prayer and intercession. Prayer is what you do for yourself: you pray for blessing, health, protection. Intercession is when you stand in the gap for others.

Abraham was such an intercessor: praying for Sodom and Gomorrah. Moses interceded for others.

What about you?

Intimate fellowship with God is possible for everyone, but it is not to be taken for granted. To serve God whilst living in sin is impossible. We must show by our words and our deeds that we follow and obey the Lord.

## David

*LORD, who may dwell in your sanctuary? Who may live*
*on your holy hill?*
*He whose walk is blameless and who does what is*
*righteous, who speaks the truth from his heart*
*and has no slander on his tongue, who does his neighbor*
*no wrong and casts no slur on his fellow-man,*
*who despises a vile man but honors those who fear the*
*LORD, who keeps his oath even when it hurts,*
*who lends his money without usury and does not accept*
*a bribe against the innocent. He who does these*
*things will never be shaken.* (Psalm 15)

*You will fill me with joy in your presence* – part 1.
(Psalm 16:11b)

## Horacio Herrera

One of the members of my church had been in prison for his faith for more than 15 years. I had not seen him since his release. But one day we met. He told me: 'Pastor, only the presence of Christ kept me alive; in the nights of shadow and fear He was at my side.'

I knew this was true, because He had been that near to me also when I was in prison.

'In His presence' is not just a theological and theoretical truth. No, it may be experienced. Or should I say: 'I speak from experience.'

Those painful experiences, horror, bitterness, doubts (yes, doubts too!) are forgotten when the presence of God comes and fills us with joy and peace – even under the most horrible circumstances.

Do we need to be in prison to experience His presence? No, we have the privilege to enter the most Holy Place by the blood of Jesus ... let us draw near to God ... (Hebrews 10:19–22).

The darker the place (prison) the clearer the light of His presence will shine. Let us draw near to God always – in times of hardship and in times of prosperity – in times of sorrow and in times of joy.

'You will fill me with joy in your presence, with eternal pleasures at your right hand.'

*You will fill me with joy in your presence* – part 2.

(Psalm 16:11)

## Horacio Herrera

Thirty years of labor for God in an atheistic country have taught me a secret. For that bad hour, that dark night, that gloomy day, that time of temptation, that moment of trial and those years of persecution ... just one moment in His presence will compensate for all.

The presence of God makes us conscious that everything worldly is trivial, and temporary.

After 'Marah' (place of bitter water) there will always come an 'Elim' (an oasis) where the bitterness of hardship will be changed in the sweetness of His presence. After the desert of terrible trials will come the Canaan – a land of flowing with milk and honey.

It reminds me of a song we often sang in our church. It has been present in my soul for all these years and I hope to live it till the end of my days.

'We will be faithful to the one that bought us with His blood. We will follow Christ, even if a thousand voices all around us call. If the road is full of thorns and the cross is heavy, a moment in His presence will compensate for all.'

## April 10

*He who dwells in the shelter of the Most High will rest in*
*the shadow of the Almighty.* (Psalm 91:1)

## Horacio Herrera

While ministering to the believers in Cuba during a time of
crisis we came across Joshua 20. It talks about the 'cities of
refuge' and we compared it with God – who is our eternal
refuge.

The cities of refuge in Joshua 20 were for those who had
killed somebody accidentally or unintentionally. They could
flee to those cities and find protection until they had stood
trial (Joshua 20:6). Psalm 91 speaks about God – our eternal
refuge.

We may flee to Him in times of trouble. We do not have
to stand trial, because that trial has already taken place: 'He
forgave us all our sins, having canceled the written code, that
was against us and that stood opposed to us: he took it away,
nailing it to the cross' (Colossians 2:14).

We can therefore call on the Lord in days of trouble and
say: 'You are my refuge and my fortress, my God, in whom I
trust' (Psalm 91:2).

And listen to the promise: 'He will save you from the
fowler's snare ... He will cover you with his feathers and
under his wings you will find refuge; his faithfulness will be
your shield and rampart. You will not fear the terror of the
night, nor the arrow that flies by day ... I will be with him in
trouble, I will deliver him and honor him. With long life will I
satisfy him and show him my salvation' (Psalm 91).

Is there anything troubling you? Flee to Him – your eternal refuge, and rest in the shelter of the Most High – your
Abba – your Father.

*I, John, your brother and companion in the suffering and kingdom and patient endurance that are ours in Jesus, was on the island of Patmos because of the word of God and the testimony of Jesus.* (Revelation 1:9)

## Horacio Herrera

To live on an island is very interesting and challenging. Having been born on an island myself (Cuba) I find it interesting to meditate on John who was on the isle of Patmos.

It was not an interesting place for him. He was sent there to be imprisoned, lonely, isolated. No contact with other countries, without the support of friends and family. That must have been very, very difficult for a 90 year-old man.

Yet, John not only survived, he was also given revelations that no man had ever been given before.

Our God is not limited. Distances are no problem to Him. He sometimes allows us to get into a prison to reveal something very special. That sounds strange – yet true.

Is it that God could not reveal these wonderful things when John was still going around preaching, teaching in freedom? That he was so busy for the Lord that there was hardly any moment to relax and listen to God?

I do not know if I understand John's attitude correctly. He must have taken much time to be with God. Yet God allowed him to be sent to a lonely place to reveal the future to him. John transformed the island into a sanctuary. His loneliness into the company of millions of angels and his exile into the entrance of heaven.

Yes, God can change our problems into His plans.

*On the Lord's Day I was in the Spirit, and I heard behind me a loud voice like a trumpet, which said: Write...* (Revelation 1:10)

## Horacio Herrera

John was in the Spirit on the Lord's Day. He must have been in prayer – worshipping God – interceding for his 'spiritual children' in Turkey.

He must have been in tune with God. God can only reveal eternal truths to us when we are in touch with Him.

No room for complaints: Lord get me out of this prison, Lord rescue me from this island of isolation, Lord I am of no use here, deliver me please.

If this would have been John's attitude, God would surely have revealed other things to him: His presence, His peace. But John was in touch with God. He was 'in the Spirit'. Despite the circumstances, suffering and loneliness, John was in tune with the Lord.

We too need to move our eyes away from circumstances and look up to God. 'Let us fix our eyes on Jesus' (Hebrews 12:2).

Not on problems, not on defeats, but on Him whose eyes 'range throughout the earth to strengthen those whose hearts are fully committed to Him' (2 Chronicles 16:9).

Maybe you are often lonely, in despair, in darkness. Be encouraged by John's situation and attitude. Be in the Spirit and transform your horrible Patmos into a beautiful place of worship. Then you will hear the voice of the Lord.

What more can we desire?

*But you will receive power when the Holy Spirit comes upon you and you will be my witnesses . . .* (Acts 1:8)

*And surely I am with you always, to the very end of the age.* (Matthew 28:20)

## Horacio Herrera

There are various reasons why we so often feel alone. We feel alone when we lose a loved one. Or when we go through times of suffering, spiritual or physical. We feel alone when we are forgotten or feel rejected, sometimes ignored or even despised.

The Lord exhorts us to hold on to Him; and He holds on to us. The disciples were saddened when Jesus went back to heaven. They felt alone, but the angel of the Lord gave them a wonderful promise, together with a great task 'This Jesus will come back'.

One day, the Lord will return in glory. We will be changed into His likeness and we shall be like Him.

What a day that will be – a day without end.

Christians do not have a hopeless end, but an endless hope.

In the meantime He will guide us by His Spirit, who lives in us and who will be with us, until we meet our Savior.

We certainly can face the future with these promises. But that is not the end. He also gives us something to do. God's promises are connected to a task; they always are.

'And you shall be my witnesses.'

No time to sit back and spend all our time lamenting and complaining. There is work to be done.

Work till He comes.

When we do so we will experience this great truth:

'And surely, I am with you always, to the very end of the age.'

# April 14

David's life is in danger. We do not know of which danger he speaks. He does not think it necessary to mention that. What is important to him is that the believer is always safe in God's hand, under all circumstances.

## David

*Keep me safe, O God, for in you I take refuge.*
*I said to the LORD, 'You are my Lord; apart from you*
*I have no good thing.'*
*I will praise the LORD, who counsels me; even at night*
*my heart instructs me.*
*I have set the LORD always before me. Because he is at*
*my right hand, I will not be shaken.*
*You have made known to me the path of life; you will*
*fill me with joy in your presence, with eternal*
*pleasures at your right hand.*

(Psalm 16:1–2, 7, 8, 11)

*If we are distressed, it is for your comfort.*

(2 Corinthians 1:6)

## Horacio Herrera

There is an infinite and glorious harmony enclosed in these verses which is a reality for the Body of Christ, worldwide. If one is distressed, it is for the comfort of somebody else.

What does Paul mean by this? The answer is found in the preceding verses (2 Corinthians 1:3–4). God comforts Paul in his troubles so that he can comfort those in trouble with the comfort he himself received from God.

If we have never been poor, how can we fully understand the situation of those who are?

If we have never been in pain, how can we help those who are? Having experienced it ourselves, we can feel with others who go through that hardship today.

What a wonderful unity in the body. Even if it is dispersed throughout the world, it keeps a harmonious unity. If any one is troubled, the other is comforted. It is almost a mystery.

Our present times of suffering become your encouragement. Because we share with you – even through this book – how God has strengthened us in times of trouble. So that you can be assured that God has not forsaken us and that He will not forsake you if you may ever have to endure the hardships we have already endured.

'And surely I am with you always' (Matthew 28:20).

*If one part suffers, every part suffers with it.*

(1 Corinthians 12:26)

## Horacio Herrera

Luke informs us in Acts 12 that Peter was imprisoned, but the church was earnestly praying to God for him. The church felt that Peter was an integral part of them and thus they felt prisoners with him.

We are a universal Body of Christ. We feel joy or affliction, happiness or sadness, freedom or persecution with all the members of that Body, wherever that part of the Body may be.

The affliction of our brothers in Eastern Europe are ours, the struggles of the Christians in Muslim countries are our struggles also. The victories of the Christians in any part of the world, are also our victories.

'Remember those in prison as if you were their fellow prisoners and those who are ill-treated as if you yourselves were suffering.'

Another translation says: 'Since you are also in the Body.' Let us remember them today in our prayers – stretching out our hands of fellowship to them. In doing so, we can bless those who are still in prison for their faith in Jesus Christ. While praying, we feel their burdens, their hardships and their pain.

'Carry each other's burdens, and in this way you will fulfill the law of Christ' (Galatians 6:2).

*By the rivers of Babylon we sat and wept when we remember Zion.* (Psalm 137:1)

*About midnight Paul and Silas were praying and singing hymns to God.* (Acts 16:25)

## Horacio Herrera

Liberty is a gift of great value to humanity, which you realize best when it is lost.

For the followers of Christ there is always liberty, joy and victory whatever the circumstances may be.

Jeremiah gives an example of a situation when liberty is lost. There is mourning, crying, desolation and bondage (Jeremiah 33).

The captured in Babylon echo this feeling of mourning when they remember Zion and the destruction of their homeland.

'How can we sing the songs of the Lord while in a foreign land?' (Psalm 137:4). 'We sat and wept' (Psalm 137:1).

But what a different picture of glory, joy and hope is presented by Isaiah when he announces the end of captivity (Isaiah 12).

Sing with joy, and feast, for captivity has ended. There will be no more slavery. What Isaiah is saying is that we need to leave our bondage behind and live in optimism, even if all the circumstances are against us.

That is what Paul and Silas did. They changed night into day from the prison in Philippi. They turned their prison into a church and their crying into a song of joy.

Let us acknowledge our painful conditions – yes – but let us not stop there. The more we concentrate on our sorrows, the more we will cry.

Let us lift up our eyes to the Lord. He will change our wailing into dancing. He will remove our sackcloth and clothe us with joy (Psalm 30:11).

Lord open our eyes – that we may see.

# April 18

*I have been crucified with Christ and I no longer live, but Christ lives in me.* (Galatians 2:20)

## Horacio Herrera

During the time that rebels in Colombia attacked Christians and churches, the following happened: A group of Christians were meeting in their church in the hills, when all of a sudden a man came running to the church, shouting: 'A group of killers are on their way to this church.' For a moment fear filled the church. Should they all run away and hide? At this moment of despair a brother stood up and said: 'Fear not, you are not in Colombia, you are in Christ.'

It had such an impact on the believers that instant calm returned to the group. Or, as another Christian leader in Latin America stated: 'In order to be a Christian here, you have to recognize the truth, that any extra day you live will be considered a bonus.'

Yes, we have died already. Death is not awaiting us. We have experienced it already – in Christ – and have been raised to life eternal. The coming death of the body is therefore just a passage, a pass-through.

Let us use the bonus time we have to live for Him.

'He died for all, that those who live should no longer live for themselves, but for him . . . ' (2 Corinthians 5:15).

*PS* Climatic circumstances (a tropical rain storm) did not allow the group of rebel killers to reach the church in the hills. ' . . . He sends rain on the righteous and unrighteous' (Matthew 5:45). Hallelujah.

*These are written that you may believe that Jesus is the Christ, the Son of God, and that by believing you may have life in His name.* (John 20:31)

## Horacio Herrera

The Gospel of John offers great encouragement to us, not only in times of prosperity but also in times of hardship and trial.

To the disoriented, thirsty Samaritan woman He offers water that will quench her thirst (John 4).

To the spiritually hungry He gives the bread of life (John 6).

To the ones that walk in darkness without any sense of destination He provides the light of the world (John 8).

To the defenceless who suffer from the wolf and the lion He assures that He is the good shepherd (John 10).

To the ones that see no way out He says that He is the door to freedom (John 10).

To the ones that have lost the meaning of life He says: 'I am the way, the truth and the life' (John 14).

To the ones that are afraid of death He says: 'I am the resurrection and the life. He who believes on me will live, even though he dies' (John 11).

The 'I AM' comes to us today, to do just that for us.

*That at the name of Jesus every knee should bow ... and every tongue confess that Jesus Christ is Lord.*

(Philippians 2:10–11)

## Horacio Herrera

When Paul wrote to the churches in Rome, he knew about their situation. They had no reason to comfortably celebrate their new life in Christ Jesus. On the contrary, they experienced painful separation from family members when they were discovered in their religious practices. They knew how real the lion's den was in their own city. But he had a message of hope for them (Romans 8:28–39). Death would not be able to separate them from Christ. Fallen angels or demons had no power over them. Worldly powers are under God's control.

The present – is passing by.

The future – is in Christ's hands.

The heights – are still under the King.

The depths – cannot keep those who die in Christ.

Anything else in all creation, can do no harm to those who belong to the family of believers.

We – and they – will one day bow down before the King of Kings and confess that Jesus Christ is Lord. They will have to confess, we will do so with all of our hearts: you are the Christ, our Savior and our Lord.

People are seeking David to take his life. He has gone through this many times before. Three times David professes to be innocent. Three times he asks God to listen to his prayer. He does that, knowing that God knows what he needs and is willing to hear his prayer.

I call on you, O God, for you will answer me.

---

### David

*Hear, O LORD, my righteous plea; listen to my cry. Give
    ear to my prayer, it does not rise from deceitful lips.
May my vindication come from you; may your eyes see
    what is right.
I call on you, O God, for you will answer me; give ear
    to me and hear my prayer.
Show the wonder of your great love, you who save by
    your right hand those who take refuge in you from
    their foes.
Keep me as the apple of your eye; hide me in the
    shadow of your wings
from the wicked who assail me, from my mortal enemies
    who surround me.* (Psalm 17:1–2, 6–9)

# April 22

*Some trust in chariots and some in horses, but we trust in the name of the Lord our God. They are brought to their knees and fall, but we rise up and stand firm.*

(Psalm 20:7–8)

## Andrés Noriega

We live in a time where materialism is defended, where being an atheist is normal, and being a Christian abnormal.

Many people criticize our faith saying it is a remnant of the past, of colonialism and exploitism. They conclude that the Church is for the weak, a shelter for the defeated.

According to their philosophy our faith is a failure and the Christian race will soon become extinct – to make place for a new, perfect society.

Communism nevertheless, has lost its grip. They are the ones that have failed. The new, perfect society turned out to be an utopia. The Church, on the other side, has grown. The weak Christians turned out to be so strong that all atheistic teaching could not destroy them. The so-called faint-hearted, turned out to be people full of hope, joy and power.

Today's society is in a bad shape, while the Church of Jesus Christ awaits the return of the King of kings – Jesus our Lord.

'They are brought down and fall – but we rise and stand firm.'

Trust in the name of the Lord our God and stand firm with us.

*It is not good for the man to be alone.* (Genesis 2:18)

## Gustavo Figueroa

Many novels have been published about the ordeal of people who managed to survive in lonely places.

Think of *The Count of Monte Cristo* which describes the ordeals of a man who was confined to a cell in a fortress, where he spent many years in complete isolation. Or think of *Robinson Crusoe*, surviving on an island, or *Treasure Island* which tells the story of a man who was abandoned on an island.

We enjoy these books and admire the people who survived, despite extreme problems and circumstances, often feeling forgotten and very, very lonely.

To feel lonely, however, does not mean that you are without company. One can live among crowds of people and still feel very, very lonely.

Our Scripture for today says: 'It is not good for the man to be alone.'

The Lord wants us to pay attention to those who are lonely, forgotten, alone.

Let us pray for them today, especially for those who are in prison for their faith in Jesus Christ. Let us pray for a believer who stands alone in a Muslim village.

Let us do something for a person in our own neighborhood who has no friends, or for one who experiences great sorrow or pain, for whom we can become a blessing in a time of need.

# April 24

*I will be with you.*                    (Exodus 3:12)

## Gustavo Figueroa

Many great men of God experienced loneliness. In the coming days we will take a closer look at some of them.

Moses was such a man. Though we remember him as a man who spoke to God face to face (Exodus 33:11), we also know from the Scriptures that he was a very lonely man.

From the time he was a baby – lying in a basket – until the time he climbed Mount Nebo to see the Promised Land, he walked alone.

Though he was living in a palace, he felt alone, because his heart was with his people, Israel. While tending the sheep in the desert, he was lonely, living in exile for forty years.

It was on one of those days, while tending the flock on the far side of the desert, that the Angel of the Lord appeared to him. Moses must have thought many times that he was alone, that God must have forgotten him – but he was never alone. The Lord accompanied him wherever he went.

The experience at the burning bush was imprinted in such a way that he realized: I never walk alone.

Whether we experience God's presence, or walk in the desert alone, His word says: 'I will be with you – now and always.'

*At my first defence, no-one came to my support, but every-one deserted me ... But the Lord stood at my side and gave me strength.* (2 Timothy 4:16–17)

## Gustavo Figueroa

Do you hear Paul's disappointment in these words? And rightly so. He had led hundreds, if not thousands of people to the Lord. Churches were planted, the lordship of Jesus Christ was proclaimed and the Gospel was preached in many towns and countries. That led to his imprisonment and trial.

When he entered the courtroom he must have looked around to see where his friends, the Christians, were sitting. He saw no-one. What a disappointment that must have been. The moment he needed them most, they were absent. In fact, it was even worse. Not only were they absent, they had deserted him.

One can find excuses for not being in the courtroom. Too dangerous, to busy with other things, maybe even praying for Paul at home. But 'everyone deserted me' is done voluntarily. They wanted nothing to do with Paul.

We, who live in countries where we also have to appear in court, often feel like Paul. Forgotten, even deserted. 'But the Lord stood at my side and gave me strength.' This wonderful experience does not relieve us of our responsibility. We have a part to play – willingly, lovingly. And so encourage a lonely brother in need.

# April 26

*I am unworthy of all the kindness and faithfulness you have shown your servant.* (Genesis 32:10)

## Gustavo Figueroa

I have a tendency to dislike Jacob. I always think of him as the liar, deceiver and crook. Indeed a man who was unworthy of God's kindness and faithfulness. And yet that is exactly what the Lord did show to Jacob. Instead of looking at Jacob's failures, let us look at God's goodness and realize that we, who are not any better than Jacob, may experience the same goodness of our loving Father.

When Jacob was running away from home, after lying to his old, blind father, and after deceiving his brother, he stopped '... because the sun had set...' (Genesis 28:11).

'...Taking one of the stones there, he put it under his head and lay down to sleep: He had a dream in which he saw a stairway resting on the earth, with its top reaching to heaven, and the angels of God were ascending and descending on it. There above it stood the Lord, and he said: "I am the Lord, the God of your father Abraham and the God of Isaac ... I am with you, and will watch over you wherever you go..."'.

What an experience. Jacob felt alone (and we would add, rightly so!) but he was still accompanied by angels and in the presence of God himself. That's why he testified: 'Surely the Lord is in this place, and I was not aware of it' (Genesis 28:12).

It strikes me when I read: 'The angels of the Lord were ascending and descending...' (Genesis 28:12). We would have figured that they were descending (from God to Jacob) first. But no, they were already with Jacob – the deceiver, the liar, the crook. Not to approve his actions, but because the Lord said: 'I will not leave you...' Great is His faithfulness.

*But while Joseph was there in the prison the Lord was with him.* (Genesis 39:20–21)

## Gustavo Figueroa

If ever there was a man who could have doubted God's plans for his life, it was Joseph. Sold by his brothers, thrown into prison, in a foreign land; surely a man without future. In spite of it all, this young man remained faithful to God. He stood firm in times of temptation, and paid the price for it: imprisonment.

Humanly speaking he should have been rewarded by God for his faithfulness. It seems so difficult to understand God's ways. For us, who know the end of the story, it is easy to understand. But Joseph did not know the final outcome. The only thing he experienced was sorrow, pain and punishment.

But Joseph changed his prison into a place of worship. 'But while Joseph was in prison, the Lord was with him.'

It is very possible that you too have experienced times of seeming defeat, loneliness, lack of support. You have concluded that nobody cares about your situation. But remember: The God who was with Joseph is with you today, whatever the circumstances.

*He came to a broom tree, sat down under it and prayed that he might die.* (1 Kings 19:4)

## Gustavo Figueroa

From the mountain of victory, to the mountain of despair. That was the experience of Elijah and often our experience as well.

'Elijah was a man just like us' (James 5:17). He had just witnessed God's power at Mount Carmel. Fire had come down from heaven in a miraculous way. Instead of repenting before God, Jezebel was furious. 'May the gods deal with me . . . if by this time tomorrow I do not make your (Elijah's) life like that of one of them' (the priests who died).

Elijah did not fear the threats of 850 prophets of Baal and Asherah, but he feared the threat of one woman.

He was so downcast that he wanted to die. At least, that is what he said. But did he really want to die? If so, all he had to do was show himself to Jezebel. She would have loved to accommodate him.

'Elijah was a man just like us', knowing the joy of victory and experiencing the pain of defeat. But the Lord had more work for him to do. 'Go back the way you came.'

No time to complain. Let's get up and do what God expects us to do.

In this beautiful psalm David thanks God for deliverance from his enemies, especially King Saul. This mighty God has always helped in the past. David trusts in Him, also for the future.

## David

*I love you, O LORD, my strength.*
*The LORD is my rock, my fortress and my deliverer; my*
*God is my rock, in whom I take refuge. He is my*
*shield and the horn of my salvation, my stronghold.*
*I call to the LORD, who is worthy of praise, and I am*
*saved from my enemies.*
*The cords of death entangled me; the torrents of*
*destruction overwhelmed me.*
*The cords of the grave coiled around me; the snares of*
*death confronted me.*
*In my distress I called to the LORD; I cried to my God*
*for help. From his temple he heard my voice; my cry*
*came before him, into his ears.*        (Psalm 18:1–6)

### Remarkable Remarks
#### *Attitude of Christians Under Pressure*

*Romanian pastor:*

'Christians are like nails; the harder you hit them, the deeper they go.'

*Nijole Sudanaite* – Russian Christian under pressure, when asked whether she would like to emigrate:

'Absolutely not. My commission is to stay here and take care of God's people who are in great need.'

*Young Chinese lady preacher* – when asked if she might get into trouble for her preaching:

'It is the way of the cross.'

*Wong Ming Dao – China:*

'We are soldiers under the banner of Jesus Christ in a spiritual battle. We can only advance and never retreat.'

*Galina – Siberia:*

'All my suffering is worthwhile, even if I were to reach only one person for Christ.'

*Proverb:*

'Crosses are ladders that lead to heaven.'

*'Whoever loses his life for my sake will find it.'*
(Matthew 10:39)

# May

## Writers for the month

*Mehdi Dibaj* from Iran. While this book was being compiled, Mehdi Dibaj had been in prison for nine years. Early in 1994 he was released, but was murdered six months later. His courtroom defense was edited to form part of this book.

*. . . The Lord said to Joshua . . . Moses' assistant.*

(Joshua 1:1)

*After these things, Joshua, son of Nun, the servant of the Lord, died . . .*

(Joshua 24:29)

## Joshua

The book of Joshua starts with: 'Joshua, the servant of Moses.' It ends with: 'Joshua, the servant of God.'

Joshua was willing to be a servant of men. That qualified him to become a special servant of the Lord.

Servanthood was a very special aspect of Joshua's life. Many Christians are willing to serve God, but not each other. The disciples disputed who was the greatest among them. Christ looked right through their carnal problem. Whoever is willing to be the smallest among you will be honoured by God. That can be said of Joshua. It took a long period of preparation. Servanthood of men has a price tag attached to it. If we are not willing to pay that price, we can never become a real servant of God.

The secret of Joshua's success can be found in Exodus 33:11.

'The Lord would speak to Moses face to face, as a man speaks with his friend. Then Moses would return to the camp, but his young assistant Joshua son of Nun did not leave the tent.'

Joshua delighted to be in the presence of God. His walk with God in secret (revealed by his willingness to serve Moses!) prepared Joshua for his very special leadership.

Raised as a slave, trained as a servant, developed into a leader – Joshua, the servant of God.

Are you willing to go that same path?

*The Amalekites came and attacked the Israelites at Rephidim. Moses said to Joshua Choose some of our men and go out to fight the Amalekites. Tomorrow I will stand on top of the hill with the staff of God in my hands.*
(Exodus 17:8–9)

*As long as Moses held up his hands, the Israelites were winning, but whenever he lowered his hands, the Amalekites were winning. When Moses' hands grew tired, they took a stone and put it under him and he sat on it. Aaron and Hur held his hands up – one on one side, one on the other – so that his hands remainded steady till sunset. So Joshua overcame the Amalekite army with the sword.* (Exodus 17:11–13)

## Joshua

In this chapter, Joshua is mentioned for the first time in the Bible. A young man, appointed Commander-in-Chief in a war between Israel and Amalek.

Joshua was one of the youngest generals ever to serve in the Israelite army. General Douglas McArthur listed Joshua among the greatest generals of world history. President Theodore Roosevelt's favorite book in the Bible was the book of Joshua.

Already in this first encounter with Joshua, we see a spiritual principle in the Kingdom of God: Not by might, nor by power, but by My Spirit. 'Hands were lifted up to the throne of the Lord' (Exodus 17:15).

That does not eliminate human responsibility. Joshua still had to battle against the enemy in the valley. But the secret of the victory must be found in the spiritual battle that was fought. Hands uplifted to God. 'My help comes from the Lord' (Psalm 121).

Work as if everything depends on you. Pray as if everything depends on God.

*Ora et Labora* – Pray and work.

*Be strong and courageous. Do not be terrified; do not be
discouraged, for the Lord your God will be with you wherever you go.* (Joshua 1:9)

## Joshua

'Be strong and courageous.' Four times these words are
repeated in the first chapter of Joshua. That can only mean
one thing: Joshua was afraid. He needed the encouragement.
But when you think about it, how strange. If anybody could
be expected to show courage, it would had been Joshua. After
all, he was the youngest general in the Israelite army, which
says it all. He and Caleb were the only spies who came back
with a positive report after their expedition to the Promised
Land. While the other ten spies were full of fear, Joshua and
Caleb were full of faith and courage.

But now fear seems to have caught up with Joshua. Yet
it is not fear of man that bothers him. Neither is it fear of
danger, or fear to enter into battle. Joshua is frightened by
the enormous spiritual responsibility which rests upon his
shoulders: to take the people of Israel to the Promised Land
is not a small thing. This responsibility intimidates Joshua.
Such a task frightens him. That is why the Lord encourages
him over and over again by telling him: 'The Lord your God
will be with you!'

Then no wall proves to be too high and no giant too
strong.

Are there similar walls and giants in your life? Do you feel
small and weak like Joshua did? Today the Lord is saying to
you: 'be strong and courageous, for I, the Lord your God will
be with you wherever you go.'

*. . . are you for us or for our enemies? Neither, he replied.*
*. . . Then Joshua fell face down to the ground in reverence*
*and asked him: 'What message does my Lord have for his*
*servant?'* (Joshua 5:13, 14)

## Joshua

Shortly before the first big confrontation with Jericho, Joshua
had a very strange encounter himself.

He had only just been called to be the leader of his people,
and now he has been asked to surrender his leadership to the
commander of the army of the Lord.

Joshua's spiritual maturity is proven by the fact that he
would rather be second-in-command in God's army, than
first-in-command of his own.

When asked if the man was for or against the Israelites,
his only reply was: 'neither'. What the messenger of the Lord
was really saying was 'I have not come to take sides. I have
come to take over.'

Whoever is willing to surrender the leadership to God,
will experience that no wall is too high for God, no river too
deep, no problem too great.

Got any rivers you think are uncrossable?
Got any mountains you can't tunnel through?
**God** specializes in things thought impossible
He does the things others cannot do.

*By faith the walls of Jericho fell, after the people had marched around them for seven days.* (Hebrews 11:30)

## Joshua

After Joshua's voluntary surrender of his leadership to the commander of the army of the Lord, some more strange orders followed. 'March around the city.' 'Make seven priests carry trumpets in front of the Ark.' 'Do not give a war cry, do not raise your voices, do not say a word until the day I tell you to shout.'

Very unusual military commands. An army does not show itself to the enemy. You don't ask the chaplains to walk in the front lines, waving their Bibles.

It seemed so illogical, unprofessional, un-military. God's way of doing things often seems unreasonable.

Joshua had to learn that this was not going to be his war, done in his way, but God's war, done in God's way. He responded with an unquestioning obedience.

Faith expressed in obedience to God's Word is always the key to victory. And victory came, because Joshua and his people fully trusted God.

When you face a 'Jericho' in your life, you too may see the walls tumble down as you trust in God and in His way of handling a crisis situation.

*Then choose for yourself this day whom you will serve . . .*
*But as for me and my household, we will serve the Lord.*

(Joshua 24:15)

*Now then, throw away the foreign gods that are among*
*you and yield your hearts to the Lord, the God of Israel.*

(Joshua 24:23)

## Joshua

Once again Joshua addressed the nation. He reminded them of God's faithfulness and deliverance. Through his farewell message he stressed the grace of God. 'I gave,' 'I brought,' 'I destroyed,' 'I delivered.' Not once did he mention his own achievements because, simply, he acknowledged God's hand in it all.

He challenged the people to follow that God. He himself set the example; 'As for me and my household, we will serve the Lord.' He practised what he preached. His mind was made up, his course was clear: we will serve the Lord.

The people responded. 'We too will serve the Lord.' It was then that Joshua challenged them to prove their sincerity by their works. 'Throw away your idols.' We can only serve God fully if we throw our idols away! Idols of any kind. Any idol blocks the way to full communication with God. A price needs to be paid. A reward is awaiting: To walk with God – to the land of promise.

The God who came brought deliverance in the past, will continue to do so in the future, for He is the living God.

The Lord lives! Praise be to my Rock! Exalted be God my Savior! (Psalm 18:46).

---

### David

---

*As for God, his way is perfect; the word of the LORD is flawless. He is a shield for all who take refuge in him.*

*For who is God besides the LORD? And who is the Rock except our God?*

*It is God who arms me with strength and makes my way perfect.*

*He makes my feet like the feet of a deer; he enables me to stand on the heights.*

*He trains my hands for battle; my arms can bend a bow of bronze.*

*You give me your shield of victory, and your right hand sustains me; you stoop down to make me great.*

*You broaden the path beneath me, so that my ankles do not turn.*                               (Psalm 18:30–36)

*Remember those in prison as if you were their fellow prisoners, and those who are ill-treated as if you yourselves were suffering.* (Hebrews 13:2)

## Mehdi Dibaj

These days there are celebrations everywhere. People outside celebrate the day of the Revolution and you, my son, are celebrating your birthday today (17 years old).

Inside my prison cell I am celebrating my forty-third year of becoming a Christian and today I am celebrating the entering of the eighth year of the test of my faith in Jesus Christ our Lord.

There is a celebration and joy within my heart. I thank my loving God ever so much that He accounted me worthy to be here in prison for more than seven years now because of my love and faith in the Lord Jesus Christ. I thank my Christian brothers and sisters who have supported me with their prayers and love, so that the victory should belong to the Lord.

Victory is yours, risen Jesus, Son of the Creator, our Redeemer.

*If anyone would come after me, he must deny himself and take up his cross and follow me. For whoever wants to save his life will lose it, whoever loses his life for me will find it.* (Matthew 16:24–25)

## Mehdi Dibaj

One of my guards in prison once asked me: 'Does Jesus Christ know that He has someone in this prison who loves Him?' I told him: 'Jesus Christ our Lord has millions of people all over the world who love Him and who wish to sacrifice their lives for Him. I too wish to one of them.'

How sweet it will be if one day my life is sacrificed for Him. When my spirit with joy and purity will fly towards Jesus. I don't want to hide from you my dear son, that I always envied those Christians who all through Church history were martyred for Christ Jesus our Lord. Because for a Christian it is a loss to leave this world by natural death. What a privilege to live for our Lord and to die for Him as well. And I am prepared for the name of Jesus Christ our Lord not only to remain in prison but to give my life in His service as well. Because living is an opportunity for me to serve Christ and death is a better occasion to be with Christ.

*Never will I leave you; never will I forsake you.*
(Hebrews 13:5)

## Mehdi Dibaj

Jesus said: 'For whoever wants to save his life will lose it, but whoever loses his life for me will find it' (Matthew 16:25).

Every Christian should be willing to be such a sacrifice for God that he gets cleansed by the fire of hardships and sufferings. 'To this you were called, because Christ suffered for you, leaving you an example, that you should follow in his steps' (1 Peter 2:21).

> My heart rejoices as I walk with Jesus
> the world behind me, the cross before me
> I will follow Him for ever ... everyday.

He will never leave us. He will never forsake us. It is the wish of every father and child to walk together. God too wishes that we walk with Him – that is to obey Him.

'I am God Almighty; walk before me and be blameless.' Two people can only walk together if they agree together.

In the triumphal procession of Christ we will go forward by the power of God.

*God is our refuge and strength, an ever-present help in trouble. Therefore we will not fear, though the earth give way.* (Psalm 46:1–2)

## Mehdi Dibaj

In the story of Daniel's friends in the fiery oven, God teaches us an important spiritual truth: if we want to walk close to our Lord we must be willing to go into the fire because it is the safest place for us. Not only will our socks not burn, but our clothes will not even smell of fire.

I praise God that during these seven years that I have been in prison for my faith, the Lord Jesus Christ has been my strength in a wonderful way. I not only may walk close to Him in the midst of the fire, but I go forward as well.

He leads me through water and fire
He leads us in the way of the Cross.

Yes, God is our refuge and strength an ever-present help in trouble.

*Praise be to the Lord, to God our Savior, who daily bears our burdens.* (Psalm 68:19)

## Mehdi Dibaj

On a busy road with strong winds and heavy traffic, the crossing of such a road is a frightening experience. A child would be very scared and cry: 'Daddy carry me, daddy carry me.'

In our walk with God we often experience the same storms and danger. Sometimes the pressures are so intense that it seems impossible to go forward anymore.

In such storms, what should our attitude be? Is there any hope or help from God?

The Lord says; 'Call upon me in the day of trouble. I will deliver you and you will praise me.'

Yes, we may cast all our burdens upon Him, for He cares for us. He daily bears our burdens.

*Taste and see that the Lord is good; blessed is the man who takes refuge in him.* (Psalm 34:8)

## Mehdi Dibaj

In days of trouble I have learned to pray – listen – praise.

### Pray

'Keep me as the apple of your eye; hide me in the shadow of your wings from the wicked who assail me, from my mortal enemies who surround me' (Psalm 17:8).

### Listen

'Be still and know that I am God' (Psalm 46:10). 'It is good to wait quietly for the salvation of the Lord' (Lamentations 3:26).

### Praise

'I sought the Lord, and he answered me, he delivered me from all my fears. Those who look to him are radiant; their faces are never covered with shame. This poor man called and the Lord heard him. He saved him out of all his troubles. The angel of the Lord encamps around those who fear him and he delivers them. Taste and see that the Lord is good' (Psalm 34:4–8a).

David honors the God of creation. In His creation God reveals His glory. But not just in creation. Above all God speaks to us through His Word.

Beholding God's greatness in nature and in His Word, leads David to one prayer: May your greatness be seen through my life as well.

## David

*The heavens declare the glory of God; the skies proclaim the work of his hands.*

*Day after day they pour forth speech; night after night they display knowledge.*

*There is no speech or language where their voice is not heard.*

*Their voice goes out into all the earth, their words to the ends of the world. In the heavens he has pitched a tent for the sun,*

*The law of the LORD is perfect, reviving the soul. The statutes of the LORD are trustworthy, making wise the simple.*

*The precepts of the LORD are right, giving joy to the heart. The commands of the LORD are radiant, giving light to the eyes.*

*The fear of the LORD is pure, enduring forever. The ordinances of the LORD are sure and altogether righteous.*

*May the words of my mouth and the meditation of my heart be pleasing in your sight, O LORD, my Rock and my Redeemer.* (Psalm 19:1–4, 7–9, 14)

*Cast all your anxiety on him because he cares for you.*
(1 Peter 5:7)

## Mehdi Dibaj

What a joy for a little child to sit on the broad and strong shoulders of his father. From that height he watches the passing of people, the business in the streets. He has fun and feels safe. When he does get frightened he clenches his arms even tighter around his father's shoulders. He knows he can trust his father.

Is this not our position in Christ Jesus? In the day of trouble He hides us in His shelter.

'He who dwells in the shelter of the Most High will rest in the shadow of the Almighty. I will say of the Lord, "He is my refuge and my fortress, my God, in whom I trust"' (Psalm 91:1, 2). The everlasting Father is our refuge. His immortal arms are our support.

Whatever our situation may be, He is always our refuge. During these past nine years in prison for my love for Him I have had the joy again and again of experiencing His strong arms of support.

Have faith in God.

## May 16

*Though the mountains be shaken and the hills be removed, yet my unfailing love for you will not be shaken nor my covenant of peace be removed, says the Lord, who has compassion on you.* (Isaiah 54:10)

## Mehdi Dibaj

The Almighty God not only gives us strength to walk with Him, to go forward with Him or to go up with Him but also to come down with Him to the valley of the battle.

Or should I say: I may go up to Him – He will come down to me.

I may sit, in the heavenly places, on His 'broad shoulders', He will kneel down with me in the valley of battle and hold my hand. The more I visit Him up there – the more I experience His help down here.

The mountains of life may be shaken, the pains of being separated from my beloved family may hurt, the prison cell may be dark – His unfailing love for me is not shaken and my love for Him is growing stronger every day.

*Like clay in the hand of the potter, so are you in my hand.*
(Jeremiah 18:6)

## Mehdi Dibaj

It is to the humble that God gives His grace.

It is in the fire that gold becomes pure.

It is the rubbing and cutting that makes the diamond brilliant.

It is in high temperatures that the rust of the pot is burnt.

It is through the narrow gate that we enter the Kingdom of Heaven.

It is in great difficulties that men of God are made.

Lord, make me such a man.

*You hem me in – behind and before; you have laid your
hand upon me. Such knowledge is too wonderful for me,
too lofty for me to attain.*                    (Psalm 139:5–6)

## Mehdi Dibaj

Truly, living with God is glorious.

The darker the night, the closer the dawn.

The darker the clouds, the more plentiful the life-giving rains.

The narrower the way, the more God's unlimited help!

The greater the troubles, the more the comforts from God. Though the waves of the sea get higher, this can never disturb the calm of the depths!

Though the storm be violent, it cannot displace the mountain. Those who trust in the Lord are like mountains that cannot be shaken.

The person who lives in the shadow of the Almighty will never be disturbed by the heat.

*For no matter how many promises God has made, they are 'Yes' in Christ. And so through Him the 'Amen' is spoken by us to the glory of God.* (2 Corinthians 2:20)

## Mehdi Dibaj

'My soul clings to you; your right hand upholds me' (Psalm 63:8).

'When anxiety was great within me, your consolation brought joy to my soul' (Psalm 94:19).

'I will lie down and sleep in peace, for you alone, O Lord, make me dwell in safety' (Psalm 4:8).

'Even youths grow tired and weary, and young men stumble and fall, but those who hope in the Lord will renew their strength. They will soar on wings like eagles; they will run and not grow weary, they will walk and not be faint' (Isaiah 40:30).

'He gives strength to the weary, and increases the power of the weak' (Isaiah 40:29).

Blessed are we Christians, for we are God's children. I will thank Him forever for His loving kindness. I shout for joy in the night with my thankful heart. 'No eye has seen, no ear has heard, no mind has conceived what God has prepared for those who love Him – but God has revealed it to us by His Spirit' (1 Corinthians 2:9, 10).

What a good God! What an incredible Savior.

# May 20

*If we live, we live to the Lord; and if we die, we die to the Lord. So, whether we live or die, we belong to the Lord.*

(Romans 14:8)

## Mehdi Dibaj

My dear son, does it ever happen to you that you weep all night? But morning comes and joy flows.

Very soon we will see the fruit of the hard things in our lives and we will be satisfied.

This is our hope, the blessed hope that Christ is coming. He will lead us to life-giving springs.

To be with you, O Lord, is Paradise
To live in the Spirit is sweet and full of fruits
To die in your way, O Christ, is life itself.

They once asked: 'What will you do in the day of hardship and pressure?'

The answer: 'I welcome the difficulties with joy, because I can do all things through Christ who strengthens me.'

In the triumphal procession of Christ
We will go forward by the power of God
And spread the good news of His salvation.

This is a prayer for the king. We could also say: a prayer for the government. Paul writes about this in 1 Timothy 2:1–3. He exhorts us to pray for those who have been placed in authority over us, that we may lead peaceful and quiet lives in all godliness and holiness.

### David

*May the LORD answer you when you are in distress;*
*    may the name of the God of Jacob protect you.*
*May he send you help from the sanctuary and grant you*
*    support from Zion.*
*May he remember all your sacrifices and accept your*
*    burnt offerings.*
*May he give you the desire of your heart and make all*
*    your plans succeed.*
*We will shout for joy when you are victorious and will*
*    lift up our banners in the name of our God. May the*
*    LORD grant all your requests.*
*Now I know that the LORD saves his anointed; he*
*    answers him from his holy heaven with the saving*
*    power of his right hand.*
*Some trust in chariots and some in horses, but we trust*
*    in the name of the LORD our God.*
*They are brought to their knees and fall, but we rise up*
*    and stand firm.*
*O LORD, save the king! Answer us when we call!*
*                                                    (Psalm 20)*

# May 22

*'But when they arrest you, do not worry about what to say
or how to say it. At that time you will be given what to
say, for it will not be you speaking, but the Spirit of your
Father speaking through you.'* (Matthew 10:19)

## Mehdi Dibaj defense – part 1

Not long ago, Mehdi Dibaj had to appear before the judge in
Iran. In the courtroom, a defense written by Dibaj himself
was read. It sounded like the testimony of a modern Paul. In
the next few days we will copy this testimony in abridged
form, without trying to rewrite it in devotional form. The
testimony speaks for itself.

'With all humility I express my gratitude to the Judge of all
heaven and earth for this precious opportunity and with
brokenness I wait upon the Lord to deliver me from this
court trial according to His promise. I also beg the honored
members of the court present to listen with patience to my
defense and with respect for the name of the Lord.

I am a Christian, a sinner who believes that Jesus has
died for my sins on the cross. Jesus paid the penalty for our
sins by His own blood and gave us new life so that we can live
for the glory of God. He has asked me to deny myself and to
be His fully surrendered follower and not fear people even if
they kill my body.

I have been charged with "apostasy". In Islamic law an
apostate is one who does not believe in God, the prophets or
the resurrection of the dead. We Christians believe in all
three.'

This is the first part of Dibaj's defense, full of courage and
faith. That is what the Lord will give to all who are not
ashamed of the name of Christ.

*He predestined us to be adopted as his sons through Jesus Christ, in accordance with his pleasure and will.*

(Ephesians 1:5)

## Mehdi Dibaj defense – part 2

'They say: "You are a Muslim and you have become a Christian." (In many Islamic countries a Muslim who becomes a Christian may receive the death penalty.)

'No, for many years I had no religion. After searching and studying, I accepted God's call and I believed in the Lord Jesus Christ. People choose their religion, but a Christian is chosen by Christ. He says "you have not chosen me but I have chosen you."

People say: "You were a Muslim from your birth." God says: "You were a Christian from the beginning." A Christian means one who belongs to Jesus Christ.'

In this part of his defense, Dibaj once again reaffirms his relationship with Jesus Christ, the Son of the Living God. Islam teaches that Jesus was only a prophet, not the Son of God. God does not have a Son, the Koran teaches. This is the most essential difference between Islam and Christianity. Dibaj witnesses of Jesus Christ, the Son of God. Such a witness can result in the death penalty. Dibaj realizes that, but he refuses to deny Christ.

About such people Christ says: 'Whoever acknowledges me before men, I will also acknowledge him before my Father in heaven' (Matthew 10:32).

# May 24

*Who shall separate us from the love of Christ?*

(Romans 8:35)

## Mehdi Dibaj defense – part 3

'I would rather have the whole world against me, but know that the Almighty God is with me, or be called an apostate but know that I have the approval of the God of glory. Who can destroy the relationship between the creator and the creature, or defeat a heart that is faithful to God? He will be safe and secure under the shadow of the Almighty. Our refuge is the mercy seat of God. I know in whom I have believed, and He is able to guard what I have entrusted to Him to the end, until I reach the Kingdom of God. That is the place where the righteous will shine like the sun, but the evildoers will receive their punishment in hell.'

At the time of this trial, Dibaj had already spent almost nine years in prison for his faith in Jesus Christ. If 'only' he would deny Jesus Christ, he could be free tomorrow. Dibaj would rather lose his freedom and life than his peace with God.

'I know in whom I have believed.'

Do you know that too? Whatever the consequences may be?

*Lord, to whom shall we go? You have the words of eternal life.* (John 6:68)

### Mehdi Dibaj defense – part 4

'They tell me: "return!" But who can I return to from the arms of my God? Is it right to accept what people are saying, instead of obeying the Word of God? I have now been walking with the God of miracles for 45 years. His kindness to me is like a shadow and I owe Him so much for His fatherly love and concern.

The love of Jesus has filled all my being and I feel the warmth of His love in every part of my body.

The test of faith is a clear example. The good and kind God tests us in preparation for heaven. The God of Daniel, who protected Daniel's friends in the fiery furnace, has protected me for nine years in prison. All the bad things that have happened to me have turned out for my good and gain. So much so, that I am filled with joy and thankfulness.'

*Answer me when I call to you, O my righteous God. Give me relief from my distress; be merciful to me and hear my prayer.* (Psalm 4:1)

## Mehdi Dibaj defense – part 5

'The God of Job has tested my faith and commitment in order to strengthen my patience and faithfulness. During these nine years He has freed me from all my responsibilities so that I could spend my time in prayer and study of His Word, with heart searching and brokenness, and grow in the knowledge of my Lord. I praise the Lord for His unique opportunity. He gave me space in my confinement, my difficult hardships brought healing and His kindness revived me. Oh what great blessings God has in store for those who fear Him.

People object to my evangelizing, but "If you find a blind person near a well and keep silent than you have sinned." (A Persian poem.)

It is our Christian duty, as long as the door of God's mercy is open, to convince evil doers to turn from their sinful ways and find refuge in Him, in order to be saved from the wrath of a righteous God and from the coming dreadful punishment.'

*Salvation is found in no-one else, for there is no other name under heaven given to men by which we must be saved.* (Acts 4:12)

## Dibaj defense – part 6

'Jesus Christ says: "I am the door. Whosoever enters through me, will be saved." "I am the way, the truth and the life. No-one comes to the Father except through me."

Among the prophets of God, only Jesus Christ rose from the dead, and He is our living intercessor for ever. He is our Savior and He is the Son of God. To know Him means to know eternal life.

I, a useless sinner, have believed in Him, and I have committed my life into His hands. Life for me is an opportunity to serve Him, and death is a better opportunity to be with Christ. Therefore, I am not only satisfied to be in prison for the honor of His holy name, but am ready to give my life for the sake of Jesus my Lord and enter His Kingdom sooner. May the shadow of God's kindness and His hand of blessing and healing be upon you and remain for ever. Amen.

With respect
your Christian prisoner
Mehdi Dibaj'

'What, then, shall we say in response to this? If God is for us, who can be against us?'

Dibaj was set free two months after he wrote this 'defense' – but was killed soon afterwards. Yet, even though he is dead, he still speaks.

*Make the most of your chances to tell others the good news.* (Colossians 4:5)

## Open Doors Contact Person – part 1

Pastor J and his wife were travelling by car from the southern part of Malawi back to Blantyre. Suddenly their car came to a standstill in front of an Islamic secondary school. Pastor J, thinking that his car was overheated, walked to a big rock nearby and sat on it, waiting for the engine to cool down. The scene attracted people from the vicinity, so Pastor J asked his wife to fetch the tambourine from the car and they began to sing some choruses. They saw the incident as an opportunity to share the Gospel. Eleven people surrendered their lives to the Lord – two of whom were Muslim students from the secondary school.

God can turn problems into opportunities, always – everywhere.

*But whatever was to my profit I now consider loss for the sake of Christ. What is more, I consider everything a loss compared to the surpassing greatness of knowing Christ Jesus my Lord, for whose sake I have lost all things. I consider them rubbish that I may gain Christ.*

(Philippians 3:7–8)

## Open Doors Contact Person – part 2

The two Muslim students who accepted the Lord Jesus Christ started an outreach amongst the other students of the Islamic Secondary school. Eight months later one hundred and seventeen students had become Christians. All of them were sent away from the Islamic school. Many of them experience severe persecution from the community and their parents. Some parents have refused to pay for their tuition in other schools. Many young people had to leave their parents' home and now find themselves in a dilemma. Yet they are prepared to pay the price.

Let us pray for them and others who suffer for His name. Are we available to be an instrument or channel of His love in our own environment?

Not just suffering, but also the presence of the Lord is the central theme of this impressive psalm. Even though this may sound contradictory.

'My God, my God, why have you forsaken me?' (v. 1).

'O my God, I cry out by day, but you do not answer' (v. 2).

'But He has listened to his cry for help' (v. 24).

The One who seems absent is there, always, in all circumstances, even in the 'why?'

## David

*My God, my God, why have you forsaken me? Why are you so far from saving me, so far from the words of my groaning?*

*O my God, I cry out by day, but you do not answer, by night, and am not silent.*

*Yet you are enthroned as the Holy One; you are the praise of Israel.*

*In you our fathers put their trust; they trusted and you delivered them.*

*They cried to you and were saved; in you they trusted and were not disappointed.*

*But you, O LORD, be not far off; O my Strength, come quickly to help me.*

*Deliver my life from the sword, my precious life from the power of the dogs.*

*Rescue me from the mouth of the lions; save me from the horns of the wild oxen.* (Psalm 22:1–5, 19–21)

## Remarkable Remarks
### *The Word of God*

---

*Josif Trifa – Romania:*
> 'A Christian without a Bible, is like a soldier without a gun.'

*Russian Christian* after receiving his first Bible:
> 'The more I read, the more I want to read.'

*Another Russian Christian* after receiving a Bible:
> 'I could go to prison for having this book, but this book can also set men free.'

*Siberian Christian* who had only one page of the Bible:
> 'I wish I knew what is on the next page.'

*Koran:*
> 'God forbid that He should have a son!' (Sura 4:172).

*Bible:*
> *'For God so loved the world that He gave his one and only Son, that whoever believes in Him shall not perish but have eternal life.'*                    (John 3:16)

*William H. Houghton:*
> 'Lay hold on the Bible, until the Bible lays hold on you.'

> *'The Word became flesh and made his dwelling among us. We have seen his glory, the glory of the One and Only, who came from the Father, full of grace and truth.'*
>                                                         (John 1:14)

---

# June

## Writers for the month

**Sister Maria** from Mozambique. She had been imprisoned under severe circumstances. Because of the present danger she uses a pseudonym.

**Brother Jacob** from Mozambique. He and Open Doors work closely together.

**Grace Dube** from South Africa. Her husband was stabbed to death. She continues to preach his message of forgiveness.

*But because my servant Caleb has a different spirit and follows me whole-heartedly, I will bring him into the land he went to, and his descendants will inherit it.*

(Numbers 14:24)

## Caleb

Although Caleb was not an Israelite by birth, he was an Israelite indeed.

His name is derived from a Hebrew word, meaning faithful, alert and obedient.

The name Caleb is also an animal name, meaning 'dog', in which faithfulness, alertness and obedience are prominent features. You may never call your dog Caleb – or your child. We don't call our children after a dog, do we? But are the qualities of Caleb's name present in our lives? Faithfulness, alertness and obedience?

Such a Caleb not only has a bright future, but also the strength to face today's conflicts. Maybe we should turn it around. Whoever faces today's problems in a spirit of faithfulness, alertness and obedience will have a bright future. He may count on God's promise: I will be with him and with his descendants.

What a promise – for the future – and for today.

*Then Caleb silenced the people before Moses and said,*
*We should go up and take possession of the land, for we*
*can certainly do it.*                    (Numbers 13:30)

## Caleb

It takes courage to stand alone. It is much easier (and safer!?)
to follow the crowd. Nobody will notice you. As the saying
goes: 'By stepping out of the crowd, you become the target.'

Yes, whoever has courage to stand up for his convictions
will soon become a target.

Caleb was such a man. While the other ten spies said that
it was impossible to possess the promised land, Caleb (and
Joshua) said it could be done.

It is easy to say that it is impossible. Everybody can say
that. It requires courage and faith to say, 'it can be done.'

God seeks people today who dare to stand up for their
faith and convictions, even though the consequence may be
that they will soon stand alone.

Remember that the crowd never reached the promised
land. They never will. Only those who do not follow the
crowd in doing wrong (Exodus 23:2) will receive God's fullest
blessing. Caleb was such a man.

The former Queen of Holland, Wilhelmina, was such a
woman, when she said, 'I am lonely, but never alone'.

Martin Luther was such a man, when he said, 'One plus
God equals a majority'.

You can be such a person, because such a God is standing
by. At school, at work, in your family – always, everywhere.

*. . . and do not be afraid of the people of the land, because
we will swallow them up. Their protection is gone, but the
Lord is with us. Do not be afraid of them.*

(Numbers 14:9)

## Caleb

What was the difference between Joshua and Caleb and the
other ten spies? All twelve of them had been in the promised
land. All of them had seen the fruit of the land. All knew of
the giants who lived there. The latter, the presence of giants,
separated Joshua and Caleb from the other ten. They had all
seen the same, but they differed in their judgement of the
situation.

The ten compared their own strength to that of the
giants. The two compared the strength of the giants to that
of the Lord. The ten viewed themselves as grasshoppers in
comparison to the giants. The two viewed the giants as grasshoppers in comparison to God.

Yes, Caleb even added that the giants would serve as food
for them, 'we will swallow them up.' So, the bigger the giant,
the greater the meal.

Yet Joshua and Caleb were not super-spiritual. They
acknowledged the presence of giants, the enemy for they had
seen them for themselves. But . . . they saw more; they saw
God.

When you see God in His greatness, even giants look as
small as grasshoppers.

It is good to acknowledge your problems, but it is wrong
and dangerous to focus all your attention on them. There is
another reality. There is a God, whom Caleb refers to as: 'The
Lord is with us, do not be afraid of them!'

'Lord, open our eyes so that we can see. Really see!'

*. . . but those who hope in the Lord will renew their strength. . They will soar on wings like eagles; they will run and not grow weary, they will walk and not be faint.*

(Isaiah 40:31)

*Train a child in the way he should go, and when he is old he will not turn from it.* (Proverbs 22:6)

## Caleb

This typifies the life of Caleb. When he was young he had the courage to stand alone. In middle-age he had the patience to walk alone with his God. In old-age he had the strength to climb mountains.

The foundation was laid in his youth. He was courageous enough to stand up for his faith. He was not intimidated by the unbelieving masses. Not even when they threatened to stone him. Rather be dead than a coward. Rather be obedient to God than be popular with men.

It did mean that at the age of forty, he had to wander around in the desert for forty years, as a result of the unbelief of the people. Maybe Caleb often said to himself during those years: 'Forty lost years in the desert and it was not necessary.'

Yet he was patient enough to wait on God's promise and he continued to walk with his God. After that, when his years increased, he did not move downhill but uphill. And that at the age of eighty-five.

In which phase of your life do you find yourself today? In your youth? Then be steadfast in obedience. In your middle years? Be patient and continue to trust. In old age? Be strong in your faith. You can still be of great value to the Kingdom of God.

Caleb was strong at the age of eighty-five. For those who wait upon the Lord will renew their strength.

*Now give me this hill country that the Lord promised me that day. You yourself heard then that the Anakites were there and their cities were large and fortified, but, the Lord helping me, I will drive them out just as he said.*

(Joshua 14:12)

## Caleb

In claiming his inheritance Caleb, willingly and voluntarily, asked for the most difficult part of the country: the mountains where the giants lived.

Those were the giants who scared the other spies. They were the very reason for unbelief among God's people, resulting in forty years of isolation in the desert.

Caleb could have asked for an easier part of the country. At the retiring age of eighty-five he took upon him the greatest challenge of his life. Caleb never thought in terms of fences or walled cities. The higher the mountain the greater the challenge to conquer it. The stronger the enemies, the greater the opportunity to trust God to defeat them.

All the other tribes received an easier part of the country, but they could not drive out the people from their territory. Only Caleb could do that. He drove out the giants. His faith resulted in conquering power. No challenge too great, no problem too difficult. His secret: faith in God. Not a great faith in God, but simply faith in a great God. Have faith for 'your mountain'. It can be done.

*I, however, followed the Lord my God wholeheartedly.*
(Joshua 14:8)

*You have followed the Lord my God wholeheartedly.*
(Joshua 14:9)

*He followed the Lord, the God of Israel, wholeheartedly.*
(Joshua 14:14)

## Caleb

We learned yesterday that the secret to Caleb's success was faith. Today we will learn about the condition of having such faith. It can be summed up in one sentence: Caleb followed the Lord wholeheartedly. No reservations, no compromise. Only undivided allegiance to God.

We read this statement three times in Joshua 14. The first mention comes from Caleb himself. This was not proud boasting, but a sober statement of fact. Dare we, can we say this about our walk with God? Some people never dare say this. Others say it too easily. The second mention comes from Moses, saying the same words. That is even more important than Caleb's own statement. What do other people see of Christ in me? How do they sum up my life? But the most important testimony comes from God himself. The God who discerns the hidden secrets of the heart.

'O Lord, you have searched me
and you know me...
you perceive my thoughts from afar...
you are familiar with all my ways.'   (Psalm 139:1–3)

There can only be one response to this statement.

'Search me, O God, and know my heart;
test me and know my anxious thoughts.
See if there is any offensive way in me
And lead me in the way everlasting.'
(Psalm 139:23–24)

In the first part of this psalm, David wrestles with the question of why God forsook him. God does not answer him and does not seem to hear his prayers. He feels lonely and miserable.

After a difficult and profound struggle, David's spirit is lifted again. Even in the deepest pit God was with him, even though he did not notice it. The Lord *did* hear him when he called out to Him (v. 24).

Because of that, David now gives thanks to his God. Lonely, but never alone.

### David

*I will declare your name to my brothers; in the congregation I will praise you.*
*You who fear the LORD, praise him! All you descendants of Jacob, honor him! Revere him, all you descendants of Israel!*
*For he has not despised or disdained the suffering of the afflicted one; he has not hidden his face from him but has listened to his cry for help.*
*From you comes the theme of my praise in the great assembly; before those who fear you will I fulfill my vows.*
*The poor will eat and be satisfied; they who seek the LORD will praise him – may your hearts live forever!*
*All the ends of the earth will remember and turn to the LORD, and all the families of the nations will bow down before him,*
*for dominion belongs to the LORD and he rules over the nations.*                    (Psalm 22:22–28)

# June 8

*This is my Gospel, for which I am suffering even to the point of being chained like a criminal. But God's Word is not chained.* (2 Timothy 2:8–9)

## Sister Maria

In all the time that I was imprisoned I never felt alone. When loneliness threatened, I started to talk to my Lord. It was within those thick walls, cutting me off from my contact with everyone else, that I experienced, more than ever before, that nothing could cut me off from God.

I also realised that God must have allowed my imprisonment for a purpose – to bring other people the message of salvation in Christ Jesus, those who otherwise might never have heard it.

Instead of looking at my difficult circumstances, God lifted me above them. His Spirit filled my whole being, enabling me to testify to the other prisoners. Within one year twenty five of them accepted Christ as their Saviour. 'God's Word is not chained'. It even sets our spirit free in times of bondage and imprisonment.

A criminal in the eyes of men, an ambassador in the eyes of God.

'Open our eyes, Lord, that we may see.'

*Save me, O God, for the waters have come up to my neck.
I sink in the miry depths, where there is no foothold. I
have come into the deep waters; the floods engulf me. I
am worn out calling for help; my throat is parched. My
eyes fail, looking for my God. Those who hate me without
reason outnumber the hairs of my head; many are my
enemies without cause, those who seek to destroy me. I
am forced to restore what I did not steal.*

(Psalm 69:1–4)

## Sister Maria

These are the words of David, the man after God's heart, but
at the same time the fugitive king of Israel, calling out to God
while fleeing his enemies. He called to God in times of peace
and in times of persecution.

I often thought of these verses when I was imprisoned.

I was also reminded of Jesus' warning:

'You must be on your guard. You will be handed over
to the local councils and flogged in the synagogues.
On account of Me you will stand before governors and
kings as witnesses to them . . .
Whenever you are arrested and brought to trial, do
not worry beforehand about what to say. Just say
whatever is given you at the time, for it is not you
speaking, but the Holy Spirit.'         (Mark 13:9–11)

I am so glad that I memorised so many scriptures beforehand, for when my turn came to be persecuted for Christ,
they really sustained me through all the difficult times.

'Let the word of Christ dwell in you richly' (Colossians
3:16).

If that is the case, you will always experience the previous
verse 'Let the peace of Christ rule in your hearts . . . and be
thankful' (Colossians 3:15).

# June 10

*If you make the Most High your dwelling ... then no harm will befall you, no disaster will come near your tent.*

(Psalm 91:9–10)

## Sister Maria

If we fear persecution and its consequences, it simply means that we do not believe He is strong enough to see us through our times of trial.

This marvellous psalm could have been written especially for me. 'Surely, he will save me from the deadly pestilence' (v.3).

Under those terrible conditions in prison I became desperately ill in my pregnant condition. (I was four months pregnant when I was arrested.) Two months before the baby was due to be born I thought I was going to die, as would my baby. But God instilled sympathy into a doctor's heart to have mercy on me. He sent me to a hospital where the baby was born.

Later, when my baby became ill, he was taken away from me. My husband was allowed to take care of him for the next seven months.

Thank God, neither myself, nor my child, suffer from any ill-effects today.

'You will not fear the terror by night, nor the arrow that flies by day' (v. 5).

When I was interrogated, they tried to force me to deny my Lord. A loaded gun was pointed at my chest, with my interrogator threatening to shoot me. I was shaking, but I just could not deny my Lord.

I was weak, but He was strong.

'He will cover you with his feathers, and under his wings you will find refuge' (v. 4).

We never need to fear, whatever the circumstances – for He is with us.

The Psalmist speaks from experience – so do I – and so may you.

*Dear friends, do not be surprised at the painful trial you are suffering, as though something strange was happening to you. But rejoice that you participate in the sufferings of Christ.* (1 Peter 4:12–13)

## Sister Maria

Many Christians today live with the false hope that peace will come to this world one day, that famine and persecution will end.

This utopia is not in accordance with God's Word.

When I was arrested, His words immediately came to me: When these things begin to happen, '...be on your guard' (Mark 13:9).

Instead of peace on earth we see hunger, disease and war. This happened in my country too. We were promised food, health and peace, but we soon discovered that there was no room for God in an atheistic environment. Our churches were closed, our Bibles burnt and our pastors arrested. Because I taught children about the Lord, I, too, was arrested. Only when the heavy cell door shut behind me and I was left naked in the cold darkness, did the words of Jesus make real sense to me: 'Be on your guard.'

I do not want to be negative and frighten you. I only say: '...be on your guard.'

Even when things look like improving in the world today, we do not have any guarantee of freedom from persecution.

Together with the warning: '...be on your guard' comes this other truth: 'Rejoice'. Peter said it, Paul wrote about it from prison: Jesus exhorted us: 'Rejoice'.

I can only add: you can.

*Blessed are you when people insult you, persecute you and falsely say all kinds of evil against you because of me.* (Matthew 5:11)

*Come you who are blessed by my Father; take your inheritance . . . for I was hungry and you gave me something to eat . . .* (Matthew 25:34–35)

## Sister Maria

In these scriptures I see an inseparable bond.

Blessed are the persecuted and . . . blessed are those who help the persecuted.

Although there were times, when in prison, that I doubted God's love, many opportunities arose when my faith was strengthened again and again through the support of other people. Their good deeds came spontaneously, because they loved the Lord . . . and me.

It reminded me of Paul's words: 'If one part suffers, every part suffers with it; if one part is honored, every part rejoices with it.'

If your leg is injured, you are supplied with a crutch. Without that crutch you cannot walk. In our walk with the Lord, one may be persecuted, but another supports and strengthens.

We need one another, and thus we fulfil the law of Christ. In doing so we all will be blessed, because: 'he who refreshes others will himself be refreshed.'

*I rise before dawn and cry for help; I have put my hope in your word.* (Psalm 119:147)

*Very early in the morning, while it was still dark, Jesus got up, left the house and went off to a solitary place, where he prayed.* (Mark 1:35)

## Sister Maria

With our full schedules today we have little time to study the Word of God and pray.

We have either been so busy – and thus too tired to pray – or we slept in the next morning (because we went to bed so late!) so we always seem to have an excuse for not praying.

Satan does not mind if we work overtime – even if it is for the Lord – as long as he can keep us away from praying and studying the Word of God.

Somebody once said: 'If the first minute is for God, the whole day will be. If the first minute is not spent with God, neither will the remainder of the day.'

There is never an excuse for not praying. Let us get our priorities right. We will soon discover that the time spent in fellowship with God, will enable us to face the remainder of the day in peace and victory.

Have you lost your peace, your victory?

It can be found again.

Take time to pray and to read God's Word.

# June 14

Throughout the ages, this psalm, more than any other psalm, has been an encouragement and comfort to countless people. David knows prosperity and adversity. He has experienced 'the valley of the shadow of death.' But he also knows the God who is always with him. His faith in that God makes him triumph over all suffering and pain. 'For you are with me.'

## David

*The LORD is my shepherd, I shall not be in want.*
*He makes me lie down in green pastures, he leads me*
*beside quiet waters,*
*he restores my soul. He guides me in paths of*
*righteousness for his name's sake.*
*Even though I walk through the valley of the shadow of*
*death, I will fear no evil, for you are with me; your*
*rod and your staff, they comfort me.*
*You prepare a table before me in the presence of my*
*enemies. You anoint my head with oil; my cup*
*overflows.*
*Surely goodness and love will follow me all the days of*
*my life, and I will dwell in the house of the LORD*
*forever.* (Psalm 23)

*Then I heard the voice of the Lord saying: 'Whom shall I send? And who will go for us?'* (Isaiah 6:8)

## Brother Jacob

I was very burdened by the problems of my people who suffered so much under a communist government. Pastors were executed, Bibles were burnt and many Christians thrown into prison.

I decided to visit the Christians in some remote areas, to encourage them and give them new Bibles. I had to travel by car to a remote area in a convoy, because it was too dangerous to travel alone.

At a road block the convoy was stopped. Some armed soldiers came up to my car and arrested me. Everything was confiscated – my car, my personal belongings, my money and all the Bibles.

The soldiers put me into an army vehicle and took me to prison. My first question was: 'But Lord, why me? I want to serve you, but how can I serve you in prison?'

Then I remembered a meeting I had had with some pastors in that part of the country. They were burdened with the many people in prison. We decided to pray and ask the Lord to burden someone with a love for these people and to send such a person to them with the Gospel of salvation.

Little did I realize at that time, that I was to be the man to bring them the Gospel.

We can become the answer to our own prayers.

Are you willing?

*The Spirit of the Sovereign Lord is on me, because the Lord has anointed me to preach good news to the poor. He has sent me to bind up the brokenhearted, to proclaim freedom for the captives and release from darkness for the prisoners.* (Isaiah 61:1)

## Brother Jacob

After being thrown into prison I had to undergo hours of harsh interrogation. Finally I was brought to a dirty cell in which a number of other prisoners were sitting or standing around.

It was a group of pathetic, dirty and hungry human beings – my co-inhabitants for an undisclosed time.

One man looked at me and asked: 'What are you here for?' Yes indeed, why was I there? For no other reason than for the Gospel of Jesus Christ.

I realized that the Lord had placed me amongst these captives because they were there without hope. They were not just physically hungry, but also spiritually. I started to witness to them and the response was beyond belief!

Two of the prisoners were back-slidden Christians. As soon as I started to speak about love and forgiveness they started to cry. They fell on their knees, confessing their sins, weeping bitter tears of repentance. Others followed their example and in the following three months many accepted the Lord Jesus as their Savior.

That dark, dirty, smelling prison cell became a place of light. Such was the change that two prison wardens also accepted the Lord. The place of curses changed into a holy sanctuary, filled with songs of praise and hope.

We all can be fruitful in the place where we are. To the glory of God. And to the salvation of others.

*So Peter was kept in prison, but the church was earnestly praying to God for him.* (Acts 12:5)

## Brother Jacob

With me in the cell was a man accused of co-operating with a rebel group in our country. This was never proven however, but in a Marxist country, proof is not essential. Even the least suspicion is enough for you to face a firing squad.

We all knew that within the next week this man would be executed. He was filled with fear and listened very attentively to the Gospel.

One day we decided to stand around him and pray for him. His heart cried to God. We worked out a plan to get him out of prison. We did not know if our plan would work, but we prayed and planned his escape.

Every morning we were taken from the cell under armed guard to wash. When an armed soldier opened the door, we were marched down the corridor. Another soldier, with a machine gun, stood at the entrance to the washroom.

As agreed, we all turned straight into the washroom, except our friend who kept walking straight on, into freedom.

The two armed guards did not make a move to prevent him from escaping, for at that moment their eyes were blinded, just as we had prayed.

Joy filled our hearts when we witnessed this miracle. Yes, miracles can still happen if you stand in prayer around those in captivity.

*The Lord provides food for those who fear him.*

(Psalm 111:5)

## Brother Jacob

When I was arrested I was worried about my family. How would they cope without me? I realized however that to worry about them would not solve their problems; neither would it make prison life easier for me. At the same time I had to prove to my fellow prisoners that, as a Christian, I had no reason to worry. I prayed for my family, that the Lord would take care of them.

Some weeks after my arrest, a woman brought some food to me in prison. This is a custom in our country. The food was nicely prepared: a bowl of rice with meat on top. I started eating the food with great enjoyment. When I got close to the bottom I saw that something was hidden there.

I carefully scraped the rice away with the spoon to find a tiny plastic bag. Inside the bag was only a piece of paper. My hands shook as I pulled the scrap of paper from the plastic. It was a very short note from the lady who had brought me the food, saying: 'Your family is fine. Other Christians are looking after them. We pray for you.'

Peace and joy flowed into my heart.

Worry breaks us down.

Trust builds us up.

Put your trust in the Lord – for yourself, your loved ones and for your fellow Christians, because He cares.

*The prayer of a righteous man is powerful and effective.*

(James 5:16b)

## Brother Jacob

That short message on a piece of paper, hidden in a rice bowl was a tremendous assurance of God's faithfulness – to me and to my family.

At the same time I was well aware of the prayers of others for me.

What encouraged me greatly was the news – which I received through local Christians who visited me in prison – that brothers and sisters around the world were praying for me.

When someone was led away from the prison cell we would often hear the muffled gunshots somewhere in the prison complex. I often thought that it could be my turn tomorrow.

'Father, please tell your children around the world to pray for me.'

I believe He did. I believe they did.

Oh, how I could rest in the knowledge and comfort of those prayers, regardless of what tomorrow would bring.

May I encourage you today with these words:

Your prayers are heard –

Your prayers are answered –

Your prayers for us are experienced by us.

What a great spiritual bond – all over the world.

*I waited patiently for the Lord; he turned to me and heard my cry.* (Psalm 40:1)

## Jan Pit

One day I visited the cave prisons in Kampala, Uganda. A place of horror, where the dictator Idi Amin punished and killed innocent prisoners.

One of the men about to be killed was Joshua, a pastor of a Full Gospel Church in Kampala. Joshua had always preached a message of love and forgiveness. Miracles had taken place in his church. God was at work.

Idi Amin's secret police reported the tremendous growth of the church to the dictator, who in turn ordered the arrest of Pastor Joshua. He was thrown into this cave prison, waiting to be executed. He cried to the Lord: 'Lord, I am scared. Help me Lord. No, I am not afraid to die, but I am afraid of the torture that will take place before they kill me.' (Many prisoners were not killed by a bullet, but by a sledgehammer.)

'Lord, let the first hit be fatal . . . please.'

A miracle took place in that dark cell.

Joshua described it as follows:

'All of a sudden a light shone into my dark cell. I heard a voice say, "You are not alone – I am with you – always."

All fear disappeared, I knelt down praising the Lord. I must have sung at the top of my voice, because suddenly the door to my cell opened and two policemen dragged me out. I thought the moment had come to be killed, but I kept on praising my Lord. When the officer saw me and heard me singing, he said to the two policemen, "This man is insane – it is no use killing him. Throw him out." A moment later I was a free man.

May I share with you what I learned?

1    We are never alone – never – never.

2    There is power in praising God.

3    God is always in control.'

What more can a man desire?

Some Bible expositors think this psalm was sung when the Ark was brought back to Israel.

Others see in this psalm a type of Christ.

In both views, the Lord is central.

Real peace is not the absence of war, but the presence of the Prince of Peace – Christ the Lord.

## David

*The earth is the LORD's, and everything in it, the world,*
*and all who live in it;*
*for he founded it upon the seas and established it upon*
*the waters.*
*Who may ascend the hill of the LORD? Who may stand*
*in his holy place?*
*He who has clean hands and a pure heart, who does not*
*lift up his soul to an idol or swear by what is false.*
*He will receive blessing from the LORD and vindication*
*from God his Savior.*
*Such is the generation of those who seek him, who seek*
*your face, O God of Jacob.*
*Lift up your heads, O you gates; be lifted up, you*
*ancient doors, that the King of glory may come in.*
*Who is this King of glory? The LORD strong and*
*mighty, the LORD mighty in battle.* (Psalm 24:1–8)

# June 22

*There is no fear in love.* (1 John 4:18)

## Grace Dube

A Marxist leader once stated that Christian love is an obstacle in the development of the communist revolution. 'We need hatred, not love,' he said.

These words were also used when a mob of people in Soweto 'visited' my husband Benjamin. The Lord had called Benjamin to preach a message of forgiveness, love and hope in our troubled township. Many people came to listen, but others were angry. 'You are black yourself' they cried, 'why then do you talk about loving the white people?' Benjamin's answer was always the same: 'We should not hate people, because Jesus loves us all – white or black.' 'If you do not stop preaching love we will kill you,' was the reaction.

One night Benjamin woke up and called our family together in the middle of the night. He told us about the threats and said, 'I believe they will kill me soon.' We could not believe our ears.

I knew he did not say these things lightly, and that I could never persuade him to stop preaching about love and forgiveness.

That night he prayed with us all. A prayer meeting that I will never forget. 'Remain faithful to Jesus' he said, 'love those who will kill me – because Jesus loves them.' It all sounded so strange and yet so true.

A few days later his car was stopped by fellow black people. He was dragged out of the car and beaten to death. His murderers took his Bible and drenched it in his own blood. 'We want hatred,' they shouted. But Benjamin was a messenger of love.

What about me? What about you?

*Father, forgive them, for they do not know what they are doing.* (Luke 23:34)

## Grace Dube

Benjamin was not alone when he was killed. One of my sons was with him, Benjamin Jr. He was only 12 years old and managed to escape. From behind a barrel he saw what they did to his father.

He came running home to Soweto to tell me what had happened. Even though my husband had predicted what would happen I could not believe it had happened.

My son Benjamin went to his room and wept and wept, all night. Then the Lord did something in the heart of my boy. He heard a wonderful voice, like his father had heard. His father had often told him: 'Benjamin, you must take my place to sing for the Lord if anything happens to me.' Early the next morning I heard singing, coming from my son's bedroom. At first it was a broken voice, but then, it became clearer and clearer. I could hear my boy sing to the Lord. He sang a verse from the Scripture: 'Father forgive them, for they do not know what they are doing.'

I could hardly control myself. O Lord, make me like my children. Help me to forgive.

My son and I have sung this wonderful song together ever since, in many meetings, in many countries, to many people who are hurt – and who need to forgive also.

Father forgive us, because we too do not always know what we are doing.

*Seventy-seven times.* (Matthew 18:22)

## Grace Dube

A couple of years after my husband died my son and I were singing in a meeting in Soweto. We gave our testimony about the hurt and about God's provision. There was a wonderful spirit in that meeting. We sang our love-song again. 'Father forgive them...'

The audience was listening spellbound. Then I was asked to speak. I read from Matthew 18:21–22: 'Lord, how many times shall I forgive my brother when he sins against me? Up to seven times?' Jesus said to him: '...seventy-seven times.'

I spoke for some time and then I invited people to accept the Lord Jesus as their Savior. Some people came forward and asked me to pray for them. One man however hesitated. He seemed to be scared. I encouraged him to tell me what was bothering him so much.

He said: 'I need your Jesus, I need forgiveness. I ... I was one of the mob who killed your husband.' I was trembling, scared, confused. What should I do? Singing: Father forgive them, is one thing, but now ... Then the Lord must have touched me, deeply, very deeply. Because He gave me strength and courage to put my arms around the killer, and forgive him – as Jesus forgives us.

'You are now my brother,' I whispered. He left, a brand new person. And so was I.

*I see four men walking around in the fire, unbound and unharmed.* (Daniel 3:25)

## Grace Dube

Living in Soweto means that people expect you to make choices: spiritual as well as political choices.

We had made a spiritual choice which had political implications:

- to preach Christ instead of systems;
- to preach love instead of hatred.

This choice made us a friend of some and an enemy of many. The more so because my children formed a music group which became rather popular in South Africa. Yet we realized that it is better to be faithful than to be popular.

The radical black political groups wanted us to join forces with them. When we refused to take sides, we became a target. This is always the case in spiritual warfare. When we follow the crowd we are no danger to the devil, but when we step out of the crowd for our faith in Jesus Christ, we become a threat to the devil. That puts us in dangerous situations. It seems to be safer to stand in the background and watch other people fight than to be in the front line where the battle is being fought.

Yet I would rather stand in the front line. That's the place where you experience blessing, victory and peace. Yes, peace in the middle of the fight.

I would rather stand with Daniel's friends in the middle of the fiery oven, than to be outside and get killed by the heat – it is a matter of choice.

When you make that choice you are not bound anymore but you will be (Daniel 3:24) 'loose, walking around in the midst of the fire.'

The only heat you will experience is the warmth of His presence.

Hallelujah.

# June 26

*I will lie down and sleep in peace, for you alone, O Lord, make me dwell in safety.* (Psalm 4:8)

## Grace Dube

That night, in June 1991, it was impossible to lie down and sleep in peace. Soweto was in chaos. Fighting, looting, killing, all through the night.

I was alone in my house. The children (all married by now) had visited me that evening, but had already returned to their own houses, elsewhere in Soweto.

All of a sudden some bandits came to my house. They banged on the door and shouted: 'Come out, we want you to join us in the battle.' I crept out of my bed and peeped through the window. I saw all the young men, with sticks in their hands. 'Lord, be my shield,' I prayed. I confess I trembled. But the Lord was in control. All of a sudden I heard the leader of the gang shout to his friends: 'Hey, leave that house alone. There is an old woman living there, all on her own. Her children are married and live elsewhere.'

When the gang hesitated about leaving, the leader shouted: 'I don't want any of you to ever come near this house again.' I could not believe what I heard. That man had always been against us, and now this . . .

'For you alone, O Lord, make me dwell in safety.'

'The angel of the Lord encamps around those who fear him, and he delivers them' (Psalm 34:7).

A short time later I went back to bed. Not nervous anymore, but: ' . . . in peace I will lie down and sleep' (Psalm 4:8).

The peace of the Lord be with you.

*These commandments that I give you today are to be upon your hearts. Impress them on your children.*

(Deuteronomy 6:6–7)

## Grace Dube

It is not always easy to be a father and a mother at the same time. After the death of my husband I had to take that responsibility upon me. That is not easy, especially in turbulent times of political chaos and without financial security.

I once heard somebody say: 'We can win the world – yet lose our family.' How true these words are. We can become so involved in preaching the Gospel to others, that we forget our first priority: our family.

Of course, the Lord wants us to witness for Him, but it starts at home. We must let our light shine, that it may give light to all **in the house**.

What do our own children see of Christ in us?

I thank God that He showed me this priority. And although this is not an easy task – He does help.

Some children do not get enough attention because the parents are too busy making money. They have their priorities wrong as well.

The Bible says: 'Train a child in the way he should go, and when he is old he will not turn from it' (Proverbs 22:6).

Do we see this priority? And act accordingly?

May God help you and me to serve Him faithfully – starting at home.

*The Lord watches over you – the Lord is your shade at your right hand.* (Psalm 121:5)

## Jan Pit

One who made a deep impression on me is Kosie, a young South African, suffering from Down's Syndrome.

I wish you could have heard him pray; it was childlike, simple and full of faith. When he prayed I had the impression that he was so near to God that he could touch Him.

One day I asked him, 'Kosie, how do you picture God?' He looked directly at me. Was my question too difficult for his simple mind? No, because his eyes began to twinkle. 'As a shade, Uncle Jan, as a shade – look there he is . . . '

He pointed to his shadow and then he stood and jumped and ran all the time pointing to his shadow. 'Look, Uncle Jan, He is always there!'

What a deep truth. 'The Lord is your shade at your right hand.'

Always visible when you walk in the light! Sometimes invisible when everything around is dark – either through sin or circumstances. But the shade is still there.

Matthew Henry, in his Bible commentary says, 'The God of Israel is sometimes a God who hides Himself, but never a God who absents Himself; sometimes in the dark, but never at a distance.'

In the light and in the dark, in storm and shine: 'The Lord watches over you – the Lord is your shade at your right hand.'

David prays for forgiveness and deliverance. He is surrounded by enemies, but he does not ask the Lord to destroy them. He asks for forgiveness instead, as if the enemy had been able to come near because of his own mistakes. Forgiveness is central. Only after that, he talks about deliverance.

## David

*To you, O LORD, I lift up my soul;*
*in you I trust, O my God. Do not let me be put to*
*    shame, nor let my enemies triumph over me.*
*No one whose hope is in you will ever be put to shame,*
*    but they will be put to shame who are treacherous*
*    without excuse.*
*Show me your ways, O LORD, teach me your paths;*
*guide me in your truth and teach me, for you are God*
*    my Savior, and my hope is in you all day long.*
*Remember, O LORD, your great mercy and love, for they*
*    are from of old.*
*Remember not the sins of my youth and my rebellious*
*    ways; according to your love remember me, for you*
*    are good, O LORD.*                    (Psalm 25:1–7)

## Remarkable Remarks
### *Protection*

*Corrie ten Boom – Holland:*

'When the devil knocks at my door, I ask Jesus to open it.'

*Unknown:*

'God allows the storm to prove He is the only shelter.'

*Vietnamese Pastor:*

'The more violently the storm rages, the more diligently people seek shelter under God's wings.'

*Unknown:*

'The will of God will never lead us where the grace of God can not keep us.'

*Unknown:*

'The safest place on earth is in the centre of the will of God. The most dangerous place is to be outside His will.'

*Charles H Spurgeon:*

'As sure as God allows His children to enter into the fiery furnace, He will be in the fiery furnace with them.'

*He who dwells in the shelter of the Most High will rest in the shadow of the Almighty.* (Psalm 91:1)

# July

## Writers for the month

*Menes Abdul-Noor* from Egypt. A respected leader of the Christian Church in Cairo.

*Ghassan Khalaf* from Lebanon. Amidst bombings and destruction, Brother Khalaf faithfully visited victims of war to encourage them in their faith.

*Mona Khauli* from Lebanon. Instead of leaving her country to seek peace, she chose to stay at great risk. She testifies of God's miracles.

*The Lord is with you, mighty warrior.*     (Judges 6:12b)

*For when I am weak, then I am strong.*
(2 Corinthians 12:10b)

## Gideon

Gideon a mighty warrior? When you read Judges, the opposite seems to be the case. Gideon was a timid, disappointed Israelite. Yet, God called him a mighty warrior.

Was God being cynical? No, God is never sarcastic. God did not see what Gideon was, but what he could become. God sees us in a different way than we view ourselves. God chooses the weak to confound the wise (1 Corinthians 1:27).

He can turn a weak and frightened Gideon into a hero and leader.

Don't look upon yourself in a negative way. 'I can't do anything, I am a nobody. I have nothing to offer.'

Whoever dares to answer 'Yes' when God calls, will be anointed by Him.

For the weak are strong. For the weak can count on God's help. And will receive it. Even today.

*. . . Tear down your father's altar to Baal and cut down
the Asherah pole beside it. Then build a proper kind of
altar to the Lord your God on the top of this crag. Using
the wood of the Asherah pole that you cut down, offer the
second bull as a burnt offering.* (Judges 6:25–26)

## Gideon

Servanthood starts at home. Before Gideon could lead the
people back to their God, he had to get rid of the idols in his
own home.

Serving God does not start on the mission field but at
home, in your own church and family. That is often the hard-
est place to serve. It seems much easier to take the Gospel to
far away peoples than to share Christ with your family and
friends. But those who are ashamed of Christ at home, will
never be able to serve Him abroad.

Conversion starts with 'turning your back on . . .' Coming
to Christ means turning your back on your idols, whatever
they may be. With this command Gideon's mission started.
'Tear down your father's altar.' That could cause a very negative reaction from his father. But Gideon was obedient to
God. It is true that Gideon was afraid to be so radical. He did
it at night, but he did it . . . 'Then the Spirit of the Lord came
upon Gideon' (Judges 6:34).

It will always be that way. Is there a Baal idol in your
life? Whatever it may be, tear it down, get rid of it. Then God
will fill you with a new spirit, the Holy Spirit.

*I will place a wool fleece on the threshing-floor. If there is dew only on the fleece and all the ground is dry, then I will know that you will save Israel by my hand, as you said.*                                    (Judges 6:37)

## Gideon

Was it alright for Gideon to ask for a sign? Wasn't he filled with the Holy Spirit? Hadn't he heard God's voice already? What more did he want?

The fact that God granted Gideon's request, does not mean He agreed with him. But God understands our human weaknesses and treats us with godly patience. God goes to meet us and meets us just where we are.

So to 'put down a fleece' and ask for a sign time and time again, is this right?

God gave us His Word as a light for our path and a lamp unto our feet (Psalm 119:105).

If God's Word is God's will for your life, He will guide you by that Word. That is no mysterious or magic act. It means: walking with God.

Whosoever follows Him, communicates with Him and keeps His Word, will be guided by Him in all truth.

# July 4

*The Lord said to Gideon: 'You have too many men for me to deliver Midian into their hands.'*  (Judges 7:2)

## Gideon

You cannot be too small for God to use, but you can be too big. That is what the story in Judges 7:2 teaches us.

When we no longer depend upon ourselves He takes us by the hand and tells us that we can trust Him completely. We have to learn to be dependent on God. Without Him we can do nothing. We will also discover that He can do the impossible.

It is not our responsibility to understand how He will perform His work in and through us. He only asks us to trust Him and do what He tells us to do.

It may seem absurd. To win a war with just empty jars. 300 soldiers against 135,000. Numbers are not important to God. He is looking for empty vessels, in which He can pour out His treasures.

'But we have this treasure in jars of clay to show that this all-surpassing power is from God and not from us' (2 Corinthians 4:7).

This way we will get the victory and God the honor. Honor to whom honor is due.

*Now the Ephraimites asked Gideon, 'Why have you treated us like this? Why didn't you call us when you went to fight Midian?' And they criticized him sharply.*

(Judges 8:1)

*Then make my joy complete by being like-minded, having the same love, being one in spirit and purpose.*

(Philippians 2:2)

### Gideon

It is sad but true that many times persecution comes from within, from fellow-believers. That hurts the most.

After the great victory, Gideon is taken up roundly. Not by his enemies but by his own people. 'Why didn't you call us when you went to fight Midian?'

It is easy to say this when the battle is over. When Gideon needed them, his own people were nowhere to be seen. But now that the war is won, they surface, full of criticism.

It's an old trick of the devil – then and now. Satan delights in us fighting each other instead of him. He is a master at causing division and Christians are very willing subjects. At least in this area.

Be aware of this today. Don't listen to the devil and don't allow him to misuse you. Put on the whole armor of God. Then you will not only be able to withstand the attacks, but also be victorious.

*Gideon made the gold into an ephod, which he placed in Ophrah, his town. All Israel prostituted themselves by worshipping it there, and it became a snare to Gideon and his family.* (Judges 8:27)

## Gideon

The story of Gideon does not have a happy ending.

Gideon put himself in a spiritual position which was impossible for God to bless. The ephod was a precious tunic, worn by the priests when they were seeking God's will for the people. That robe Gideon acquired for himself. He installed his own worship service. Not in Shiloh, as God had ordained, but in Ophrah. Not performed by the Levites but by Gideon himself.

In doing so, Gideon disobeyed God's order. He had been called to be a leader, not a priest. God anoints whom He appoints. It is very dangerous to take upon ourselves all the different ministries that God has appointed in His Church. That can lead to pride and dictatorship. It became a snare to Gideon, however well-intentioned it may have been.

Work with whatever talents God has given you and do not covet other people's gifts.

God will reward that attitude with His full blessing.

This psalm can be divided into three parts. In all three, David prays for forgiveness. Only then can he have intimate fellowship with God. Real deliverance is the result of intimate fellowship with the Lord. To those people He will reveal His covenant.

**David**

*The LORD confides in those who fear him; he makes his
   covenant known to them.
My eyes are ever on the LORD, for only he will release
   my feet from the snare.
Turn to me and be gracious to me, for I am lonely and
   afflicted.
The troubles of my heart have multiplied; free me from
   my anguish.
Look upon my affliction and my distress and take away
   all my sins.
See how my enemies have increased and how fiercely
   they hate me!
Guard my life and rescue me; let me not be put to
   shame, for I take refuge in you.
May integrity and uprightness protect me, because my
   hope is in you.*       (Psalm 25:14–21)

# July 8

*He cuts off every branch in me that bears no fruit, while every branch that does bear fruit he trims clean so that it will be even more fruitful ... This is to my Father's glory, that you bear much fruit, showing yourselves to be my disciples.* (John 15:2, 8)

## Menes Abdul Noor

God works in the heart of the believers, not on their outward appearances (1 Samuel 16:7). He does not sew a piece of unshrunken cloth on an old garment (Mark 2:21). He makes you a new creation, so you joyfully shout, 'the old has gone, the new has come!' (2 Corinthians 5:17).

As a result of this new life you bear fruit. The Father prunes you so you produce much fruit. We all need pruning to lay aside every weight and sin which so easily ensnares us (Hebrews 12:1). We have bad habits, like weights burdening us. We also have evil surroundings ensnaring us. Our abiding in Christ is the condition to bear fruit, as the branch cannot bear fruit of itself (John 15:4). Our fruit should increase as we grow in knowing Christ.

The greatest fruit is to live victoriously, defeating Satan and having a successful witness for Christ (Acts 1:8). It glorifies the Father, since it declares the kindness of His care, the goodness of His laws and the abundance of His grace.

Jesus has chosen you that you should go and bear fruit, and that your fruit should remain (John 15:16). He chose you for salvation, and for a service. What an honor!

*If you remain in me and my words remain in you, ask whatever you wish, and it will be given you.* (John 15:7)

### Menes Abdul Noor

A bored father scolded his son saying, 'When will you quit asking?' The smart son answered, 'When you quit giving!' God is never a bored Father, and He gives to all liberally and without reproach (James 1:5).

When you abide in Christ He makes you pure-hearted. He tells you, 'You are already clean because of the word I have spoken to you' (John 15:3). God testifies to you that He has found you a person after His own heart, who will do all His will (Acts 13:22). If you do God's will as if it were your will, He does your will as if it were His will. 'What the righteous desire will be granted' (Proverbs 10:24).

When we abide in Christ we come to the Father in the merits of Christ. We hear Jesus saying, 'And I will do whatever you ask in my name, so that the Son may bring glory to the Father. You may ask me for anything in my name, and I will do it' (John 14:13, 14). God says to His repentant people, 'Then you will call upon me and come and pray to me, and I will listen to you. You will seek me and find me when you seek me with all your heart. I will be found by you,' declares the LORD, 'and will bring you back from captivity. I will gather you from all the nations and places where I have banished you,' declares the LORD, 'and will bring you back to the place from which I carried you into exile' (Jeremiah 29:12–14).

Let us abide in Him, and experience answered prayers!

# July 10

*As the Father has loved me, so have I loved you. Now remain in my love.* (John 15:9)

## Menes Abdul Noor

What a privilege to abide in the love of Jesus, so we love Him because He first loved us (1 John 4:19), and love our brothers and sisters in Christ because the love of God has been poured out in our hearts by the Holy Spirit who was given to us (Romans 5:5).

The love of God to us was giving, forgiving, accepting – continuous and sacrificial. The Bible says that God reconciles us to Himself, but it never says that we reconcile ourselves to God, because God was never in enmity with us. Jesus said, 'I have called you friends' (John 15:15) because on His part He was full of love to us, though we were enemies of Him.

When we abide in Christ He teaches us His will. He does not call us 'servants' for the servant does not know what his master is doing. He only knows the master's orders, but not the master's plan. 'The LORD confides in those who fear him; he makes his covenant known to them' (Psalm 25:14). God said to Abraham, 'Shall I hide from Abraham what I am about to do?' (Genesis 18:17). Jesus said, 'If any one chooses to do God's will, he will find out whether my teaching comes from God or whether I speak on my own' (John 7:17).

Let us love Him with all our hearts, imitate Him and learn from Him.

*If you obey my commands, you will remain in my love,
just as I have obeyed my Father's commands and remain
in his love ... You are my friends if you do what I
command.* (John 15:10, 14)

## Menes Abdul Noor

When we abide in Christ we receive blessings exceedingly
abundantly above all that we ask or think (Ephesians 3:20).
We experience that Jesus has given us life to live more abundantly (John 10:10). The Lord reminded the Israelites how
He saved them from bondage, and this is why they should
have no masters except Himself (Exodus 20:1, 2). We feel the
same obligation, and say, 'I have been crucified with Christ
and I no longer live, but Christ lives in me. The life I live in
the body, I live by faith in the Son of God, who loved me and
gave himself for me' (Galatians 2:20).

Whoever receives Jesus accepts His kingship on his life.
He knows that he ought to obey Jesus rather than man (Acts
5:29). He asks Jesus, 'Lord, what do you want me to do?'
(Acts 9:6). Sometimes we say, 'Not so, Lord!' (Acts 10:14). If
He is Lord of life He should not take a 'no' for an answer.

What a blessing for us to receive from Him and obey
Him!

'Then you will be prosperous and successful' (Joshua 1:8).

# July 12

*I have told you this so that my joy may be in you and that your joy may be complete.* (John 15:11)

## Menes Abdul Noor

The joy of the world is the result of what people get or achieve. When the getting and achievements end, this kind of joy ends. The joy stays as long as its source remains.

Not so with the joy of Christ. He abides in us and guarantees to us that He gives us not as the world gives us (John 14:27). What He gives is everlasting, guaranteed and full.

When we abide in Christ we find the way, the truth and the life (John 14:6). Of His fullness we all receive, and grace for grace (John 1:16). In Jesus the life was manifested, and we have seen and bear witness, and declare that Jesus is the eternal life who gives us fellowship with the Father and with Himself, that our joy may be full (1 John 1:1–4).

When we abide in Christ we love Him and keep His word. The Father loves us. The Father and the Son come to us and make their home with us (John 14:23). What a privilege and what a joy!

When we abide in Jesus He guarantees to us an eternal abode. He says, 'Do not let your hearts be troubled. Trust in God; trust also in me. In my Father's house are many rooms; if it were not so, I would have told you. I am going there to prepare a place for you. And if I go and prepare a place for you, I will come back and take you to be with me that you also may be where I am' (John 14:1–3).

We have all the right to be joyful, because we abide in Christ. All His privileges become ours.

*If the world hates you, keep in mind that it hated me first.
If you belonged to the world, it would love you as its own.
As it is, you do not belong to the world, but I have chosen
you out of the world. That is why the world hates you.*

(John 15:18–19)

## Menes Abdul Noor

The greatness of Jesus is seen in the clarity and openness of His teachings. He tells us that the world gives privileges to its followers. It loves its own. It hates the believers in Jesus because it hates their Master. The world hates the Father because it does not know the Father (John 15:21, 23). The world has no excuse for its sin, because Jesus spoke clearly about the consequences, but they refused His testimony.

Those who abide in Christ should know who they are. They are not of the world. They are chosen by Jesus to go out of the world. The world hates their leader.

Jesus teaches us that if persecution comes to us, it should come because we are loyal to Him, and not because of our mistakes. When the apostles of Jesus were beaten they departed from the presence of the Jewish council rejoicing that they were counted worthy to suffer shame for Jesus' name (Acts 5:41).

Jesus warned us of coming persecutions (John 15:20). We should not be shocked. If we suffer for His name's sake, then persecution is normal. We should not think that the Lord had deserted or forgotten us (Isaiah 49:14–16). 'Rejoice and be glad, because great is your reward in heaven' (Matthew 5:12).

This beautiful psalm consists of two parts. In the first part, the writer speaks *about* the Lord (27:1–5). In the second part he talks *to* the Lord (27:7–14, see July 21).

David trusts in the Lord his God, who draws near in every desperate situation. Safe under God's protection.

## David

The LORD is my light and my salvation – whom shall I fear? The LORD is the stronghold of my life – of whom shall I be afraid?

When evil men advance against me to devour my flesh, when my enemies and my foes attack me, they will stumble and fall.

Though an army besiege me, my heart will not fear; though war break out against me, even then will I be confident.

One thing I ask of the LORD, this is what I seek: that I may dwell in the house of the LORD all the days of my life, to gaze upon the beauty of the LORD and to seek him in his temple.

For in the day of trouble he will keep me safe in his dwelling; he will hide me in the shelter of his tabernacle and set me high upon a rock.

(Psalm 27:1–5)

*In the beginning was the Word, and the Word was with God, and the Word was God. He was with God in the beginning.*

*Through him all things were made; without him nothing was made that has been made. . . .*

*He came to that which was his own, but his own did not receive him. Yet to all who received him, to those who believed in his name, he gave the right to become children of God – children born not of natural descent nor of human decision or a husband's will, but born of God.*

*The Word became flesh and made his dwelling among us. We have seen his glory, the glory of the one and only Son, who came from the Father, full of grace and truth.*

(John 1:1–3, 11–14)

### Ghassan Khalaf

It was one of the darkest periods of war in Lebanon. Beirut was like an open hell. Gun shells were showering over a vast area for several days. Many people were killed.

After the fighting stopped, I went to visit a young lady to bring her my sympathy. She had lost her husband in the final skirmish and was left with three little children. She was weeping and grieving – friends were trying to comfort her. When she noticed me, she shouted: 'I don't believe in God, don't speak to me about Him. He does not care for us. He let us die. He is just watching us.'

A wave of compassion came over my soul. Thousands of people in my country say the same words. After she calmed down, I said: 'Dear lady, what you have said about God would have been all true, if He had not become flesh and died on the cross to redeem us and to prove that He does care. God in Christ was involved in our situation and because He has passed through suffering, He is able to help those who suffer. Do you believe that?'

She nodded.

*Jesus was in the stern, sleeping on a cushion. The disciples woke him and said to him, 'Teacher don't you care if we drown?'* (Mark 4:38)

## Ghassan Khalaf

Often in life we go through times of troubled circumstances; like the disciples of Jesus at the sea of Galilee. Our distress becomes very severe to the degree that we do not see Jesus who is very near to us; like the disciples in the boat who were so overwhelmed by the stormy sea, that they couldn't see the peaceful face of the Savior who was asleep on the cushion in the stern of the boat.

We feel that God does not care; that He has forsaken us. We begin to make the loudest noise we can to attract the attention of Heaven. We even wish to disturb God and make Him see our need. Just as the disciples, who lost their patience and disturbed Jesus while He was resting: 'Teacher, do you not care that we are perishing?' Jesus woke up and rebuked the wind and said to the sea: 'Be still.' But He also rebuked His disciples: 'Why are you afraid? Have you still no faith?' So let us in our turmoil be quiet. Let us have faith and not disturb Jesus. He is with us. He is closer to us than we think He is.

*Let us fix our eyes on Jesus, the author and perfecter of our faith, who for the joy set before him endured the cross, scorning its shame, and sat down at the right hand of the throne of God.* (Hebrews 12:2)

## Ghassan Khalaf

When we suffer or see people suffering, a cry from the depth of our being comes up: 'Where is God?' Especially when suffering lasts for years and years, then our morale deteriorates and our situation becomes frustrating. We begin to question even the essential attributes of God: His love, wisdom, and faithfulness. And still worse comes when we begin to question the reality of God's existence. I am sure many people, even Christians, are shaken by these doubts when their prayers have gone unanswered for years.

How can our faith be sustained in such circumstances? Our faith will be as deep as the cross is in our belief. People tend to look to heaven in the midst of their suffering and say, where are you God? They feel that God is on His Throne up there in heaven, far away and uncaring. Those who have the cross as the centre of their theology will not look up to a distant heaven as if to get help for their suffering, but will look to the crucified Jesus down here on Golgotha, and from His suffering, their hearts find healing in the midst of their suffering.

# July 18

*You sympathized with those in prison and joyfully accepted the confiscation of your property, because you knew that you yourselves had better and lasting possessions.* (Hebrews 10:34)

## Ghassan Khalaf

Complete surrender is the only way to overcome anxiety. During the black days of Beirut the sky was continuously raining mortar shells and rockets. No place was spared from their shrapnel. Everyone was in danger of having his house burned, or losing his money, his possessions, library, car, or life.

Anxiety was about to rob me of my peace in Christ. Confusion hovered over me for days. In a period of meditation I put all I had before the Lord and asked His victory over the feelings of anxiety, and about losing material possessions. I prayed: 'Oh Lord! I am resolved, by your grace, to accept with all contentment, with total surrender and joy, whatever physical or material harm may come to me.'

I dreamed one night that my car was stolen. Feelings of resentment attacked me. A struggle began in my soul between complaint and contentment. After a cruel struggle I accepted the loss with pleasure and complete surrender. Then I woke up.

I was happy it was only a dream. But a thought captured me: It is beautiful to be victorious in a dream, but it is more glorious to be victorious over anxiety in real life while awake.

*Blessed is the man who perseveres under trial, because
when he has stood the test, he will receive the crown of life
that God has promised to those who love him.*

(James 1:12)

## Ghassan Khalaf

Frequently after wars, there emerges a class of people called
'the war rich'; those who seize the opportunity and improve
their own conditions. This is exactly what happened after the
war in Lebanon. But what about God's children? Do we
accept the hard times as opportunities to prove the genuineness of our faith which is more precious than gold, so we
might receive the crown of life?

Believers in Lebanon benefited much from passing
through the fire of war. They became 'war rich' on the spiritual plane. Those who love God collect spiritual fortunes and
plenty of practical experiences. In times of distress the
cyclone shakes us so that our dry leaves and rotten fruit fall
down. At the same time, trials increase our stability by
extending our roots into the depths. After the storm you see
believers still holding their hands high, and roses in their
hands. Because, if you see a person who has passed through
the valley of terror and reached the land of peace, with a
flower plucked from that valley in his hand, then you will
know that God was with him and that his soul has kept the
freshness of faith.

*We love because he first loved us. And he has given us this command: Whoever loves God must also love his brother.* (1 John 1:19, 21)

## Ghassan Khalaf

Christianity is distinguished by the word 'love'. This is the only way to describe the Christian faith in just one word. We think always of God's love for us, and our love for others, and forget a very essential element which is that we can love God too. Love is a mutual relationship between Him and us. He loves us and we love Him.

If we are to understand fully the deep meaning of this relationship, we need to compare love with mercy. Here the full meaning of this love relationship with God will appear. Mercy contains the meaning of 'a higher to lower' relationship and not vice-versa. God can say: 'I will have mercy on you, people;' but we can not say back: 'We will have mercy on you Lord!' But God can say: 'I love you my people,' and we can say to Him: 'We love you, Lord.' Mercy language is between a lord and his slaves. Love language is between a father and his children. There is nothing in the world like this loving mutual relationship between us and God through His Son Jesus Christ.

In this second part, David does not talk *about* the Lord but *to* the Lord.

People feel sorry for David. He is in great need. His faith in the almighty God is his comfort and hope.

## David

*Hear my voice when I call, O LORD; be merciful to me
and answer me.*
*My heart says of you, 'Seek his face!' Your face, LORD,
I will seek.*
*Do not hide your face from me, do not turn your servant
away in anger; you have been my helper. Do not
reject me or forsake me, O God my Savior.*
*Though my father and mother forsake me, the LORD will
receive me.*
*Teach me your way, O LORD; lead me in a straight path
because of my oppressors.*
*Do not turn me over to the desire of my foes, for false
witnesses rise up against me, breathing out violence.*
*I am still confident of this: I will see the goodness of the
LORD in the land of the living.*
*Wait for the LORD; be strong and take heart and wait
for the LORD.* (Psalm 27:7–14)

*. . . who through faith conquered kingdoms, administered justice and gained what was promised.* (Hebrews 11:33)

## Mona Khauli

Few people would choose to live a life of danger and risk. Those who do are either professional stuntmen or terrorists, for whom it is a way to make a living.

In our case, however, life at constant risk has been our experience for fifteen years now. Our beautiful country of Lebanon is paying a high price. Terrorism, bombings and shelling of residential areas have victimized thousands of innocent civilians. Our Christian community is being confronted with a great dilemma: flee the country and live in peace elsewhere, or stay to serve the people and accept the risk of getting killed. We have decided to stay and take a stand for our Lord. By serving people in distress and sheltering the displaced we have been able to light their path and motivate their tenacity for survival against the odds.

We experience great danger, but we also experience the presence of our God in a wonderful way. What more can we desire?

Are you faithful in your own situation serving God and men as He directs?

In doing so you will experience God's guidance and blessings. Be available, be grateful, rejoice in the Lord always. Whatever your situation may be. If we can do it – you can.

Pray for peace in the Middle East.

*The God we serve is able to save us . . . but even if he does not, we want you to know, O king, that we will not serve your gods . . .* (Daniel 3:17, 18)

## Mona Khauli

Throughout the fifteen-year old war, God has moved in our midst, and through us to others.

The most recent example of God's miraculous protection involved a young couple. One day heavy artillery bombing took them by surprise, when a Syrian offensive was launched against Christian areas. Before they could run to take shelter, a phosphorous shell penetrated the roof of their bedroom and exploded, setting the place on fire. They were both severely injured and burnt. The woman, a few months pregnant, was miraculously saved. Her husband, however, was pronounced clinically dead on arrival at the hospital as he had sustained serious injuries from head to toe. His parents and church brethren pleaded with hospital staff to give him emergency care, while they committed themselves to the bedside in prayer. For months, he 'existed' by way of instruments that pumped life into his shredded body, bandaged together like a cocoon.

But God intervened and performed a miracle. Six months later he was released from hospital a walking miracle, only in need of surgery to restore sight in one of his eyes. Doctors and nurses saw him off with these words; 'Lazarus has risen from the dead.'

Pray and trust. Have faith in God to perform a miracle. God is in control.

# July 24

*Faith by itself, if not accompanied by action, is dead.*

(James 2:17)

## Mona Khauli

In our present world, with so much pain and suffering, it is imperative that faith should lead to action in order to create change. This process of change must start in our own lives and attitudes. We have no right to excuse ourselves for lack of potential, as we have been empowered by Christ for the task that lies before us. Though we stand helpless against the wiles of political manipulation in Lebanon we do not stand idle. With faith and perseverance our Christian community has given emergency assistance, year after year, to the orphaned and homeless.

As peacemakers they heal the wounds of war with love. As people who care they take immense personal risks when penetrating military checkpoints to insure medical help to the displaced. Though facing unprecedented levels of torture and violence, they refuse a life of safety in exile.

We do not share these facts with you to show you how good we are. We simply share this to show you it can be done.

Our Christian community in Lebanon wants to demonstrate faith through deeds.

What about you?

*. . . we also rejoice in our sufferings because we know that suffering produces perseverance; perseverance, character; and character, hope. And hope does not disappoint us, because God has poured out his love into our hearts by the Holy Spirit, whom he has given us.* (Romans 5:3–5)

## Mona Khauli

These words are so rich and meaningful; yet they are so difficult to put into practice.

To glory in tribulation? How can this be? It is neither human nor tactful to rejoice in suffering, especially when it concerns people around us. What does Paul really mean?

The best way to explain is to quote a Christian woman in my country, Lebanon. She was facing one family hardship after another. When asked how she managed to cope with all these hardships she answered: 'Troubles are challenges to me. Even difficulty that comes my way is a perpetual source of wonder. I am so eager to see how the Lord will get me out of it.'

She had found the secret. Not theoretically but through pains and problems. 'In all these things we are more that conquerors through him who loved us' (Romans 9:37). Her secret was Paul's secret. Paul's experience became her experience. What about you?

It is no secret what God can do, what He has done for others He will do for you.

*Though I walk in the midst of trouble, you preserve my life; you stretch out your hand against the anger of my foes, with your right hand you save.* (Psalm 138:7)

## Mona Khauli

Throughout and despite the war in Lebanon, the Lord has been my strength and my salvation. Nevertheless in moments of emotional despair, I have often asked myself; 'Given a choice to relive those years would I perhaps opt for a change of course?'

My answer is **no**. I would never exchange the intimate fellowship with God for a more peaceful period of earthly existence. It is also true that I have often been near breaking point. During these times of distress Psalm 138:7 has been a great encouragement for me.

'You stretch out your hand against my foes, with your right hand you save me.'

Both aspects are so real. The danger is that we too often only see the stretched out hand of our foe. May God continuously open our spiritual eyes for the other truth: 'with your right hand you save me.'

*By faith . . .* (Hebrews 11:3)

**Mona Khauli**

Faith is:
- expecting God to accomplish miracles through my five loaves and two fishes. He can use me.
- rejecting the feeling of panic when things seem out of control. He is in control.
- confidence in God's faithfulness to me in an uncertain world. He holds the future.
- depending on the fact that God loves me, not on my ability to figure out how or why. He can be trusted.
- thanking God for his gift of emotional health, not assuming it all stems from my ability to cope with stress. He provides.

'. . . I do believe; help me to overcome my unbelief' (Mark 9:24).

*And now, dear children, continue in him, so that when he appears we may be confident and unashamed before him at his coming.* (1 John 2:28)

## Menes Abdul Noor

The Apostle John writes to the 'little children' as people who are close to him. They are also close to the Heavenly Father. They are weak and small. They are dependent on Divine grace and care. This is why they should abide in Christ and in His Word. They can trust in Him here and now, and forever.

Jesus has come, born in a manger in Bethlehem. He also comes to us, knocking at the door of our hearts (Revelation 3:20). He comes to those who ask for His help, as He came to His disciples walking on the water to rescue them (Matthew 14:22–33). He will come again in the last day to judge sinners and take His followers to be with Him forever. If we abide in Him we will await His second coming eagerly. We hear Him say, 'Yes, I am coming soon.' And we cry, 'Amen. Come, Lord Jesus' (Revelation 22:20).

When He appears, we may have confidence because He saved us and abides in us. We will fall down before Him who sits on the throne and worship Him who lives forever and ever, and cast our crowns before the throne, saying, 'You are worthy, our Lord and God' (Revelation 4:11).

Let us be ready, little children!

*When the foundations are being destroyed, what can the righteous do?* (Psalm 11:3)

## Ghassan Khalaf

During wars, moral and spiritual foundations are liable to be undermined and people tend to be permissive. They abandon God's laws and government laws. In Lebanon when militiamen dominated, the government was dissolved. A state of chaos and complete confusion emerged. The foundations were destroyed. In a situation like this, what can the righteous do?

Learning from our situation the righteous can prove that He is the foundation when moral and spiritual foundations are destroyed. The Christian is the law in the absence of law, and he is the conscience of the nation when morals deteriorate. The example of Christ is reflected in our lives in humanity's darkest hours. Christ is the light of the world, and we should let Him shine through us.

When foundations are destroyed, the righteous should not stand still. He must rebuild what is destroyed. Our call is not just to stand by and observe the destruction. Our call is to share in building up whatever is destroyed, especially in the moral and spiritual realm. What if what we have rebuilt is destroyed again? The righteous should be determined to build it again and again and again.

## July 30

David knows the balance between asking God for things and offering up prayers of thanksgiving. He calls on God for help, but he does not forget to thank Him for answered prayer.

### David

> *To you I call, O LORD my Rock; do not turn a deaf ear*
> *to me. For if you remain silent, I will be like those*
> *who have gone down to the pit.*
> *Hear my cry for mercy as I call to you for help, as I lift*
> *up my hands toward your Most Holy Place.*
> *Do not drag me away with the wicked, with those who*
> *do evil, who speak cordially with their neighbors but*
> *harbor malice in their hearts.*
> *Praise be to the LORD, for he has heard my cry for*
> *mercy.*
> *The LORD is my strength and my shield; my heart trusts*
> *in him, and I am helped. My heart leaps for joy and*
> *I will give thanks to him in song.*
> *The LORD is the strength of his people, a fortress of*
> *salvation for his anointed one.*
> *Save your people and bless your inheritance; be their*
> *shepherd and carry them forever.*
>
> (Psalm 28:1–3, 6–9)

## Remarkable Remarks
### *Victorious Under Pressure*

---

*Chinese Evangelist* writing from prison:

'I am not afraid of being looked down upon by people, because, when I look up I see the smiling face of God.

*George MacDonald:*

'No man ever sank under the burden of the day. It is when tomorrow's burdens are added to the burden of the day, that the weight is more than a man can bear.'

*John Trapp:*

'God has one Son without sin, but none without sorrows.'

*Somebody:*

'Persecution for Christ's sake is not a mark of defeat, but of victory.'

*Wong Ming Dao:*

'Stand firm in your faith, live the Christian life you confess; God can use you wherever you are.'

*William Orchard:*

'It may take a crucified Church to reach the world with the message of a crucified Christ.'

*For we do not have a high priest who is unable to sympathise with our weaknesses, but we have one who has been tempted in every way, just as we are – yet was without sin.* (Hebrews 4:15)

*Let us, then, go to him outside the camp, bearing the disgrace he bore.* (Hebrews 13:13)

---

# August

## Writers for the month

*Lung Singh* from Laos. He did not write his own contributions, but Jan Pit has edited his experiences and remarks and printed them under his name in this devotional. His life story is recorded in the book *No Turning Back* by Jan Pit, Marshall Pickering, 1985. According to rumors Singh was killed by his brother because of his faith in Jesus Christ.

*Yang Zhang* from China. A fiery evangelist from China writing under a pseudonym for his protection.

*Li An* from China. Because he is well known in China he requested his real name not to be published, so we have used a pseudonym.

(The meditation of August 27 was edited from the booklet *Morning Light* compiled by Jonathan Chao, Chinese Research Centre.)

*. . . and I questioned them about the Jewish remnant that survived the exile, and about Jerusalem.*

(Nehemiah 1:2)

## Nehemiah

Though Nehemiah lived in exile, his conditions were pleasant. He enjoyed a comfortable lifestyle, had a good job and as the King's cup-bearer he held a high place of honor in the palace.

He had every reason to be content – but he was not. Not because of his own circumstances, but because of the circumstances of his fellow Jews in Jerusalem. His heart and mind were with them. When he met someone who had just come from Jerusalem he eagerly enquired how the people were doing.

Many Christians today dare not ask questions about the situation of the Body of Christ under persecution. Because, if they would ask, they would have to do something about it. Knowledge leads to responsibility, to love and to action.

As for Nehemiah, it was not enough for him to live a life of comfort, while his brethren lived a life of discomfort.

May we be people who are grateful for what we may possess, and who are willing to do something for those who lack freedom of worship.

Nehemiah sets the example: pray and work. If you follow his example, God's people will be encouraged. And so will you.

*When I heard these things, I sat down and wept.*

(Nehemiah 1:4)

## Nehemiah

When Nehemiah learned that God's people were in great trouble, something happened within him.

He could have said: 'It's too bad, but what can I do about it?' He did not react that way. When he heard the bad news he sat down and wept.

Night and day Nehemiah sat and wept, mourned and fasted, thus to share the sorrows of his countrymen.

'By the rivers of Babylon we sat and wept when we remembered Zion ... If I forget you, O Jerusalem, may my right hand forget its skill' (Psalm 137:1–5).

Paul states in 1 Corinthians 12:26 'If one part suffers, every part suffers with it ...

Nehemiah suffered with that other part.

The suffering of other people will be lifted in the same measure in which we share in their suffering. If we are willing to lift part of their burden, they do not need to bear that part any more. In doing so we not only become part of their problem, but also part of the solution.

*I confess the sins we Israelites, including myself have committed against you. We have acted very wickedly towards you. We have not obeyed the commands . . . you gave your servant Moses.* (Nehemiah 1:7)

## Nehemiah

Nehemiah had a burden. The burden of his people became his own burden. What could he do about it?

Had his response to the bad news been only grief, it would have been nothing more than an expression of sentiment.

Nehemiah's response was different. It started with grief, it led to prayer and was followed by action. A few things stand out in his prayer.

In the first place he mentioned the reasons for Israel's troubles.

In the second place he acknowledged that he himself was not any better than his fellow countrymen. Instead of only accusing others, he confessed that he too had sinned. His confession was both corporate and personal.

In the third place he reflected upon the promises of God. He reminded God of His promises. His whole prayer was rooted in these promises: God, You have said . . .

When we point our finger at others, we must remember that three fingers will point back to ourselves. We are not any better. We too, do not deserve the grace of God. We too have sinned. In confessing their sins and ours, we may count on God's promises.

'If my people, who are called by my name, will humble themselves and pray and seek my face and turn from their wicked ways, then will I hear from heaven and will forgive their sin and will heal their land' (2 Chronicles 7:14).

There is hope, for our nation, for ourselves, and for those who suffer in captivity.

# August 4

*The king said to me, What is it you want? Then I prayed*
*to the God of heaven and I answered the king: If it*
*pleases the king ... let him send me to the city in Judea*
*... so that I can rebuild it.*                    (Nehemiah 2:5)

## Nehemiah

'*Ora and labora*' – pray and work.

That's what Nehemiah did. Whoever prays for people in
need, also does something for them. Prayer always leads to
action. Where there is no action there is probably no prayer.
Where there is prayer, people automatically become acti-
vated.

Those who are unable to go on account of bodily disabil-
ity or age can pray that God will call others to offer real help.
Their prayer sets God and men in movement. Those who have
no restrictions, should also have no objections to doing something themselves.

Nehemiah could have invented all sorts of objections. He
had a distinguished and trustworthy position in the palace
and would be missed. He was also no expert building engin-
eer. He was a waiter, not a carpenter, and carpenters, not
waiters, were needed.

But Nehemiah did not hide behind his lack of expertise.
'He has made us competent' (2 Corinthians 3:6).

Therefore he can say: 'Come, let us build the wall of Jerusalem again. The God of heaven will give us success. We his
servants will start rebuilding, but as for you, you have no
share in Jerusalem or any claim or historic right to it'
(Nehemiah 2:17, 20). God sought such builders.

Pray and build. He will prosper you.

*Remember me with favor, O my God, for all I have done for these people.* (Nehemiah 5:19)

*I had rebuilt the wall and not a gap was left in it . . .* (Nehemiah 6:1)

### Nehemiah

Nehemiah was a man of prayer – and a man of action. There are seven mentions of prayers in the Book of Nehemiah. He prayed all the time, all the way through, about everything he did, and he prospered because he prayed. To Nehemiah prayer was fundamental, not 'supplemental'. He did not just pray for his work, his work grew out of his praying.

We can summarise his noble work by stating:
- So I prayed.
- So we built.
- There is power in prayer.

'I looked for a man amongst them who would build up the wall and stand before me in the gap on behalf of the land, so that I would not have to destroy it, but I found none' (Ezekiel 22:30).

In Nehemiah's case: God looked and found. What about you? Today?

*Nehemiah said: Go and enjoy choice food and sweet drinks and send some to those who have nothing prepared.* (Nehemiah 8:10)

## Nehemiah

When the wall was rebuilt it was celebrated with a feast. All the people gathered together to listen to the word of God. After years of suffering and shame the word of the Lord was being read again.

The people wept when they heard the word of God. Tears of happiness, but also tears of sorrow. Sorrow over sins they had committed. It is good to grieve over a sinful past, but there should also be happiness because of the forgiving love of God.

'Be still, for this is a sacred day. Do not grieve' (Nehemiah 8:11).

After that Nehemiah called the people to think about others also, those for whom there was nothing to celebrate.

'Send something to everyone for whom nothing is prepared, a portion.'

Real happiness and thankfulness is characterised by sharing.

The people understood the command. They counted their blessings and shared them with those who had received nothing. There is still a blessing in giving. 'A generous man will prosper; he who refreshes others will himself be refreshed' (Proverbs 11:25).

The Lord has blessed David in many ways.

Unfortunately, success makes David presumptuous.

He takes the Lord's blessing for granted.

He is so concentrated on the gift that he forgets about the giver.

Prosperity and blessing come from God. Whosoever forgets that, trusts in his own strength and performance.

David realises that, and acknowledges his dependence upon God.

---

### David

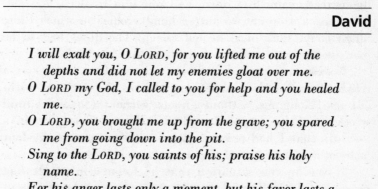

*I will exalt you, O LORD, for you lifted me out of the depths and did not let my enemies gloat over me.*

*O LORD my God, I called to you for help and you healed me.*

*O LORD, you brought me up from the grave; you spared me from going down into the pit.*

*Sing to the LORD, you saints of his; praise his holy name.*

*For his anger lasts only a moment, but his favor lasts a lifetime; weeping may remain for a night, but rejoicing comes in the morning.*

*You turned my wailing into dancing; you removed my sackcloth and clothed me with joy,*

*that my heart may sing to you and not be silent. O LORD my God, I will give you thanks forever.*

(Psalm 30:1–5, 11, 12)

# August 8

*If the Son sets you free, you will be free indeed.*

(John 8:36)

## Lung Singh

He came from the eastern part of Laos, near the border of North Vietnam. A witch doctor and addicted to opium. When he was still a baby he had already received his first opium. Liquid opium, which his father would give him when he cried, to calm him down and put him to sleep. A small dose, just a drop or two onto a handkerchief on which Lung Singh could suck until he fell asleep. The doses had to be increased over the years to come to satisfy his needs.

Now he came to our village – in western Laos – as a refugee from the Communist part of Laos. A poor man, without any belongings, without a home, without a future. A total wreck – at the age of forty-five. Addicted to opium in a measure that I had never seen before. More than forty-four years of drug-taking had asked a price, a high price.

It was in this situation that he found Christ. He had never heard the Gospel before, but when he heard about Jesus, for the first time in his life he made a decision: to follow that Jesus. I never forget his first prayer. He did not know how to pray, or even to whom he should pray. It was just a simple prayer – but coming from the heart of a desperate man: 'Devil I have followed you for forty-five years. I have been your slave.' Then Lung Singh turned around, looked to the heavens and said: 'God, I want to follow you. Please accept me. I want to be your slave, forever more.'

God did not make him His slave ... He made him His child, and delivered him from opium and evil spirits.

If the Son sets you free – you will be free indeed. Nothing is too hard for **Him**.

*Will a man rob God? Yet you rob me. In tithes and offerings. Bring the whole tithe into the storehouse, that there may be food in my house. Test me in this ... and see if I will not open the floodgates of heaven and pour out so much blessing that you will not have room enough for it.*

(Malachi 3:8–10)

## Lung Singh

Lung Singh was sitting in his little bamboo house, reading the Bible, while his wife Bunmah was preparing a meal. It was not much of a meal because they had hardly any food left. Being poor refugees she tried to divide the little rice that was left over into seven portions, so that they would have at least some food for the rest of the week.

All of a sudden Lung Singh called his wife: 'Bunmah, we have stolen from God' and read to her from Malachi 3.

'What do you think God means that he wants ten per cent of what we have? Everything we have comes from Him anyway, so why does He want it back?'

'Of course not' his wife said, 'We don't even have enough rice for ourselves to eat. If we give God some of it we will starve ourselves.' 'Maybe we have so little because we give so little' Singh replied. When he came to my house telling me this story, I looked at him. A poor man, should I tell him that we don't live under the law of the Old Testament anymore but under the grace of the New Covenant? I am glad I did not tell him that. Singh would have replied that the grace of God is worth more than ten per cent!

That evening Lung Singh sold ten per cent of his rice, two chickens and one duck (out of twenty chickens and nine ducks – his total belongings) and put the money in the offering the next Sunday. Not because he had to but because he wanted to.

No wonder he was such a happy, spiritual man.

# August 10

*If anyone is in Christ, he is a new creation, the old has gone, the new has come.*     (2 Corinthians 5:17)

## Lung Singh

It was a beautiful day when Singh was baptised in the Mekong River. Many people listened to his testimony which he gave before his baptism. Among the spectators were Buddhist priests who knew Singh. They knew about his addiction to opium, about his conversion and deliverance from drugs and evil spirits. Singh finished his testimony by quoting from his love-song (he dare not sing, so he quoted from it).

'I have decided to follow Jesus
No turning back, no turning back.
The world behind me, the cross before me
I will follow Jesus – no turning back.'

The congregation started to sing that song as Singh stepped into the river. After his baptism he looked at the fast flowing water in which he was baptised and said: 'There goes my old life – the old has gone, the new has come.'

Some days later, the Buddhist priests came to our house and wanted to know how Lung Singh had managed to break with the old way of life. 'It is impossible that a man can break with opium after forty-five years,' they said. 'How did he do it?' Lung Singh looked at them and smiled. 'I didn't do it – God did. All He asked of me was a willingness to break with my sin and when I said "yes" – **He** did it in me.' Christ can set us free – me and you.

From that day on, Lung Singh – at the request of the Buddhist priests, spoke in the Buddhist temple to other drug addicts about his deliverance – to the glory of God!

*I am the light of the world.* (John 8:12)

*You are the light of the world.* (Matthew 5:14)

## Lung Singh

Every Sunday afternoon was set aside for evangelism. The whole congregation was encouraged to take part. In the morning we would have our Sunday worship meeting, in the afternoon the Sunday service meeting: evangelism in unreached villages of Laos. Some villages were free – others were controlled by the Communist soldiers in the area.

When we entered a village where the Gospel had never been preached before, some people recognised Lung Singh. 'Is that not the man who was more addicted to opium than anybody else?' they would ask. I called Lung Singh and asked him to speak to the crowd. By now the whole village had gathered around us. Lungh was not a great speaker – but he was a great example! He stood up and simply said this: 'Look at me. Look at me. Don't I look great?' I felt uneasy about his remarks. I almost told him to change his testimony: 'Don't say "look at me", you should say: "Look at Jesus".' Before I could say anything, Singh had already sat down ... and the crowd was astonished, they wanted to know what had happened to Singh. Many hours later we left ... leaving a new group of Christians behind. They had **seen** the power of God. 'You are the light of the world.' They saw that light – and gave glory to the heavenly Father.

Does the world see the change of conversion in us? 'Let your light shine before men, that they may see your good deeds and praise your Father in heaven.'

*If we live, we live to the Lord; and if we die, we die to the Lord. So whether we live or die, we belong to the Lord.*

(Romans 14:8)

## Lung Singh

Singh's brother was the leader of a Communist group in the area where Singh lived. He was furious about Singh's conversion – and especially about Singh's continued Christian 'propaganda'. The reason why he decided to visit Singh was to warn him not to be actively involved in evangelism. 'I can't stop you believing in your religion' he told Singh, 'but I warn you, don't talk about it. If you do, the consequences will be yours.'

That evening Singh and his wife discussed the situation. They realised what the consequences would be if they continued to witness for Christ. Should they decide to only believe in their hearts – and thus escape arrest? Their discussion did not take long. They had made up their minds. 'If we live, we live for the Lord, whatever the consequences might be. And if we die, we die for the Lord.' They finished their discussion with a time of prayer together, followed by singing their love-song;

'We have decided to follow Jesus, no turning back.'

When Singh's brother learned about their decision he went over to their house again, taking some Communist soldiers along – and arrested Lung Singh and his wife Bunmah. They were taken into the forest, from where they never returned.

'Whether we live or die, we belong to the Lord.'

'Be faithful, even to the point of death, and I will give you the crown of life' (Revelation 2:10).

'Well done, good and faithful servant ... come and share your master's happiness' (Matthew 25:21).

In this first part of the psalm, David cries out to God for help. He is surrounded by enemies. Even his own health is suffering because of it. In the midst of this sickness and strife, David calls on God for help. The Lord knows, the Lord sees. We can trust such a God under all circumstances.

## David

*In you, O LORD, I have taken refuge; let me never be put to shame; deliver me in your righteousness.*
*Turn your ear to me, come quickly to my rescue; be my rock of refuge, a strong fortress to save me.*
*Since you are my rock and my fortress, for the sake of your name lead and guide me.*
*Free me from the trap that is set for me, for you are my refuge.*
*Into your hands I commit my spirit; redeem me, O LORD, the God of truth.*
*I hate those who cling to worthless idols; I trust in the LORD.*
*I will be glad and rejoice in your love, for you saw my affliction and knew the anguish of my soul.*
*You have not handed me over to the enemy but have set my feet in a spacious place.* (Psalm 31:1–8)

*The friendship of the Lord is for those who fear him and he makes known to them his covenant.* (Psalm 25:14)

## Lung Singh

The Suffering Church is a praying Church. Persecuted Christians pray a lot. When it comes to praying, they even seem to be leading figures, for their prayers seem to be much more powerful and intensive than the prayers of many in the 'free' world.

Many times when I listened to their prayers, I was deeply moved. And strange as it may seem, I often watched them while they were praying. I felt that they were so close to God that they could almost touch Him.

These were prayers without verbiage, without shame, without searching for sentences. Prayers with a deep realization of being in the presence of the living, holy God.

Their prayers were characterized by genuineness, simplicity and ... tears. Not from emotion, for the Suffering Church has learned to restrain emotion long ago, but because of the consciousness of their own sinfulness and weakness when meeting God. Is this the reason why their prayers are so powerful? And yet they know and address this holy God as 'Our Father'.

True friendship with God is brought about by intimate contact with Him, the Holy One ... Our Father.

'Lord, teach us to pray' (Luke 11:1).

*In quietness and trust is your strength.*     (Isaiah 30:15)

## Lung Singh

In spite of the sorrow, a burial in Laos often looks like a celebration. Immediately after the death of the sick person, when the ceremonial dirges are over, there is a feast – apparently. Sometimes a film is presented in front of the house of the dead person, preferably a comedy. Inside, people play cards or dice, and there is drinking and talking. It looks as if they are trying to laugh away their distress.

Of course this is not the case. There is sorrow – great sorrow, and they show it when the dirges are sung. But after this, the spiritual world must be given the impression that the dead person has already been received by the good spirits, while the evil spirits must be misled by pretending as if nothing has happened – by means of a comedy, drink and gambling games.

The night after the death, the so-called 'death watch', the whole family sits around the dead body, while outside there is the film and inside there is the drinking and gambling. For Christians, the 'death watch' is an opportunity to testify to the hope and eternal life through Jesus Christ, the risen Lord.

That is what Lung Singh did that night. Outside there was a high wind and Singh looked worried. He called me to a 'quiet' place behind the house. 'Will you pray for me?' he asked. 'The storm frightens me. I am not afraid myself, but I am worried about my wife and child and our little pile house. I want to stay here and testify, but I can't keep my mind on it.' I prayed for him and Singh prayed too.

After we prayed he got up and said: 'Well, I can go and testify in peace now.' He had presented the problem to the Lord and it was off his shoulders now. Childlike trust – mature faith – and a divine answer.

'Cast all your anxiety on him, because he cares for you' (1 Peter 5:7).

# August 16

*As the heavens are higher than the earth, so are my ways higher than your ways and my thoughts than your thoughts.* (Isaiah 55:9)

## Lung Singh

An answer to prayer does not necessarily mean that God always gives you what you have asked for. Yet His motivation is always love, though we may not always understand Him.

After Singh had prayed, he calmed down. But the wind didn't abate. It seemed to get even more stormy. I looked at Singh while he testified of his faith in Jesus Christ. The wind of which Singh had been so afraid of was whining around the house. I called Singh and told him that the wind was really very strong now and I offered to bring him home in my land-rover, so that his wife and child and he himself didn't have to be afraid anymore. Singh looked at me in astonishment: 'But I am no longer afraid. We just prayed about it, didn't we? It's alright now.'

Outside the wind was howling, but Singh was quiet. At home, his wife was sound asleep and their child was safe also. The wind didn't drop as I had expected it to. God answered our prayer by bestowing peace in the hearts of those who needed it. I had learned my lesson.

For today's storms the Lord has His own solution.

*The Lord is close to the broken-hearted and saves those who are crushed in spirit.* (Psalm 34:18)

## Lung Singh

Singh and Bunmah had been married for eleven years when their deepest wish came true: they had a child. It was not a child of their own, it was adopted from an orphanage. They felt they were the happiest family in the world. Unfortunately their happiness lasted only nine months – then the child's real father suddenly showed up. It turned out that the man, a soldier, was not killed in battle as the orphanage had assumed. He was still alive and he wanted his child back, though, since his wife's death two years before, he had never concerned himself about it.

It was the beginning of the biggest crisis in Sing and Bunmah's life. 'Why did the Lord allow this to happen?' they asked. 'We prayed for a child so long and now this. Why?'

They asked many questions but they received no answer. Until one day Singh and Bunmah were praying for 'their' child again: 'Lord, you know where she is now. You are with her. You love her and You will look after her better than we ever could. Bless her, dear Lord, and do not forget us either. We need You more than ever now. Amen.'

Singh looked at his wife. He didn't say anything but softly sang: 'We have decided to follow Jesus, no turning back.' There was a brief silence, then Bunmah also joined in the song – uncertainly at first, but then with growing conviction.

They missed their child. They suffered a great loss, but yet victory had returned. Victory through acceptance – peace through submission. Again and again. Not just for Singh and Bunmah, but also for you.

*Therefore I tell you, do not worry about your life, what you will eat or drink; or about your body, what you will wear. Is not life more important than food and the body more important than clothes?* (Matthew 6:25–26)

## Lung Singh

Is God only interested in big problems or is He also interested in our little day-to-day worries?

That was the subject of a Bible study in a small village inhabited by refugees from east Laos. All of them had had to flee the danger of war, the war between the United States and North Vietnam. Now they were living in the free part of Laos, robbed of house and home, in shabby little bamboo huts.

They had big problems, which was the reason why we had this Bible study about worries and confidence. But there were also small problems and these they often expressed in their prayers, which were sincere and uncomplicated.

A widow who had been able to take refuge with her only son was listening attentively. She had so many problems concerning many different matters. There were no social services, there was no work and every day they had to search the woods for food in order to stay alive. 'Give us this day our daily bread' was an everyday prayer for her. At the end of the meeting she asked the others to pray for her. 'Will you please pray for my pig, for it is ill.' There was no negative reaction whatsoever to this strange request. It was her only possession. So there was fervent and faithful prayer for the poor woman's pig. Why would God make an axe float on water (2 Kings 6) and not cure a pig?

God is so great yet He is also interested in small matters.

'Do not be anxious about anything, but in everything ... present your requests to God' (Philippians 4:6).

The Lord answered David's prayer and David is aware of it: 'In my alarm I said, I am cut off from your sight! Yet you heard my cry for mercy when I called to you for help' (v. 22).

For that David thanks his God.

Whatever happens: 'You are my God. My times are in your hands' (v. 16).

---

**David**

---

*How great is your goodness, which you have stored up for those who fear you, which you bestow in the sight of men on those who take refuge in you.*

*In the shelter of your presence you hide them from the intrigues of men; in your dwelling you keep them safe from accusing tongues.*

*Praise be to the LORD, for he showed his wonderful love to me when I was in a besieged city.*

*In my alarm I said, 'I am cut off from your sight!' Yet you heard my cry for mercy when I called to you for help.*

*Love the LORD, all his saints! The LORD preserves the faithful, but the proud he pays back in full.*

*Be strong and take heart, all you who hope in the LORD.*

(Psalm 31:19–24)

## August 20

*You must go to everyone I send you to and say whatever I command you.* (Jeremiah 1:7)

## Yang Zhang

God sent Jeremiah to Israel to speak on his behalf. His words were to be God's words.

God has spoken to us through His Word – the Bible.

In my country, we experience a great shortage of that word. So, for us, the verbal sharing of the Word of God has become very important.

'And He has committed to us the message of reconciliation. We are therefore Christ's ambassadors, as though God were making his appeal through us' (2 Corinthians 5:19–20).

Whether we are free – or in captivity – there will always be opportunities to share the news that Christ came to save sinners.

Do we use these opportunities or are we too afraid of the consequences: Prison, persecution, torture, even death? May we be people about whom God says:

'They overcame him by the blood of the Lamb and by the word of their testimony; they did not love their lives so much as to shrink from death' (Revelation 12:11).

*Preach the word.* (2 Timothy 4:2)

## Yang Zhang

To share the Gospel is the number one priority of the Body of Christ. New believers also have this responsibility. Not just 'mature' believers. Every believer should get involved in spreading the Word of God. The more you plant – the more you reap. Without planting there is no harvest.

God wants to see a harvest of souls. He needs laborers to plough, plant and reap. We are these laborers. We are not only His people – we are also His servants. He can send a servant as He pleases.

The servant has no excuse: I am not gifted. I am not qualified. The master knows what he does.

– When He appoints – He anoints
– When He calls – He enables
– When He sends – He goes along
– When He asks you to speak – He will give you the words
Just obey – and you will see God at work – through you.

# August 22

*. . . A man after His own heart.* (1 Samuel 13:14)

## Yang Zhang

A man who obeys God is not necessarily a man after God's heart. Of course, God wants us to obey Him. But obedience does not always come voluntarily. We can obey God because we feel we have to, whereas a man after God's heart obeys the Lord's will fully and voluntarily.

The first is a matter of will, the second a matter of the heart. David was such a man. He said: 'I desire to do your will, O my God' (Psalm 40:8).

Not because he had to, but because he wanted to. That is what made David a man after God's heart. Why? Because David knew that God wants the best for us. That God's will is perfect.

Many people say God's will is a yoke or a burden. David's assertion was: 'His yoke is easy and his burden is light.' That makes all the difference.

Such a man can face problems, overcome temptations, and be steadfast in times of persecution. Why should I not be that man?

*Here is a boy with five small barley loaves and two small fish, but how far will they go among so many?*

(John 6:9)

## Yang Zhang

This wonderful miracle tells us that God can do much with little.

If we give Him what we have He can perform miracles. The boy could have kept the little that he had. But he gave it to Jesus. That act of obedience fed 5,000 people.

We never need to complain about the little that we have. Our Lord can use it and feed the people around us.

A Chinese friend told me one day: 'Our eyes, nose, ears, mouth and heart are like five loaves. Our two hands are like two fishes. And with our two legs we go and meet the needs of the people around us.'

Let us give our body and our heart into the hands of the Lord and thus become an instrument in God's service, saving many hungry people.

# August 24

*I have hidden your words in my heart that I might not sin against you.* (Psalm 119:11)

## Yang Zhang

To lay up God's words in our hearts takes time. It means that we have to read God's Word so many times that it becomes a part of us.

Some people have the Bible, but they never read it. They have laid up God's Word on a bookshelf.

But we must lay it up in our hearts. Nobody can take that away from us. Wherever we are, we have it with us. In freedom – and in prison.

That is why we in China, read God's Word as many times as we can. We feel already privileged to have a copy of the Bible. But we also know that the Bible can be taken away from us any time – or that we may be sent to places where we cannot take a Bible along.

That's why we memorize as much as we can. One of the best known Christians was Rev John Sung. He once said: 'When I was young I was locked up in a mental hospital for 190 days. I was so glad that I could keep my Bible and I read it many times through during those six months.'

When he came out of the mental hospital his doctors expected that his spirit had been broken. But he came out a stronger Christian than ever before. None of the doctors understood – but we did!

Do you?

*Be joyful always; pray continually; give thanks in all circumstances.* (1 Thessalonians 5:16–18)

## Yang Zhang

When I was studying theology the Rev Chia was our principal. A very humble man and devoted to prayer. Prayer had become so much a part of his life that you could always call upon him to pray for you in times of need.

I remember a time when I visited him, together with some other students. During our conversation he would, unintentionally, close his eyes and pray for us.

We all felt so humble and small in his presence. This man taught me to pray, not by what he said about prayer, but by the way he prayed.

When he prayed he was in touch with God. But I also learned that the Rev Chia was not special. God is special. He has no favorites. All of us are called to pray and be in touch with God. Whenever I think of the Rev Chia I pray this prayer: 'Lord teach me how to pray.'

*... Come, you who are blessed by my Father; take your inheritance, the kingdom prepared for you since the creation of the world. For I was hungry and you gave me something to eat, I was thirsty and you gave me something to drink, I was a stranger and you invited me in, I needed clothes and you clothed me, I was sick and you looked after me, I was in prison and you came to visit me.* (Matthew 25:34–36)

## Open Doors Contact Person

Queen Wilhelmina, former Queen of The Netherlands, wrote a book after her abdication entitled: *Lonely but not Alone.*

The same title could be given to a book about the Suffering Church: 'Lonely but not Alone'.

A while ago, an Open Doors co-worker visited a church leader in Vietnam. He had brought several small presents and gave those to the pastor. They were gratefully accepted, but the pastor commented: 'The greatest present to us is your being here. Now we know for sure that we are not forgotten. We often feel lonely, but God is always with us. Your visit means more to us than the presents you brought. Thank you for coming.'

Flowers, a card, a short visit. How encouraging they can be. Those who bless the lonely will never be lonely themselves.

'You who are blessed by my Father ...'

*Produce fruit in keeping with repentance. And do not begin to say to yourselves, 'We have Abraham as our father.'* (Luke 3:8)

**Li An**

We cannot depend on tradition to be saved. For example, 'I am from such a denomination' or 'I am from such a church.' We cannot depend on spiritual heroes; 'I am a follower of...' or 'I am a co-worker with...'

We are to produce true fruit of repentance. If we do not bear such repentance, nothing else can save us.

A Christian lady in Shanghai summed it up so nicely when she said 'before the Communists came with power I was a Lutheran. Now the Communists have closed down all our churches. All I can say now is I am just a Christian.'

In the final analysis this will be the only true testimony that will count.

'When they saw the courage of Peter and John and realised that they were unschooled ordinary men, they were astonished and they took note that these men had been with Jesus' (Acts 4:13).

'For you know that it was not with perishable things ... that you were redeemed from the empty way of life handed down to you from your forefathers, but with the precious blood of Christ. Through him you believe in God ... and so your faith and hope are in God' (1 Peter 1:18–21).

*The word of God is living and active. Sharper than any double-edged sword, it penetrates even to dividing soul and spirit, joints and marrow; it judges the thoughts and attitudes of the heart.* (Hebrews 4:12)

## Open Doors Contact Person

A Chinese Communist had a Christian wife. He was very much opposed to the Gospel. He had tried his best to make his wife recant her faith. In vain.

One evening, he got so mad at his wife that he threw her out of the house in her pyjamas. The poor woman did not know where to go. The fact that she was blind made her situation even worse. She sat down on the steps in front of her house, shivering with cold, and prayed for her husband.

After a while, he started feeling sorry for her and he let her come in again. To make up, he asked her if she needed anything. She answered: 'I need encouragement and I find that in the Bible. Would you please read something from the Bible to me?' To her great surprise, he conceded and started reading to her from the Word of God.

God's Spirit started to work in the man and the prayers of his wife were answered. He continued to read the Bible and a few days after the incident he gave his life to Christ. Today he is a Bible teacher in China.

We can never expect too much from God.

*And anyone who does not take his cross and follow me is not worthy of me.* (Matthew 10:38)

*The apostles left the Sanhedrin, rejoicing because they had been counted worthy of suffering disgrace for the Name.* (Acts 5:41)

## Open Doors Contact Person

'Take his cross' – it sounds ominous. This does not sound like something that goes with faith. Victory, blessing, peace – these are things which make you happy. But struggle, the cross, suffering, these have such a negative sound to them.

Yet Christians who have endured suffering, often consider it an honor to have been counted worthy to take part in Christ's suffering.

A twenty-one year old Chinese woman from Guangzhou told us openly about the many chances she had in China to be a witness for Christ. 'Aren't you persecuted then?' she was asked. 'Yes' she answered, 'but that does not matter. It's the way of the cross.'

We are not asked to seek persecution and suffering. We are called to take up our cross.

Whoever has to carry such a cross, will be given sufficient strength to do just that.

'But rejoice' ... yes, it really is written there. 'But rejoice that you participate in the sufferings of Christ, so that you may be overjoyed when his glory is revealed' (1 Peter 4:13).

David is short of words to thank and honor his God. To thank him for answering his prayer; to honor him for his faithfulness.

He challenges others to always trust in the Lord – and never to forget to thank Him.

## David

*I will extol the LORD at all times; his praise will
    always be on my lips.*
*My soul will boast in the LORD; let the afflicted hear
    and rejoice.*
*Glorify the LORD with me; let us exalt his name
    together.*
*I sought the LORD, and he answered me; he delivered
    me from all my fears.*
*Those who look to him are radiant; their faces are never
    covered with shame.*
*This poor man called, and the LORD heard him; he
    saved him out of all his troubles.*
*The angel of the LORD encamps around those who fear
    him, and he delivers them.* (Psalm 34:1–7)

## Remarkable Remarks
### *God's Provisions – Our Responsibilities*

*Pastor Lamb – China:*

'Abraham sent Ishmael away with a water bottle, God provided a well.'

*Yiddish Proverb:*

'God gave burdens, but also shoulders.'

*Brother Andrew:*

'When I tell those who suffer: don't run away from your country, I should add: I will help you.'

*Chinese proverb:*

'Instead of cursing the darkness, light a candle.'

*Horace Bushneel:*

'What you call hindrances, obstacles and discouragements are possibly God's opportunities.'

*Corrie ten Boom – Holland:*

'God has no problems – only plans.'

*Somebody:*

'Your problems become God's plans, the moment you give the problems to Him.'

*. . . God is faithful; he will not let you be tempted beyond what you can bear . . . he will also provide a way out so that you can stand up under it.*   (1 Corinthians 10:13)

# September

## Writers for the month

In the coming month *Antonio Garrido*, *Enrique Palacio*, *Andrés Noriega* and *Gustavo Figueroa* from Cuba share about their life with the Lord. Despite the battle, their meditations witness to victory and faith. All write under a pseudonym.

*In the land of Uz there lived a man whose name was Job.*
*This man was blameless and upright; he feared God and*
*shunned evil.* (Job 1:1)

## Job

One person we could not leave out of this book is Job. In no other book of the Bible are we confronted with the problems of suffering so much. Yet the question 'why' is not clearly answered. Eliphaz and his friends had an easy answer: it was Job's own fault. For them and for many today, suffering is a consequence of sinning. Others will announce boldly their theory that those who follow God will never be in need. However, Job 1:1 puts paid to this dangerous suggestion immediately, 'this man was blameless and upright, he feared God and shunned evil.'

Job suffered so much precisely because he *was* so God-fearing. In Job chapter one, verse one, he is described as blameless, upright, God-fearing and one who shuns evil.

Those who are really blameless are also upright.

Those who really fear God, also shun evil.

Job practised what he preached. He not only came across as blameless, but was also known as an upright business man. He not only said that he feared God, but he also made a conscious effort to keep away from evil.

Such people automatically become a target of Satan. But they also become honored by God.

In Job's case God let the devil do his utmost. Incomprehensible, sometimes unacceptable. Had God such great trust in Job? And Job in God?

This is what it is all about this week. Job's secret is our instruction today: blameless and upright, God fearing and shunning evil. Then, even in evil days, you can stand fast. And in dark days you can see light. *The* light.

*When a period of feasting had run its course, Job would send and have them purified. Early in the morning he would sacrifice a burnt offering for each of them, thinking, 'Perhaps my children have sinned and cursed God in their hearts.' This was Job's regular custom.*

(Job 1:5)

## Job

Job was not only an upright believer (there was no better on earth [1:8]) and an outstanding business man (the richest in the area [1:3]), he was also a good father.

Whenever his children came together to celebrate Job sat at home and worried. He thought it was good that they kept in touch with each other regularly – that there were such close family ties. He was not aware of what took place on such occasions – he was not invited. The older generation was not invited – it was not appropriate.

Job was with his family in spirit. He knew that the prosperity of his children could easily lead to leaving God out of their lives. 'Surely they will not forget God?' Because he could not at that time speak to his children about God, he talked with God about his children. This was Job's practice.

Praying is sometimes the only thing that you can do for your children. Admonishment often brings distance rather than nearness. Children must be able to go their own way. Job had to let his children go – we must also.

The be  way to let them go is to place them in the hands of God. Job did this. You may also do this: over and over again.

*Then the Lord said to Satan, Have you considered my servant Job? There is no one on earth like him; he is blameless and upright, a man who fears God and who shuns evil.* (Job 1:8)

## Job

Satan had not expected that God would talk to him about Job. Satan had hoped that he could bring a report about all the misery he had seen during his roaming through the earth. He had his story ready, about all the hypocrites, thieves and adulterers. And about all the Christians who hate each other and who are not to be trusted. Those who sing righteous songs but do bad things. That's what Satan would like to talk about. That is what he looked forward to.

But the Lord only wanted to talk about one thing – this Job, who was so trustworthy.

Satan always wants to talk about negative things. He encourages God's children to do the same – and with much success. God points us to the positive. Although he condemns sin and is moved by the needs of men and the world, he offers forgiveness and expectations for people without hope for the future.

He is our God and Savior. We should walk in His steps. And pray:

'Search me, O God, and know my heart;
test me and know my anxious thoughts.
See if there is any offensive way in me,
and lead me in the way everlasting.'
(Psalm 139:23–24)

*Does Job fear God for nothing? Satan replied ... You have blessed the work of his hands ... but stretch out your hand and strike everything he has, and he will surely curse you to your face.* (Job 1:9–11)

## Job

These verses form the essence of the Book of Job. Many think that it is about the problem of suffering. Although the suffering of Job is central, surely the essence is this; Does Job believe in God out of love, or because He had blessed him so much?

Satan charged Job with the latter. Job had reasons for being well rewarded by God.

'Does Job fear God for nothing?' 'Yes' said God. 'Impossible', said the devil.

Job himself knew nothing of the conversation between Satan and God. If only he could have looked behind the scenes! But he could not do that. Job was, although it sounds awful, the battleground. Job was the only one who could clarify who was right: God or the devil. And Job declared who it was. Although the price was high – humanly speaking too high – Job clung to God and God to him!

When everything around Job died this witness remained; 'I know that my redeemer lives' (Job 19:25).

Job's faith was based on this. He was sustained by the living God.

The Redeemer still says: 'See I make all things new.'

May that also be your confession and comfort – now and always.

*The Lord gave and the Lord has taken away; may the
name of the Lord be praised. In all this, Job did not sin
by charging God with wrongdoing.* (Job 1:21–22)

### Job

Many sayings from Sister Basilea Slink are well known. One
of these reads: 'God's actions are always love, even if we do
not understand Him.'

Job could have written those words, or better still, this
was Job's testimony.

He did not understand God. He was full of 'whys' but he
had no doubt that God had His best in mind.

Some people say that you must never ask 'why' something has happened, but 'what for'? That may sound a little
pious, but on a more practical note hear the words of a
woman, who herself had come through many things: 'I do not
ask "why?", nor "what for", but I ask myself the question:
How am I going to get through all this?'

Job did it because he clung to God, who does not have a
hand in our suffering, but has His hands around it.

Not only in Job's situation but also in yours.

*. . . The Lord made him prosperous again.* (Job 42:10)

## Job

When did the Lord bring a change in the plight of Job? After Job had prayed for his friends.

Friends? They had been more like enemies than friends. They had pushed Job deeper in the mire. They had tried to convince Job with many pious words that his suffering was a result of his own sins. Job had to defend himself (and God!), but his pious friends appeared to know much better.

Job became angry – and God also: 'I am angry with you and your two friends, because you have not spoken of me what is right, as my servant Job has' (Job 42:7).

At least four times God referred to Job as His 'servant'.

This servant Job had to pray for his friends, otherwise God would not forgive their sins.

Would you have done that? Pray for people who say they are your friends, but in the hour of need accuse you of all sorts of sins? Perhaps for sins which they have committed themselves and not you?

Job did what God told him to do. He prayed for his enemies – and then the Lord brought about a change in his circumstances.

If Job could remain faithful, in spite of his suffering, then there is hope for us. For Job's God is also our God.

'And God is faithful; he will not let you be tempted beyond what you can bear. But when you are tempted, he will also provide a way out so that you can stand up under it' (1 Corinthians 10:13).

A song of praise to the Lord, to the God who is alive.

This God hears when His children call on him.

He seems far away sometimes, but he is never absent.

'The Lord is close to the brokenhearted and saves those who are crushed in spirit' (Psalm 34:18).

---

**David**

---

*Come, my children, listen to me; I will teach you the
fear of the LORD.*

*Whoever of you loves life and desires to see many good
days,*

*keep your tongue from evil and your lips from speaking
lies.*

*Turn from evil and do good; seek peace and pursue it.*

*The eyes of the LORD are on the righteous and his ears
are attentive to their cry;*

*the face of the LORD is against those who do evil, to cut
off the memory of them from the earth.*

*The righteous cry out, and the LORD hears them; he
delivers them from all their troubles.*

*The LORD is close to the brokenhearted and saves those
who are crushed in spirit.*

*A righteous man may have many troubles, but the LORD
delivers him from them all.*          (Psalm 34:11–19)

*So do not fear, for I am with you; do not be dismayed, for I am your God. I will strengthen you and help you; I will uphold you with my righteous right hand.* (Isaiah 41:10)

## Antonio Garrido

The events that took place in the revival in my country are an evident act of God's power.

For thirty years the government had taught that there is no God. The Christian faith was ridiculed. But just when the battle seemed to be won by the government, God sent a great revival.

People were so disappointed in Communism that they came to the very churches which the government tried to destroy.

Thousands and thousands of people would gather together in and outside the church to hear the Gospel. They would bring the sick, and God performed miracles, again and again. Even atheists came to listen and many of them acknowledged that God is alive and at work. We never need to be dismayed. God is still in control. Despite all persecution and false propaganda the church grew.

Yes, we can trust in God. He says: 'I will build my church...' (Matthew 16:18). So we never need to be dismayed whatever the circumstances.

*And the Israelites enquired of the Lord. (In those days
the ark of the covenant of God was there, with Phinehas
son of Eleazar, the son of Aaron, ministering before it.)
They asked, 'Shall we go up again to battle with Benjamin our brother, or not?' The Lord responded, 'Go, for
tomorrow I will give them into your hands.'*

(Judges 20:27–28)

### Antonio Garrido

The story of Judges 20 is not that well known. The Benjaminites had committed a crime and the Israelites had to take
revenge. Three times they asked God if they should punish
the Benjaminites. Three times the Lord told them to do so.

Yet, the first two times they suffered defeat at the hands
of the Benjaminites. After praying and fasting they tried a
third time and this time they prevailed.

We Christians in Cuba, are not going to take revenge on
those who have persecuted us and treated us so badly. Our
suffering is spiritual, not carnal. But we too, often feel
defeated, despite all God's promises.

The story of Judges teaches us a spiritual lesson. For the
children of God there will always be new opportunities to
defeat the enemy – Satan – when we keep trusting our Lord.
We too have often been defeated, but it does not mean definite loss. For the children of God it will never be too late.
There will always be new, spiritual opportunities to destroy
the work of darkness.

Let us claim, take and declare God's final victory, despite
all setbacks.

*Who shall separate us from the love of Christ? Shall trouble or hardship or persecution or famine or nakedness or danger or sword? As it is written: 'For your sake we face death all day long; we are considered as sheep to be slaughtered.' No, in all these things we are more than conquerors through him who loved us. For I am convinced that neither death nor life, neither angels nor demons, neither the present nor the future, nor any powers, neither height nor depth, nor anything else in all creation, will be able to separate us from the love of God that is in Christ Jesus our Lord.* (Romans 8:35–39)

## Antonio Garrido

The Church in Cuba has gone through many times of persecution during the last three decades.

Sometimes the enemy of God's people confronted us face to face. Sometimes the battle was more subtle, when they disguised themselves and infiltrated our churches as wolves in sheep's clothing. But they failed. We knew their plans. They tried to discourage God's people through loss of jobs, loss of education and other privileges. They infiltrated the minds of our children with diabolical materialism. But in all these things they failed.

Despite these trials and tribulations the Church of God remained: alive, growing and full of power. If God is for us – who can be against us? Who shall separate us from the love of Christ? Shall tribulation, or distress, or persecution, or famine, or nakedness, or peril, or sword?

No, in all these things we are more than conquerors through Him who loved us.

*Moses answered the people, 'Do not be afraid. Stand firm
and you will see the deliverance the Lord will bring you
today. The Egyptians you see today you will never see
again. The Lord will fight for you; you need only to be
still.' Then the Lord said to Moses, 'Why are you crying
out to me? Tell the Israelites to move on. Raise your staff
and stretch out your hand over the sea to divide the water
so that the Israelites can go through the sea on dry
ground.'* (Exodus 14:13–16)

## Antonio Garrido

The Israelites, with Moses at the front, were involved in a
very delicate situation. In front of them was the Red Sea. To
their sides the desert and behind them the Egyptian army to
capture them. A very frightening scene. A street with a dead
end.

God's people often find themselves in similar situations.
Enemies all around us with a seemingly dead end awaiting.
Wherever we look we see danger, anguish and despair. But
God permits these situations to show us that there is never
reason for despair. Certain spiritual lessons can only be
learned in streets with a dead end, where the way to God is
still open.

When things got really bad Moses obeyed the voice of
God and struck the water with his rod. And the dead end
street changed into a thoroughfare.

It always will ... if we obey and trust our Lord.

*And I heard a loud voice from the throne saying, 'Now the dwelling of God is with men, and he will live with them. They will be his people, and God himself will be with them and be their God. He will wipe every tear from their eyes. There will be no more death or mourning or crying or pain, for the old order of things has passed away.' He who was seated on the throne said, 'I am making everything new!' Then he said, 'Write this down, for these words are trustworthy and true.' He said to me: 'It is done. I am the Alpha and the Omega, the Beginning and the End. To him who is thirsty I will give to drink without cost from the spring of the water of life.'*

(Revelation 21:3–6)

## Antonio Garrido

Although we know we are 'not of the world', we need many things from this world.

When you are deprived of these daily necessities because you are a Christian, life becomes difficult and hard.

This has often been the case with Christians in my country. Not only was it hard for us to find employment, but it almost became impossible to purchase certain articles, ranging from luxury goods like cars to necessities of life such as food and clothes.

When church services are forbidden as well, you feel discriminated against as a Christian and you have to beware of despondency and hopelessness. But the words spoken by Christ in Revelation 21:5 gave us hope: 'I am making everything new!'

Is this only valid for eternity? No, God in His might is able to make all things new now. How does He do that? By changing the circumstances? Or by changing us, so that we experience that in all these things we are more than conquerors? In trouble, in loneliness and in prison. For nothing is able to separate us from the love of Christ. He holds us fast, He makes all things new. Every day – including today.

*And my God will meet all your needs according to his glorious riches in Christ Jesus.* (Philippians 4:19)

## Antonio Garrido

God shall supply every need. What a promise. And we had many needs in Cuba. For more than 30 years we had a shortage of almost everything: Food, medicine, clothing, freedom.

But we also experienced the truth of God's promise. The Lord did supply, especially in moments when there was almost nothing left.

The non-Christians were deeply touched when they saw how Christians helped each other in moments of despair.

God supplied, sometimes in a miraculous way, but also often through fellow believers. That too is a miracle of grace and love.

As is written in Galatians 6:10: 'Therefore, as we have opportunity, let us do good to all people, especially to those who belong to the family of believers.'

God can supply – are we willing to be a channel of His grace? To believers and unbelievers?

# September 14

Christians suffering for their faith in Christ, are encouraged and strengthened by this psalm of David. He speaks about what he himself had experienced: struggle, suffering, loneliness and questions. But also: victory, healing, encouragement and answered prayer.

'Awake, and rise to my defence! Contend for me, my God and Lord' (Psalm 35:23).

## David

*Then my soul will rejoice in the Lord and delight in his salvation.*

*My whole being will exclaim, 'Who is like you, O LORD? You rescue the poor from those too strong for them, the poor and needy from those who rob them.'*

*Ruthless witnesses come forward; they question me on things I know nothing about.*

*They repay me evil for good and leave my soul forlorn.*

*But when I stumbled, they gathered in glee; attackers gathered against me when I was unaware. They slandered me without ceasing.*

*O LORD, you have seen this; be not silent. Do not be far from me, O Lord.*

*Awake, and rise to my defense! Contend for me, my God and Lord.* (Psalm 35:9–12, 15, 22–23)

*And without faith it is impossible to please God, because anyone who comes to him must believe that he exists and that he rewards those who earnestly seek him.*

(Hebrews 11:6)

## Enrique Palacio

I was born in Cuba in 1945 and I heard the good news of the Gospel in the living room of my grandmother's house. When I was only 15 years old I dedicated myself to Christ. It was at that time that tribulation and hardship came to my life.

When I became a minister of the Gospel these tribulations increased, but during my 13 years of ministry, it was my faith in Jesus that sustained me. Whenever tribulations, trials, temptations and discouragements came to my life I was reminded of Hebrews 11.

When I had to leave Cuba I thought that all the tribulations would be something of the past. But I soon discovered that the same spiritual enemy was very much present in the country of freedom and prosperity.

We cannot escape from the wiles of the devil.

But we can draw near to God ... in *faith*.

'This is the victory that has overcome the world, even our faith' (1 John 5:4b).

*Now faith is being sure of what we hope for and certain of what we do not see. This is what the ancients were commended for. By faith we understand that the universe was formed at God's command, so that what is seen was not made out of what was visible. By faith Abel offered God a better sacrifice than Cain did. By faith he was commended as a righteous man, when God spoke well of his offerings. And by faith he still speaks, even though he is dead. By faith Enoch was taken from this life, so that he did not experience death; he could not be found, because God had taken him away. For before he was taken, he was commended as one who pleased God. And without faith it is impossible to please God, because anyone who comes to him must believe that he exists and that he rewards those who earnestly seek him. By faith Noah, when warned about things not yet seen, in holy fear built an ark to save his family. By his faith he condemned the world and became heir of the righteousness that comes by faith.* (Hebrews 11:1–7)

## Enrique Palacio

The first man of faith mentioned in Hebrews 11 is Abel. The Bible declares that it was Abel's faith which allowed him to get close to God.

Hebrews 11:5 talks about Enoch, who by faith, was translated because he had walked with God.

And Hebrews 11:7 talks about Noah, who by faith worked with God and for God.

Worship by faith is the most elevated function of the human soul. It is only when we worship in spirit and truth (like Abel) that we are able to walk with God (like Enoch) and work with God (like Noah).

Therefore ... 'let us draw near to God with a sincere heart in full assurance of faith, having our hearts sprinkled to cleanse us from a guilty conscience and having our bodies washed with pure water' (Hebrews 10:22).

*By faith Enoch was taken from this life, so that he did not experience death; he could not be found, because God had taken him away. For before he was taken, he was commended as one who pleased God. And without faith it is impossible to please God, because anyone who comes to him must believe that he exists and that he rewards those who earnestly seek him.* (Hebrews 11:5–6)

### Enrique Palacio

The first verse of Hebrews chapter 11 gives us a definition of faith. It is synonymous with assurance and conviction. Hebrews 11:6 indicates that faith has such importance, that it will be impossible to please God without it.

God exhorts us to be faithful unto death.

'Do not be afraid of what you are about to suffer. I tell you, the devil will put some of you in prison to test you, and you will suffer persecution for ten days. Be faithful, even to the point of death, and I will give you the crown of life' (Revelation 2:10).

A road that is 1,000 miles long begins with the first step. Likewise, the first step of faith for salvation is the beginning of your communion with God. But although the beginning is important, we must persevere, day by day, week after week, year after year, until that day when we too will be translated to be in communion with God through eternity. The continuation of our communion with God will then be rewarded: and so shall we be with the Lord forever.

# September 18

*By faith Noah, when warned about things not yet seen, in holy fear built an ark to save his family. By his faith he condemned the world and became heir of the righteousness that comes by faith.* (Hebrews 11:7)

## Enrique Palacio

True faith is demonstrated in deeds. In other words: faith must be manifested in the way we live, act and behave.

Noah gave evidence of this reality when he heard God's command and acted upon it. For many, many years Noah built in faith. No signs of rain or destruction were there. But he built and waited.

Christ compares the end times with the days of Noah: 'As it was in the days of Noah, so it will be at the coming of the Son of Man. For in the days before the flood, people were eating and drinking, marrying and giving in marriage, up to the day Noah entered the ark; and they knew nothing about what would happen until the flood came and took them all away. That is how it will be at the coming of the Son of Man' (Matthew 24:37–39).

Noah lived in a time of grace and judgement. He lived in a time of tremendous apostasy. All around him was evil, sin and unbelief. Yet Noah had faith in God. And when judgement came he was safe.

'Do not let your hearts be troubled. Trust in God; trust also in me' (John 14:1).

'Watch, therefore, for you do not know on what day your Lord is coming.'

*The LORD saw how great man's wickedness on the earth had become, and that every inclination of the thoughts of his heart was only evil all the time. The LORD was grieved that he had made man on the earth, and his heart was filled with pain. So the LORD said, 'I will wipe mankind, whom I have created, from the face of the earth – men and animals, and creatures that move along the ground, and birds of the air – for I am grieved that I have made them.' But Noah found favor in the eyes of the LORD.* (Genesis 6:5–8)

### Enrique Palacio

The work of faith is to hear the voice of God in the midst of many different disturbing voices.

It is to obey the voice of God even if it seems contradictory to circumstances. It is to do the will of God even though you are doing it alone, with no other believers around you.

It is to persevere regardless of opposition and discouragement.

It is to accept the divine judgement without asking about its justice.

It is to proclaim the message of salvation even when nobody wants to listen.

It is ... total obedience despite the circumstances.

Can it be done?

Yes, because He who calls is *faithful* – He will do it.

*Now Joseph had been taken down to Egypt. Potiphar, an Egyptian who was one of Pharaoh's officials, the captain of the guard, bought him from the Ishmaelites who had taken him there. The LORD was with Joseph and he prospered, and he lived in the house of his Egyptian master. When his master saw that the LORD was with him and that the LORD gave him success in everything he did, Joseph found favor in his eyes and became his attendant. Potiphar put him in charge of his household, and he entrusted to his care everything he owned. From the time he put him in charge of his household and of all that he owned, the LORD blessed the household of the Egyptian because of Joseph. The blessing of the LORD was on everything Potiphar had, both in the house and in the field. So he left in Joseph's care everything he had; with Joseph in charge, he did not concern himself with anything except the food he ate. Now Joseph was well-built and handsome.* (Genesis 39:1–6)

## Enrique Palacio

The story of the life of Joseph occupies more than ten chapters of the book of Genesis. It seems that God wants us to know all the details of the faith that perseveres. Joseph resisted hatred, injustice, temptations and maybe the most difficult of all: success, prosperity and power.

From his life we learn:
- faith is not moved by adversity
- faith that persists is not shaken by false accusations
- it is not blurred by promises that never seems to come true
- it is not limited to the present, but projects to the future.

The faith that persists:
- sees the invisible
- believes the impossible
- receives the incredible.

David notices that the wicked prosper while the righteous suffer. Yet he concludes that the little that the righteous have is better than the wealth of many wicked (Psalm 37:16). For the power and the riches of the wicked will vanish, but the righteous will live for ever and ever. The choice is not hard to make.

'Wait for the Lord and keep his way. He will exalt you to possess the land' (Psalm 37:34).

---

### David

*The wicked plot against the righteous and gnash their teeth at them;*
*but the Lord laughs at the wicked, for he knows their day is coming.*
*The wicked draw the sword and bend the bow to bring down the poor and needy, to slay those whose ways are upright.*
*But their swords will pierce their own hearts, and their bows will be broken.*
*Better the little that the righteous have than the wealth of many wicked;*
*for the power of the wicked will be broken, but the LORD upholds the righteous.*
*The days of the blameless are known to the LORD, and their inheritance will endure forever.*
*In times of disaster they will not wither; in days of famine they will enjoy plenty.* (Psalm 37:12–19)

## September 22

*For you are great and do marvelous deeds; you alone are God.* (Psalm 86:10)

### Andrés Noriega

Though we often felt out of touch with the Body of Christ elsewhere – we have seen and enjoyed God's hand of provision. He is in touch with His people, worldwide, and causes those who are free, to help those who are persecuted.

The following incident explains this so beautifully: I had received an invitation to attend a Christian congress in another country. Due to the fact that Cuban authorities had always refused to give permission to go, we prayed very earnestly for government clearance. While making arrangements to go I had a long list of all the things I wanted to buy in the free world, that I could bring back to Cuba. The three most urgent items were: Bibles, two tambourines for our worship group and four microphones for the church.

Then came the news: I was not allowed to go. What a disappointment and discouragement. But God was in control. Three days later a young man came to my house. He came from the country where the Christian congress was taking place. He was on a business trip to Cuba and had only arrived a day ago.

'I have some gifts for you Pastor' he told me. He did not know me, and I did not know him so I was surprised. 'A few days ago' the brother told me 'I heard about my business trip to Cuba so I quickly went to a shop to buy some things for the trip. Another customer in the shop overheard me talking about my forthcoming visit to Cuba. He came to me and said: "I know a pastor in Cuba who has great needs in his church. Would you please visit him and give him some gifts?"

'You are that pastor sir . . . and here are the gifts.' I was overwhelmed. Many, many gifts and among them . . . Bibles, tambourines and four microphones . . .

God knows our situation. He knows your problems too. He listens to our prayers and provides. Maybe in a different way than we expected, but in a wonderful way which gives glory to God. 'How great thou art.'

*The Lord will fulfil his purpose for me; your love, O Lord, endures for ever ... do not abandon the works of your hands.* (Psalm 138:8)

## Andrés Noriega

I was at the point of entering university to study Philosophy. It was like a dream come true. I would finally be able to escape from my parents and their situation. My father was a pastor. I had lived with shortages and limitations. The last thing I ever wanted was to become was a pastor. Because to me it stood for poverty, humiliation, danger and suffering. I had seen it and had lived through it. This was the time to get away from it. Go to university, learn, get a good job, become somebody. What I had forgotten ... God had not.

My mother could not have children, for various reasons. Then, through a miracle, she got pregnant. She was overwhelmed with joy. When I was still in my mother's womb, promises came from different sources that the fruit of her womb was to become a servant of God. But here I was ... entering university. I had forgotten all about the promises to my mother. In fact, instead of following the Lord at all, l lived my own life, the life of the world, with plenty of fun and pleasure. I knew I lived in sin, but I still enjoyed it much more than living the dull life of a Christian.

But just before I entered the university something happened. It was as if a film was played, showing my life story. My whole life passed before me .... and the Lord touched my heart. I saw my stubbornness and His love, my insignificant self and His majesty. I cried and confessed my sins. Everything lost its value, nothing became more important than to receive forgiveness. I renounced all and dedicated my life to His service.

Today I am a pastor, joyful and happy and with this great conviction: The little that a righteous man has, is better than the riches of the wicked.

# September 24

*We also rejoice in our sufferings, because we know that suffering produces perseverance, perseverance character and character hope, and hope does not disappoint us.*

(Romans 5:3–5)

## Andrés Noriega

Many of us believe that our faith will grow best in favorable conditions, without any resistance, without any hardships or without being put to the test. But it is not like that. Fellow Christians in my country have often said that they would be better believers, more devoted and more faithful if they could live in a country where there is freedom of religion. They make a big mistake. Our thinking is wrong when we believe that our faith would grow if the circumstances were easier. Faith, like a muscle, grows as it is exercised. The inactivity, the calm, the lack of struggle can be more dangerous to our faith than the presence of persecution. It awakens in us the sense and reality of who we really are; it helps us, or should I say it forces us to depend on God.

A church without any struggle, hardship or persecution can easily fall asleep, become inactive and then lose the victory, because in order to gain a victory you need a battle.

True faith does not need favorable conditions of peace and prosperity. True faith needs favorable (yes favorable) conditions of persecution and trials. That is Paul's message in Romans 5 that is also his experience. And by the grace of God mine too. Therefore: rejoice that you participate in the sufferings of Christ (1 Peter 4:13).

*Why are you downcast, O my soul? Why so disturbed within me? Put your hope in God.* (Psalm 42:11)

---

## Andrés Noriega

My wife and I were very confused when our third child was born. A baby without a hope of staying alive. Each day he lived was an agony.

We felt our world had been turned upside down. We were confused, upset and full of questions. The more so because I experienced a great revival in my church. People were saved, delivered from all kind of addictions, healed from various kinds of diseases. The people in my church were glorifying God. So did I ... until our child was born. 'Why Lord? Why?' we cried.

The next eighteen days were like one long nightmare. We cried, we prayed, we fainted, we argued with God until we were left without strength. It was then that we realised that we were selfish, proud and stubborn. I thought I heard the voice of the mockers saying: 'Doctor, heal yourself.' So I said: 'Lord, your will be done. If you decide to take my child it will not change my obedience to you.' That very day a miracle happened ... the peace of God entered our hearts. We had won the battle.

*PS* Late that night our child came back to life and has been healthy ever since. What a bonus.

What a secret. Put your hope in God and surrender to His love and sovereignty – even when 'the miracle' does not take place.

---

# September 26

*If any man will come after me, let him deny himself, and take up his cross and follow me.* (Matthew 16:24)

## Andrés Noriega

Denying ourselves is a voluntary and conscientious act. We make a definite decision which is equivalent to a complete and absolute surrender to our God. In doing so we accept His plan for our lives and hand over the control to Him. He can make changes in accordance with His plan and purpose for our lives. To deny oneself and follow Jesus, does not signify losing or to winning. It does not nullify oneself but rather opens the way to be raised to the most noble standard of God's plan for our lives. To follow Jesus has consequences. To take up a cross involves struggle. 'If they persecuted me, they will persecute you' Jesus said (John 15:24). It means identification with Him who was crucified. But there is also another truth involved. 'Rejoice that you participate in the sufferings of Christ, so that you will be overjoyed when His glory is revealed.'

The ultimate consequence of following the Lord is not death by crucifixion, but life eternal through resurrection.

'I am the resurrection and the life ... and whoever lives and believes in me will never die' (John 22:25).

*... Since we are surrounded by such a great cloud of witnesses, let us throw off everything that hinders and the sin that so easily entangles, and let us run with perseverance the race marked out for us. Let us fix our eyes on Jesus.* (Hebrews 12:1–2)

## Gustavo Figueroa

We know the loneliness which the great missionary David Livingstone experienced while serving the Lord in Africa. We also remember how Martin Luther spent his time in loneliness in a fortress, where he used this time to translate the Bible into the German language. No room for bitterness: 'Lord, deliver me from this place so I can serve you better.' No, he served the Lord right where he was, despite the limitations.

And what about John Bunyan, confined to a prison for 10 years, where he wrote his famous book: *The Pilgrim's Progress*?

Yes, we are surrounded by a great cloud of witnesses. From the Bible and from church history. People who lived by faith, not by sight.

At the same time we realize that sometimes we can live by sight, and not recognize God's presence. We feel like the two men on the road to Emmaus, who thought they were walking 'alone', while Jesus walked with them.

'... Were not our hearts burning within us while he talked with us on the road and opened the Scriptures to us?' (Luke 24:32).

There are numerous examples from the Scriptures and from history which tell us that a Christian will never walk the road of faith alone. Whatever the circumstances may be, even if our feelings or perception dictate the contrary, the Lord will be *with* us, *in* us and *for* us. Hallelujah.

# September 28

*Be careful, then, how you live, not as unwise but as wise, making the most of every opportunity, because the days are evil. Therefore do not be foolish, but understand what the Lord's will is.* (Ephesians 5:15–17)

## Antonio Garrido

One day a brother came to our home to learn how we reproduced cassette tapes from Bible studies. We not only told him how we did it, but also shared with him what a blessing this ministry had been to other Christians and non-Christians.

It had resulted in great encouragement for the Christians while many unbelievers accepted the Lord as well. While we shared these blessings our brother started to weep.

He then told us: 'I am so embarrassed. I received some equipment a year ago to do a similar job, but I have not used it at all yet. Now that I see how you use your old equipment, and what the results have been, I feel so guilty for not using God's provision. It could have saved so many people; it could have encouraged so many fellow believers; why did I not use God's gift?'

I sat down next to him and said: 'You feel guilty – and maybe you are – but don't stop there. Make a fresh start and use what God has given to you.'

Yes, we must take advantage of the time and gifts we have. Do not leave for tomorrow the things you can do today: 'Make the most of the time.'

The subject of this psalm, like in many other Psalms of David, is trusting the Lord when life is difficult.

Every time David's life is in danger, he trusts in his God, always thanking the Lord for His help in the past. That encourages him to also trust God for the present. Is He not the same, yesterday and today?

---

### David

*I waited patiently for the LORD; he turned to me and heard my cry.*

*He lifted me out of the slimy pit, out of the mud and mire; he set my feet on a rock and gave me a firm place to stand.*

*He put a new song in my mouth, a hymn of praise to our God. Many will see and fear and put their trust in the LORD.*

*But may all who seek you rejoice and be glad in you; may those who love your salvation always say, 'The LORD be exalted!'*

*Yet I am poor and needy; may the Lord think of me. You are my help and my deliverer; O my God, do not delay.* (Psalm 40:1–3, 16–17)

---

## Remarkable Remarks
### *Presence of God*

---

*Nepalese Christian:*

'Not: I was in prison and Jesus was with me,
but: Jesus was in prison, and I was with Him.'

*Pastor Chen – Vietnam* after five years in a re-education camp:

'Looking back, I can say that I experienced God's love in such a special way in the concentration camp, as I have not experienced at any other time in my life.'

*Pastor Mehdi Dibaj – Iran* after his release from prison:

'God gave me the privilege to spend nine years in prison for His Name sake. They turned out to be the best years of my life, because what I had believed while free, is what I experienced while in prison: Lo, I am with you always.'

*Also:*

'It is better to stay in prison with Him, than in a palace without Him.'

*Also:*

' "Close to Jesus" changes the worst prison into a paradise.'

*Remember those in prison, as if you were their fellow-prisoners, and those who are ill-treated as if you yourselves were suffering.* (Hebrews 13:3)

*So Peter was kept in prison, but the church was earnestly praying to God for him.* (Acts 12:5)

---

# October

## Writers for the month

*Hristo Kulichev* from Bulgaria. He was imprisoned and exiled for almost four years for his faith in Jesus Christ. He now has a leading function in the Bulgarian Church and is also editor of the Evangelical newspaper *Zornitza* (Morning Star).

*Nicolae Gheorghita* from Romania. He became well-known as one of pastors of the largest Baptist Churches in Europe. Despite his status, his messages are characterized by their simplicity and servitude.

*Ferenc Visky* from Romania. He and his wife write in a moving way about their life with the Lord despite heavy persecution.

*Daniel resolved not to defile himself with the royal food and wine.* (Daniel 1:8)

## Daniel

'What you learn as a child, stays with you always,' says a Dutch proverb. Such as praying at bed-time and maybe the children's songs from Sunday School.

That is what the first chapter of Daniel is all about.

The youth of Israel who were deported from Jerusalem to Babylon should have become impregnated with a pagan spirit. They were to undergo a complete brainwashing. Not under pressure but voluntarily. If they were put into a concentration camp they would have resolved to remain faithful to God. Their Babylonian captors were aware of this and so they adopted another strategy. They offered the youngsters all kinds of privileges.

The goal was clear – to influence the spirit. The method was devilish.

1  They exchanged their parental home for a palace.
2  They were given new names, for their own names reminded them too much of God. They received new names linked to the idols of Babylon.
3  They had different literature to read. Not about God but about the Babylonian religion.
4  They had a choice of different food, which had been offered to idols and so would render it unclean for the Israelites.

How would the young teenage Israelites react? Verse 8 provides the answer; they refused.

They had believing parents who had taught them about God. Because of their upbringing they dared to take a stand even though they were only teenagers. And God blessed them for their commitment. May God find many such young people in our days. Parents hold the key.

'What you learn as a child stays with you', even when things seem to go wrong.

Remember: God still has His hand on your children.

*Daniel remained there until the first year of King Cyrus.*
(Daniel 1:21)

## Daniel

'The One enthroned in heaven laughs,' says the poet of Psalm 2. God could also have laughed when Daniel 1:21 was written: 'Daniel remained there until the first year of King Cyrus' ... 76 years later. Everything was aimed at changing the young Israelites into 'real' Babylonians so that Israel as a nation would disappear. So that (and that was Satan's final goal) a Messiah could never come out of Israel. Therefore the brain-washing was an attempt to make them forget God.

In consequence Daniel must also disappear. That was Satan's plan. But according to God's plan Daniel must remain, as a man of God, as a proof of God's faithfulness, and as a hope for the future. And Daniel did stay. He came to Babylon as a young man of 14 and stayed till Cyrus became king, 76 years later.

Kings came and went – but Daniel remained. World empires rose and fell – but Daniel remained. That is history and Christian history at the same time. Satan cannot destroy Israel as a nation and neither can he destroy the Church of Jesus Christ. He can close churches: he can imprison pastors: burn Bibles and replace them with atheistic literature ... but the 'Daniels' will stay.

For Jesus has promised that He will build His Church and the 'gates of hell will not prevail against it.'

Till Cyrus came ... the deliverance.

Till Christ came ... the Redeemer.

Therefore we can laugh, even through our tears.

*If we are thrown into the blazing furnace, the God we
serve is able to save us from it, and he will rescue us from
your hand, O king. But even if he does not, we want you
to know, O king that we will not serve your gods or
worship the image of gold you have set up.*

(Daniel 3:17–18)

## Daniel

In this chapter Satan follows another tactic to draw the Jews
away from God. A clever tactic which he had already applied
frequently with success – that of compromise.

What kind of compromise?

To believe in God but also to worship other gods. In the
morning pray to God and in the afternoon kneel before idols.
By allowing such a compromise you can maintain your social
and financial standing. That is what the majority of Jews
thought anyway.

Only three refused.

They knew that any form of compromise was nothing less
than a denial of their faith in the one, true God. The other
Jews concluded that one must give and take in life, that it
would be foolish and too spiritual to risk a good career and
position. In addition, through compromise, much could be
attained. Their point of view was that you must know how to
separate work from religion.

For the three friends of Daniel every form of compromise
meant giving in to Satan himself. Therefore they refused,
although they knew that by doing so they risked death in the
fiery furnace. They would rather die for God, than live with
the devil.

The tactic of compromise is always wielded by Satan, in
the Suffering Church as well as in our prosperous society.

Will you kneel or stand?

'Therefore put on the full armor of God, so that when the
day of evil comes, you may be able to stand your ground, and
after you have done everything, to stand' (Ephesians 6:13).

# October 4

*They saw that the fire had not harmed their bodies, nor was a hair of their heads singed; their robes were not scorched, and there was no smell of fire on them.*

(Daniel 3:27)

## Daniel

All's well that ends well. Yes, it is so in Daniel chapter 3. But this does not mean that God will always protect all Christians from sorrow and suffering. The Bible exhorts us to prepare for more suffering. The fiery furnace will always keep burning. Think about the stone ovens of Egypt, where the Israelites endured much suffering. Think about the Christians going to the stake, or the silence of the prisons and concentration camps in Russia and China. The Christians in Islamic countries are continually confronted with the 'fiery furnaces' of hanging and decapitation. The Bible warns us that the Church of the future will face the fiery furnace again.

All's well that ends well? The opposite seems to happen. And yet ... the fire from the furnace did not burn the men. The only things which were consumed were the ropes with which they were bound, enabling them to walk around freely in the fire. We have not been spared from the fire, but the flames will only consume that which is to be removed from our lives.

Flames of blessing – they only burn what must be destroyed so that we may be free, truly free.

*Finally these men said, 'We will never find any basis for charges against this man Daniel unless it has something to do with the law of his God.'* (Daniel 6:5)

## Daniel

When Darius planned to introduce Daniel as vice-president it led to great dissatisfaction by the other leaders of the people. Daniel – as their boss? That must never happen. They began to plan their revenge to dethrone Daniel. The tactic was simple. To find a complaint against him concerning his work. But it was not that easy. Daniel was very fair and very honorable and they had not expected this. They anticipated that Daniel would have been like many other believers whose words and deeds were not the same. Spending Sundays in church but for the rest of the week just going on like the world – business is business. Life with two measuring rods? That is what they expected from Daniel.

But they had got it all wrong, for there lived an 'excellent spirit' in Daniel. They quickly discovered that they 'never could find any basis for charges against this man,' because 'he was trustworthy and neither corrupt nor negligent.' What a witness.

Then it seemed as if there was one more trap. What for many Christians can be the first trap, was for Daniel the last: his faith ... 'unless it has something to do with the law of his God.'

In God's children today there also lives an 'excellent spirit', the Holy Spirit.

Is He at work in our lives only on a Sunday, or also during the week?

Have your colleagues at work discovered that yet?

*Now when Daniel learned that the decree had been published, he went home to his upstairs room ... he got down on his knees and prayed, giving thanks to his God, just as he had done before.* (Daniel 6:10)

## Daniel

This text forms the climax of Satan's attack on God's people.

It began with a trick (chapter 1), followed by compromise (chapter 3) and now comes the climax; all contact with God is forbidden. Prayer must become silenced. Folded hands are an atrocity in the eyes of Satan.

Prayer has been well named the breath of the soul. If the breath is cut off you automatically die – this also applies to the spiritual life. Daniel had already fought with the lions when there was no lion to be seen. The roaring lion crept up on Daniel in his private room – not in the lions den. When Daniel was thrown to the visible lions he had already wrestled with the invisible lion and ... won. Therefore the visible lions in the den were unable to do anything to Daniel, for there was no more 'flesh' on him. Do we see the tactic of Satan – he who goes round as a roaring lion, seeking whom he may devour? The contact with God must always be there. Praying Christians are a danger to the powers of darkness. God is seeking such pray-ers.

'Lord, teach us to pray.'

When the prophet Nathan comes to David to confront him with his sin, David collapses. He realises his sin, confesses his guilt and repents deeply.

How will God react to this sin? And to such a prayer?

David hopes for, and trusts, in God's grace. 'The sacrifices of God are a broken spirit; a broken and contrite heart, O God, you will not despise' (Psalm 51:17).

**David**

*Have mercy on me, O God, according to your unfailing love; according to your great compassion blot out my transgressions.*

*Wash away all my iniquity and cleanse me from my sin.*

*For I know my transgressions, and my sin is always before me.*

*Hide your face from my sins and blot out all my iniquity.*

*Create in me a pure heart, O God, and renew a steadfast spirit within me.*

*Do not cast me from your presence or take your Holy Spirit from me.*

*Restore to me the joy of your salvation and grant me a willing spirit, to sustain me.*

*Then I will teach transgressors your ways, and sinners will turn back to you.* (Psalm 51:1–3, 9–13)

# October 8

*We know that we are children of God, and that the whole world is under the control of the evil one.* (1 John 5:19)

## Hristo Kulichev

We live in a world which is controlled by the enemy of God. And because we have become children of God, we also have become enemies of the wicked one. His goal is to destroy our souls. It makes no difference how he tries to do that: persecution or oppression; flattery or compromise; vanity or prosperity. The method is unimportant – the end result counts. Satan knows that Christians will not give up their belief in God. That is: true Christians will not. Nominal Christians easily will. We should ask ourselves again and again: am I living under the control of Satan – or does God control my life? I know I am His child – do I live likewise?

Being a child of God, I should never make friendship with the world. 'Friendship with the world is hatred towards God' (James 4:4). Friendship starts with compromise – and leads to slavery. The Christian life is not a life of compromise and slavery, but of steadfastness and freedom. 'For everyone born of God overcomes the world. This is the victory that has overcome the world, even our faith' (1 John 5:4).

'For He who is in us is greater than he who is in the world' (1 John 4:4). 'Have faith in God' (Mark 11:22).

*I delight in weaknesses, in insults, in hardships, in persecutions, in difficulties.* (2 Corinthians 12:10)

## Hristo Kulichev

These words sound strange, if not foolish in the ears of carnal man. People seek happiness and pleasure. Who wants to find that in suffering? Is it possible that someone could be happy in infirmities, in reproaches, in persecution or insults? Those who seek fulfilment of life in pleasure will always be dissatisfied. But when the meaning of life is serving Christ, then everything we do or endure will give us pleasure. Whether we are reproached or persecuted, we will rejoice because through it we can show our love for Him. And this would be the greatest pleasure for us. It will be a pleasure for us when people reproach us, or call us old-fashioned, or when they mock at us because we do not conform to this world. Any attack by the devil will be considered as a mark of true discipleship.

We delight in weakness. We accept the fact that we seem to be most vulnerable, but we claim God's promise: 'When I am weak, then I am strong' (2 Corinthians 12:10). Because 'My power is made perfect in weakness' (2 Corinthians 12:9). The weaker we are – the stronger He becomes. The more helpless we feel – the greater Helper He becomes. What a mighty God we serve.

# October 10

*Not unto us, O Lord, not unto us but to your name give glory.* (Psalm 115:1)

## Hristo Kulichev

Sometimes we get selfish in our faith. We want God to arrange our life in such a way that we will be able to live happily and comfortably. We are always thinking of our own comfort and that God is obliged to provide for it. We want Him to supply our needs (and we have plenty of them!) in such a way that we will experience pleasure in life.

But God doesn't act that way. When Joseph was in prison he wanted to get out of that place as soon as possible. But God did not answer his prayer right away. He delayed his answer in order to give glory to His own name (Genesis 41:28). Martha and Mary wanted Jesus to come quickly and heal their brother Lazarus, but Jesus did not come right away. Was He not aware of their need and prayer request? Oh yes He was – but He waited in order to glorify God's name (John 11). As long as we want things for our own pleasure – He will wait and not answer our prayers. God wants to glorify His name.

'You do not have, because you do not ask God. When you ask, you do not receive because you ask with wrong motives, that you may spend what you get on your pleasures.'

Are our motives right? Are our priorities right? That teaches us to pray:

'Father, hallowed be your name, Your kingdom come, Your will be done.'

Such a prayer will always be answered. To His glory – and that gives us the greatest pleasure.

*Your will be done.* (Matthew 26:42)

## Hristo Kulichev

There are many believers who put their desires before God's will. They expect that God will satisfy their whims and wishes. God did it for Hezekiah, didn't He?

God's will for Hezekiah was: 'Put your house in order.' Instead of obeying God's will, Hezekiah pleaded with God to let him live a bit longer. God answered his prayer and added fifteen more years to his life because Hezekiah had followed the Lord with his whole heart. But the extra fifteen years were not a blessing. Not for Hezekiah, nor for his family or his nation. It was during those extra years that Hezekiah made a terrible mistake (2 Kings 20:12) showing all his possessions and riches to visitors from Babylon. God was not honored. Hezekiah was exalted – not God.

Let us be sons and daughters of the living God whose pleasure it is to do the will of the Father instead of God having to please us.

The greatest blessing for us is not when God satisfies all our desires, but when we obey His will. Then we will find real joy and full pleasure in our complete obedience to God.

*Man shall not live by bread alone . . .*     (Matthew 4:4)

## Hristo Kulichev

God teaches us to pray for our daily bread – but He doesn't say that we have to think only about our daily bread. The struggle for bread is called 'struggle for life'. People are willing to make all kinds of compromises in order to receive bread. When I was put in prison there was hardly any food. When they gave us the prisoner's uniforms, one boy complained that his trousers were too tight. The supervisor said: 'Don't worry, very soon they will become loose.'

I knew what would follow. Every day I prayed: 'Lord, you fed five thousand people with five loaves of bread and two fishes. Only a little crumb is enough for me Lord, please give it to me.' I then realised that God can meet our needs in two ways.

1   He can give us what we need; or

2   He can set us free from what we consider a need.

God did not give me more bread. But he set me free from the feeling of hunger. I always felt satisfied. I never felt hungry – and bread and salt turned out to be a delicious meal for me.

When we trust the word which proceeds from the mouth of God we will never suffer want.

*Anyone who loves their father or mother more than me is not worthy of me.* (Matthew 10:37)

## Hristo Kulichev

Many times I was summoned by the police because they didn't allow me to preach the Gospel. When I was arrested the public prosecutor tried every possible way to exert influence on me. Satan used this man to tempt me in many different ways. The man offered me a better job. When I refused to accept it he began to remind me of the difficulties I would have to face in prison. When he realised that I was ready to suffer for God he said: 'You seem to be willing to suffer for your faith, but do you realise it will have many consequences for your children also? Your imprisonment will affect all your family and they will suffer because of you. Your daughter won't be allowed to graduate from Sofia University, and your son will not be allowed to finish at the Technical College. And you will be the only reason for that. You will destroy their future.' I know parents in my church who ceased coming to church for fear that they might hinder their children's career. I did not blame them. Fear is the strongest tool of Satan to tempt us. Fear for ourselves, fear for our loved ones. Fear, which we hid under the cover of love and care.

I turned to the prosecutor and said: 'If I love my family more than God I am not worthy of Him. I am ready to sacrifice anything for my Savior and so disarm Satan.'

When we love God with our whole heart, soul and mind, Satan will not be able to enter into our lives. God will enter and take care. He did. My children finished their education and both are now serving the Lord. God not always takes what we sacrifice, but He wants us to be ready to sacrifice everything for Him.

That gives complete and lasting victory.

# October 14

David is on the run from Saul again. He is hiding in caves, in the desert of Ziph. But the Ziphites betray him. They tell Saul where David is hiding.

'Day after day Saul searched for him, but God did not give David into his hands' (1 Samuel 23:14).

'And Saul's son Jonathan went to David at Horesh and helped him to find strength in God' (1 Samuel 23:16).

## David

*Save me, O God, by your name; vindicate me by your might.*
*Hear my prayer, O God; listen to the words of my mouth.*
*Strangers are attacking me; ruthless men seek my life – men without regard for God.*
*Surely God is my help; the Lord is the one who sustains me.*
*Let evil recoil on those who slander me; in your faithfulness destroy them.*
*I will sacrifice a freewill offering to you; I will praise your name, O LORD, for it is good.*
*For he has delivered me from all my troubles, and my eyes have looked in triumph on my foes.*    (Psalm 54)

*In humility consider others better than yourselves.*

(Philippians 2:3)

## Nicolae Gheorghita

On 17 January 1982 two laymen were ordained for the ministry without former theological training: Paul Negrut, a psychologist and Nick Gheorghita, an endocrinologist. They were to serve in one of the largest Baptist churches in Europe. I, Nick, was one of the two. On the way home from church, I suddenly heard the voice of the Holy Spirit, saying: 'He must increase, you must decrease.' And although I know that these words were spoken by John the Baptist in relationship to Jesus Christ – I also knew in my heart that it touched on the relationship between me and my newly ordained co-partner. I therefore asked Paul to stop the car and told him what the Lord has just showed me: I must be Paul's helper. There is no greater joy in my life than to see God leading Paul to victory in the valley, while I am interceding on the mountain on his behalf. I am committed to support him in what he does for the Lord.

Humanly speaking people want to be first – not second. They want to be served – not to serve. But if we allow God, through His Spirit, to control our lives we can all play our part – as leader or servants so that Christ's body will be built and His name glorified. Should that not be the goal of us all? What part does God want you to play?

# October 16

*But when they arrest you, do not worry about what to say or how to say it.* (Matthew 10:19)

## Nicolae Gheorghita

After various trials, I was once asked to go to the secretary of the county, an evil man, a committed Communist. My wife said 'It will be a miracle of God if you come back safe.' The 'comrade' party official made me wait for an hour in the hallway for him, after which I was told he wanted to see me now. I prayed (again); 'Lord please go in first. I am afraid to go without you.'

The official was sitting behind his desk. 'I could have sent you to prison for what you have done, but I wanted to see you first' he started. 'You were in Cluj and you preached without permission.' I realised immediately what he was referring to. I had indeed preached to the students of the university in Cluj. I had encouraged them to remain faithful in the week ahead. I had spoken about courage because they had been threatened with dismissal from the university if they continued to believe in God. I told the party official that it was my duty to preach the Word. He started to threaten me. Strange, the more he threatened me the more God's peace flowed into my heart. I was sitting there, full of peace, rejoicing in the opportunity to be threatened for my faith in Christ.

Suddenly, the official realised that he could not frighten me. 'Are you not afraid?' he asked. I just said: 'no'. Then he added: 'Do you have anything else to say?' I said 'yes' ... and I told him my testimony and that God loved him too. I saw him lowering himself behind the desk and he asked me to pray for his soul also. How great Thou art.

*'Son, go and work today in the vineyard.' 'I will not' he answered, but later he changed his mind and went.*

(Matthew 21:28–29)

## Nicolae Gheorghita

When asked to do something we do not like, our first reaction is often negative. In 1981 I went to visit a church that had just lost its pastor. Joseph Ton was 'asked' to leave the church by the government. I had to preach in that church that same evening. I saw sadness and confusion and many empty seats ... because of fear. I started by asking a question. 'Has Joseph Ton left?' They answered: 'Yes.' Then I asked another question: 'Has the God of this congregation left along with Joseph?' My question fell like thunder. They all answered: 'No.' 'Then let us give Him glory,' I continued.

A week later, the church committee called me on the telephone to make an appointment with me to meet with them. I realised straight away that they wanted to ask me to become their pastor. I told them that I was not interested and that I could tell them 'No' over the 'phone. 'But we still want to visit you.' Of course I could not refuse that request.

The church was fasting and praying for our meeting. The members of the committee came and we talked for a long time. All of a sudden I heard myself say 'yes' to their request to become their pastor. When I realized it was not me saying yes – it was from God, peace filled my heart. 'Father, not my will, but yours be done' (Luke 22:42).

'Teach me your way, O Lord, and I will walk in your truth' (Psalm 86).

'Here I am ... I desire to do your will, oh my God' (Psalm 40:8).

*Be self-controlled and alert. Your enemy the devil prowls around like a roaring lion looking for someone to devour.*

(1 Peter 5:8)

## Nicolae Gheorghita

I remember an exceptional day. I woke up feeling refreshed and read the text from Ephesians 6:11. 'Put on the full armor of God so that you can stand against the devil's schemes.' Everything seemed clear and peaceful. I heard myself praying: 'Anything that Satan will try to do today against me will not be successful.'

Everything went well, until one o'clock when we had a special meeting at the hospital where I was working. Prior to that meeting, a colleague was asked by a party official to stand up and accuse me. The colleague looked at me and said: 'You, Dr Gheorghita, are using office time to read and translate Christian books.' He was partly right. I read and translated books, but not during office hours. Instead of spending my lunch hour talking to the other doctors, I spent the time translating books. I knew that the man was being used to speak against me, I asked him to tell me the title of one of the books I had translated. He stuttered and could not answer. The hospital director then told the man that no further charges could be brought against me without proof.

I remembered the verses from Ephesians 6:11 and 1 Peter 5:8. The best way to be alert is in the confidence of God's presence in all circumstances. The battle is not ours but God's and then victory is assured.

*Do not be surprised at the painful trial you are suffering,
as though something strange were happening to you.*

(1 Peter 4:12)

## Nicolae Gheorghita

Sometimes God uses atheists to prove that the Bible is true.
One day the secret police came to my house and confiscated
many Christian books. I was summoned to appear for investigation the following day. A military prosecutor and four
secret police officers questioned me for 10 hours, they then
asked me if there was anything else for which I would like to
confess, so I said 'Sir, this investigation does not take me by
surprise because I knew this would happen. The Lord Jesus
Christ told His followers that they would be arrested and
suffer if they wanted to follow Him. If I would not be a dis-
ciple, would you have arrested me?' They looked at me and
said 'No.' 'So the Bible is true' I continued. 'This investigation confirms to me the biblical truth, and I am willing to face
the consequences; I am willing to pay the price. Your job is to
set the price and mine is to pay it with gladness because I love
my God – and He will strengthen me to bear this burden. But
I also want you to know that He loves you too.' They looked
at me, astonished and bewildered. They apologised to me and
told me I was free to go home. 'We were only doing our job,'
they said.

Let us never be ashamed of the Gospel. It is the power of
God for salvation.

*If you are insulted because of the name of Christ, you are blessed, for the Spirit of glory and of God rests on you.*

(1 Peter 4:14)

## Nicolae Gheorghita

Christ exhorts us to take up our cross. That is not easy. We do not want to suffer. But we need to realise that suffering is a part of our walk with God. If we only believe in God with our heads and not with our actions and deeds, we will not suffer. Only when we live up to God's standards will we face hardships. But what does the Bible teach us? 'If you are insulted because of the name of Christ you are blessed, for the Spirit of glory and of God rests on you.'

I already mentioned that I am translating Christian books from English into our own language. From the moment I started doing this I realised that sooner or later the police would arrest me for this. My wife and I had talked about the consequences. We realised that I could be put in prison and beaten for my work, that she could be left alone to raise our children. However, we decided that I should continue to serve the Lord in this way. He would take care whatever might befall us. I thank God for my wife and children. God has always been faithful. You know God not only exhorts us to take up our cross – He bears it with us. He bears the heavy part ... I am just walking along. Let us not look at the price and pain only. Let us look to Christ. He bore the cross and went all the way. What a love. What a joy to be found worthy to suffer with Him. He is worthy.

Even though David is again threatened with death, this
psalm, written by him, is full of trust in the Lord his God.

The more David speaks with God, the more the enemy
fades to the background.

The one who puts his trust in God, can remain steadfast
under all circumstances. For the enemy is not in control, but
God is.

**David**

*Be merciful to me, O God, for men hotly pursue me; all
day long they press their attack.*
*My slanderers pursue me all day long; many are
attacking me in their pride.*
*When I am afraid, I will trust in you.*
*In God, whose word I praise, in God I trust; I will not
be afraid. What can mortal man do to me?*
*Then my enemies will turn back when I call for help.
By this I will know that God is for me.*
*In God, whose word I praise, in the LORD, whose word
I praise—*
*in God I trust; I will not be afraid. What can man do
to me?* (Psalm 56:1–4, 9–11)

*Take your son . . . and sacrifice him as a burnt offering.*
(Genesis 22:2)

## Ferenc Visky

God speaks to Abraham and requires something from him.
Abraham thinks of every thing, except the fact that he has a
God who asks something from him.

Nobody is aware that God can also ask for things. People
like to ask for things and they like God to give. God asked
Abraham to sacrifice his own beloved son and with it, He
asked everything from him.

When I was deported together with my seven little children, the eldest of whom was eleven years old and the youngest only two, my biggest concern was not that all our
possessions had to be left behind, that the door was closed
behind us and that we would not return. The one thing I
worried about was the seven little ones. What would become
of them? Who would feed them and look after them?

Abraham obeyed and laid his son on the altar, though he
did not know God's purpose. He only knew God Himself, for
he believed Him and loved Him. Before Abraham sacrificed
Isaac, he laid himself on the altar – by obeying God. Because
he sacrificed himself first, he prevented the sacrifice of Isaac.

I knew I had to do the same thing. I cried for my children, but I had to lay myself on the altar first. And there, in
that fateful situation, I experienced a miraculous surprise.
Jesus had been there before. He did His Father's will and so I
found that He was there when I was prepared to sacrifice
myself and it meant salvation for me and my children.

Don't try to find an excuse when God takes you to the
altar, for it is there that He Himself is waiting for you – in
His beloved Son.

*I am God Almighty; walk before Me...* (Genesis 17:1)

## Ferenc Visky

God did not introduce Himself to Abraham like this without reason: 'I am God Almighty...' God always makes Himself clear. He calls Himself the Almighty because Abraham did not know yet that He was omnipotent. If he had known, he wouldn't have taken Hagar for his wife. He would have awaited God's plan, the birth of Isaac and it would have saved himself and others a lot of misery. Abraham was wrong about God when he thought that He would not have the power to give Sara a baby in her hopeless situation.

And Abraham was not the only one. It happens to everyone who doubts God's omnipotence and His salvation. And it is a sin.

I believe that God created man out of the dust of the earth and that the visible originated from the invisible, but when it became clear that He was able to maintain me and my family from nothing, I was dumbfounded. God proved to me that He was also the Almighty during my deportation.

He also said to Abraham: 'Walk before Me and be blameless.' I can even walk in impassable ways when I am certain about God's omnipotence and be blameless, too, that is to say that I can completely rely on God, Who is perfect, and then I can walk straight towards my goal.

Don't be afraid to lean on God's omnipotence completely. It does not mean looking on passively. It means going on. He who walks with God is carried by Him and crowned with His salvation. He did so with us. Wouldn't He be able to do so for you? 'I am God Almighty.' Do you know this God?

*So Jacob served seven years to get Rachel, but they seemed*
*like only a few days to him, because of his love for her.*

(Genesis 29:20)

## Ferenc Visky

Jacob had to serve Laban for seven years under difficult
conditions to get his wife Rachel. In fact, the whole period of
his service amounted to twenty years (Genesis 31:41). Love
delivered him from the tyranny of time. Where love is, there
is eternity, timelessness.

Convicts in prison undergo the heaviest crisis when the
last remains of a life in freedom are taken from them. I went
through that crisis together with eight other brothers: our
heads were shaved bald and we were given striped prison
clothes. Our sentences varied from eighteen to twenty-two
years' imprisonment. We had to give up the life we had led
until then. All of this was accompanied by derision and rough
abuse from the guards, between grey walls with barred
windows. All of us bore the visible signs of our readiness to
die in silence. But we also experienced the comfort of the Lord
in this desperate situation. He sent us this text: '...they
seemed like only a few days to him, because of his love for
her.' I whispered it in the ear of the brother who stood beside
me and he passed it on to the next. As if in a holy relay, it
passed the whole row: '...because of his love for her.'

God, too, loved us so much that He sacrificed His own
beloved Son with joy to save us. Jacob didn't count the
years, the only thing that counted for him was Rachel. Even
during the long years of service he was a free man. Love made
him free. When the apostle Paul speaks about his suffering for
the name of Jesus, he says that the troubles are 'light and
momentary' (2 Corinthians 4:17).

When you love the Lord, your captivity for His sake,
your suffering for Him is light and a pleasure.

*Therefore the prudent man keeps quiet in such times, for the times are evil.* (Amos 5:13)

## Ferenc Visky

Keeping silent to conceal something is quite different from keeping silent to listen to God. When we conceal something we do not hear God's voice. 'Hear, O Israel, the Lord our God, the Lord is one.'

The well-known 'sema' is attached to the doorpost of every Israelite. It is also on a small scroll on his wrist and on his forehead. God shaped and preserved His people by this 'hear, Israel'. But it is also possible not to hear correctly.

We had been in prison for a few weeks and there were eight of us in a cell that was meant for only two. We had all been convicted for the testimony of Jesus Christ. The evenings were harder than the days, because then our thoughts were with our loved ones, whom we had been forced to leave behind.

From the corridors alongside the cells, the sound of dull blows and an occasional restrained cry came to our ears. Someone was being beaten again. Our heavy, drunken guard sometimes picked out one of us and beat his victim up in the corridor. It could be our turn at any moment. We sat together like a flock startled by wolves and the beating of our hearts was audible...

The tempter wanted to make things even more difficult for us. One of us softly remarked: 'We wouldn't be here if we had kept silent, for it is written that the prudent man keeps quiet in evil times.' The words came down on us like sledgehammer blows. It is bearable to be accused by people, but when God condemns you as well, that is unbearable. We almost collapsed under the heavy load. But we were comforted again. The Holy Spirit explained the text to us through one of our brothers as follows: the prudent man keeps quiet in evil times, but he is silent in order to listen. To listen to God.

At that instant, the charge of the accuser was disproved and the terror vanished from our cell.

Listen to God and the tempter will flee from you.

*But a time is coming and has come when . . . you will
leave me all alone. Yet I am not alone, for my Father is
with me.* (John 16:32)

## Ferenc Visky

In prison, and also outside, the realization of being delivered
and then abandoned is the most difficult thing to deal with.
In our cell, we began every new morning with worship. It is
true that we had no Bible, but the Holy Spirit fulfilled the
promise from John 14:26: 'He will teach you all things and
will remind you of everything I have said to you.'

One morning, the following text came to my mind: 'The
time has come when you will all leave me alone.' I pondered
on the meaning of this text. What did it mean: leaving Jesus
all alone? Does it mean that I must let You be the only one to
stay with me, Lord? Will my brothers be taken away from me
and will I be alone in this cell? No, it can't be true, Lord.
After all, they prayed me back from death one time. They
shared their last piece of bread with me and supported me in
everything because I am the weakest of them. In my struggle,
I clearly heard Jesus' voice: 'Am I not enough for you?' I
couldn't give a negative answer. Yes, Lord, You're enough!

After this, I felt relieved. I passed this text on to my
brothers. A few minutes later, the door of the cell was opened
and some Securitatè officers came in. They read out a list of
names of people who had to move from the cell. I knew
beforehand that they wouldn't read out my name. I was on
my own now, yet I was not alone. Jesus' glowing presence
filled my heart with joy.

Jesus' presence makes up for everything. You can be sure
that He only takes something or someone away from you in
order to give Himself even more fully.

*You know that your brothers throughout the world are undergoing the same kind of sufferings.* (1 Peter 5:9)

---

## Ferenc Visky

---

God never tests us without comforting us as well. But the comfort is not always what we expect it to be.

It was the sixth year of my detention and I didn't know anything about my wife and seven little children who had stayed behind in the vicarage. The eldest of the children was only ten years old when I left them.

One evening, another group of prisoners arrived at the Szamosujvar prison. They came from the Danube delta and among them was a pastor who recognized me. He came to me and softly said to me: 'I don't want to upset you, but I have to tell you something. On good authority, I know that your family have been deported to a temporary accommodation close by the prisoners' work area.'

At first, I was deeply shocked by this message: weren't they satisfied with the sentence of twenty-two years' imprisonment? Did they also have to intrude into the lives of my wife and children? My heart was craving for strength and comfort. In this awful inner struggle, the Lord answered me. Like a flash of lightning, the words came to my mind: '...your brothers are undergoing the same kind of suffering.' An inexpressible joy filled my heart and I gave thanks to the Lord for the favor which he allowed my wife and children to share. They, too, had become bearers of Christ's wounds. Gratitude and peace filled my heart. To the present day, I experience what a rich source of blessing these four years of severe suffering have been in the lives of our children. If you say 'yes' to God's unusual comfort, your life, too, will be full of immeasurable blessing.

---

# October 28

*. . . he was taken up before their very eyes . . .* (Acts 1:9)

*. . . and seated us with him in the heavenly realms in Christ Jesus.* (Ephesians 2:6)

## Ferenc Visky

A few years ago, at the time of my enforced emeritus status, I was summoned by the Securitatè once more. I had 'sinned' against the state again. One of the interrogations happened to take place on Ascension Day. In the course of the cross-examination, this Christian holiday came up. The one who interrogated me had no idea as to the meaning of this day. He thought it was some kind of ceremonial hocus-pocus.

Unexpectedly, he was listening to what I said about this: 'Christ went to heaven to raise us above all misery and suffering that happens to us on earth and also to give us victory. He never promised to spare us suffering, fear, disease and death, but that He would raise us above it. These things do not control us, but through Christ, we control them. I am in the terrifying Securitatè building now, but I am here with Jesus and He is more powerful than anyone. It not only makes the interrogation bearable, but even a blessing. I live in a heavenly perspective here and anywhere. How small the Himalayas are when you look at it from above . . .' (a Chinese saying). My interrogator treated me humanely and tried to save me. I experienced a bit of heaven at the Securitatè, in the presence of Jesus.

Do not deny your troubles, but allow Jesus to raise you above them. You can have a glorious life while you are still on earth.

*However, I consider my life worth nothing to me, if only I may finish the race and complete the task the Lord Jesus has given me – the task of testifying the gospel of God's grace.* (Acts 20:24)

## Open Doors Contact Person

Somewhere in the Transylvanian mountains, in the little village of Livada, lived one of the great spiritual leaders of Romania: Traian Dors. He has spent more than seventeen years in prison because of his evangelistic activities. The last time he was in prison he was given so little food and water that he expected to die.

So did the Communist authorities. Expecting his imminent death, Dors was sent home to die. To make absolutely sure that he would stop all his Christian activities, he was also sentenced to 'house arrest'. 'But I need to see a doctor' he complained. His request was granted. 'You can see a doctor once a week.'

'So I chose a doctor at the other side of my country' he told us, with a twinkle in his eye. 'Even though I was very weak, I could still be taken to that doctor, enabling me to visit the brethren along the way.'

'Shouldn't you stop? You're an old man now, isn't there any one else who can do that work?' The simple old man just shrugged his shoulders. 'We are the grain of wheat that must fall into the ground and die. Only then will it produce a harvest. We must learn to die so that the Body may live.'

We may not have reached that point of commitment yet. But we can start by a willingness to live for Christ and for His Body.

'For none of us lives to himself alone and none of us dies to himself alone. If we live, we live to the Lord; and if we die, we die to the Lord. So, whether we live or die, we belong to the Lord' (Romans 14:7, 8).

# October 30

David is hiding from Saul in a cave. There is no way out. Saul is unaware of David's presence when he goes into the cave. David's men encourage David to kill Saul. 'This is the very day the Lord spoke of when he said to you, 'I will give your enemy in your hands for you to deal with as you wish.'

How does David react to this 'gift from God'? 'The Lord forbid that I should do such a thing to the Lord's anointed ... for he is the anointed of the Lord' (1 Samuel 24:3–6).

## David

*Have mercy on me, O God, have mercy on me, for in*
*you my soul takes refuge. I will take refuge in the*
*shadow of your wings until the disaster has passed.*
*I cry out to God Most High, to God, who fulfills his*
*purpose for me.*
*He sends from heaven and saves me, rebuking those who*
*hotly pursue me; God sends his love and his*
*faithfulness.*
*I am in the midst of lions; I lie among ravenous beasts*
*– men whose teeth are spears and arrows, whose*
*tongues are sharp swords.*
*Be exalted, O God, above the heavens; let your glory be*
*over all the earth.*
*They spread a net for my feet – I was bowed down in*
*distress. They dug a pit in my path – but they have*
*fallen into it themselves.*
*My heart is steadfast, O God, my heart is steadfast; I*
*will sing and make music.* (Psalm 57:1–7)

David's answer is clear.

He leaves the judgement to God. This gives peace in the midst of danger: 'My heart is steadfast, O God.'

## Remarkable Remarks
### *Counting the Cost*

*Chinese Evangelist* after spending many years in prison:

'If you accept suffering for your faith as a privilege, it becomes your friend, and brings you closer to God.'

*Iranian pastor* at funeral service of murdered Christian leader Rev Haik Hovsepian Mehr:

'Just as at the stoning of Stephen, for every stone that is being thrown, another Paul will rise.'

*Russian judge to Christian* at a trial:

'We don't mind that you believe in God, but leave living according to your Bible until you are in heaven.'

The response of the Christian:

'Your Honor, if I do not live according to the Bible on earth, I will never go to heaven.'

*Chinese Evangelist:*

'Many Christians have been killed for their faith. But because of this, more people have been raised up by the Lord.'

*G K Chesterton:*

'Christianity has died many times and risen again, because it has a God who knows the way out of the grave.'

*I have fought the good fight, I have finished the race, I have kept the faith. Now there is in store for me the crown of righteousness, which the Lord, the righteous Judge, will award me on that day – and not only to me, but also to all who have longed for his appearing.*

(2 Timothy 4:7–8)

## Writers for the month

*Sisters Chen* and *Zhu* and *Brother Li An* from China are pillars of God's house in this vast land. Due to security reasons, we cannot introduce them further to you, but their testimonies speak for themselves.

*Oswaldo Magdangal* from Saudi Arabia. This Filipino brother ministered in Saudi Arabia where he testified of his Savior even while being threatened with hanging.

(The meditation of November 20 was edited from the booklet *Morning Light* compiled by Jonathan Chao, Chinese Research Centre.)

*By faith the prostitute Rahab, because she welcomed the spies, was not killed with those who were disobedient.*

(Hebrews 11:31)

## Rahab

It states plainly enough – Rahab the prostitute. And that in the gallery of the heroes of the faith too!

It is mentioned in Joshua because it belongs there but to be stated a few thousand years later, in Hebrews 11, seems to be so unchristian.

Yet she is not called by name and surname in Hebrews to show how terrible her past had been. On the contrary, Hebrews chapter 11 tells us that Rahab, by God's grace, began a totally new life.

This sinful, pagan woman turned to faith in God. That is what it is all about. That is what it is always about. It is as if the Bible in Hebrews 11:31 is calling out – God can make all things new. Just as Paul says, 'Therefore, if anyone is in Christ, he is a new creation; the old has gone, the new has come!' (2 Corinthians 5:17).

God changes a prostitute into a saint. That is why she is included in Hebrews 11.

We find Rahab again in Matthew chapter 1 in the family tree of the Lord Jesus Christ. Rahab was the new mother-in-law of Ruth, the great-grandmother of David from whose lineage Christ was born.

Glory be to Him Who loved us,
Washed us from each spot and stain!
Glory be to him Who bought us,
Made us kings with Him to reign . . .

*So Naomi returned from Moab accompanied by Ruth the Moabitess, her daughter-in-law, arriving in Bethlehem as the barley harvest was beginning.* (Ruth 1:22)

## Naomi

The book of Ruth tells the story of three women: Naomi, Orpah and Ruth.

All three had gone through a lot of suffering. Undoubtedly Naomi suffered the most. She had lost her husband and two sons while living in a foreign country. No wonder she changed her name from Naomi (meaning pleasant) to Mara (meaning bitter). Indeed all pleasure had disappeared from her life. When you lose all your loved ones, bitterness can so easily enter one's heart. Yet bitterness is often the result of self-pity. God was blamed. 'The Almighty has made my life very bitter.'

Be careful, Naomi. Don't blame God for your own mistakes. She and her husband had voluntarily left Israel. It had been their choice to go and live in Moab, while Moab was under a curse from God (Deuteronomy 23:3). What is more, Elimelech and Naomi allowed their sons to marry Moabite women. That too was not according to God's command (Deuteronomy 7:3–4). Instead of blaming God, she should have acknowledged that she had brought much bitterness upon herself. Yet God does not reject Naomi. He fulfils His plan and puts colour back into the life of Naomi. It started when she returned to Bethlehem. The famine was over and the first harvest was being gathered. Gradually her self-pity and bitterness disappeared.

Whosoever returns to the Lord, will always end up in Bethlehem: the house of bread.

*Your people will be my people and your God my God.*
                                                    (Ruth 1:16b)

## Ruth

The story of Naomi and Ruth shows that the relationship between a woman and her daughter-in-law can be very good. Ruth's love for her mother-in-law is central in this story, but Naomi must have been a lovable and sweet mother-in-law to her as well, otherwise Ruth would undoubtedly have returned to Moab with Orpah.

Yet Ruth chose to stay with Naomi. Had she discovered something of Naomi's God through her life? She makes this clear by saying: 'Your people will be my people and your God my God.'

Ruth, the Moabite, is included in the history of Israel. She is even chosen by God to be the great-grandmother of David, the great king, from whose lineage eventually the Messiah would be born. That was every Jewish woman's dream. Yet this privilege was given to Ruth, the Moabite.

In Ruth, Jew and Gentile are brought together. The wall of partition is taken away. Ruth met Boaz in the fields of Ephrata. Years later, in those same fields their descendant, Jesus Christ the Lord, was born.

Never look down on a foreigner. God certainly does not do that.

God's curse on Moab was changed into salvation for all people. Ruth played an important part in that. That which is despised by people can still be used by God to fulfil his plan. Nobody is rejected by God. So Ruth becomes what her name means: a friend or companion.

We can move forward together towards full salvation because my God is your God.

# November 4

*And who knows but that you have come to royal position for such a time as this?* (Esther 4:14)

## Esther

The name of God is not mentioned in the Book of Esther. Yet God is present on every page. He shows us how He watches over His people Israel. And He uses people who – at first sight – appear to be 'secret' believers.

Haman, the Agagite, hated the Jews. His greatest passion was to destroy all Jews (Esther 3:6–11). The Hitler of the Old Testament.

But God watches over His people in exile. And He uses men and women like Mordecai and Esther. The Jews are not hanged, but Haman, the hater of the Jews is.

Queen Esther, imperceptibly, played an important role. She, together with Mordecai, would save the Jewish people from certain annihilation. Esther means: 'star'. In Jewish history, she still shines brightly.

Yet she did not appear to be a shining light for her environment. She never mentioned the name of God. No, God's people did not talk very much, but God did. He spoke through His deeds.

So, in this 'God-less' book we meet an almighty God who is eternally faithful and never gives up on the work that His hands started to do.

In our days, especially in Islamic countries, there are many 'secret' Christians. If they would openly profess their faith in Christ, they might even face death.

Let us not give up on them too easily, but let us pray that God's plan in their lives will be fulfilled. Through our intercession we are co-labourers of God's church, for the honor of His glory.

*And a sword will pierce your own soul too.*   (Luke 2:35)

## Mary

In our Protestant churches, we do not pay much attention to Mary. Maybe this is a counter-reaction to the over-attention that is given to Mary in the Roman Catholic Church?

Yet in this devotion we want to contemplate her life, her joy and her sorrow. It really is too much to summarize in a few words.

Shortly after Jesus' birth, while in the temple, Mary is confronted with the suffering that she will endure. 'A sword will pierce your own soul.' Just imagine what it must be like when that is said to you when your child is born!

Yes, the suffering of the child is the suffering of the mother as well.

About thirty years later, the sword pierces Mary's soul, as she watches the crucifixion and death of her son.

She suffers too, together with her child. She does not run from the place, even though it is almost unbearable to watch. She stays with her child. She sees His agony, hears the mocking, feels His pain. Which mother cannot identify with Mary?

Yet this is not the last time we meet Mary in the Bible. In Acts 1:4 she is mentioned again. She meets for prayer regularly with the other disciples. Her Lord (no longer her child) has ascended to heaven already. Her job as a mother has been completed, her task as a sister has started.

We do not worship Mary, but we do have to give her the place that she deserves. Most blessed amongst women. Bearer of **the** Child, her's and our Savior.

# November 6

*Now he had to go through Samaria.* (John 4:4)

## Samaritan Woman

Just a few words – 'He had to go through Samaria'. It is easy to overlook the deep meaning of these words. Jesus did not *have* to go through Samaria at all. True, Samaria was the short route to Galilee, but a Jew *never* went through Samaria. They treated Samaria like a contagious disease and always made a detour through the Jordan valley, through Judea to Galilee or vice versa.

But Jesus *had* to go through Samaria. That means: there was something there for Him to do. There was a person in need, a despised woman, without morals, looked down upon. Sure, it was her own fault that she had lived a promiscuous life without ever taking God into account. But her heart was empty. She longed for real peace and happiness. Jesus meets the woman at the well, about noon. Nobody ever goes to the well at that time of day, but she did. She wanted to be there before all the decent women arrived. Rather alone in the heat of day, than together with other women in the heat of their gossip.

Jesus had to go through Samaria to transform this despised woman into the first missionary to the Samaritans. She had to change inwardly first, but when that had happened she became the first witness for Christ in Samaria.

Samaritans were despised by Jews. But God is always on the lookout for the rejected. The hated 'foreign' Samaritans were visited by Christ.

He *had* to go through Samaria. Amongst millions he notices the individual person.

'But whoever drinks the water I give him, will never thirst' (John 4:13a).

'Many of the Samaritans from that town believed in him because of the woman's testimony' (John 4:39).

David is pursued by Saul continually.

Nowhere can he find rest. Nowhere is he safe.

Yet, he does find rest ... in God.

That is why he can say: 'My soul finds rest in God alone; my salvation comes from him (v. 1).

'My salvation and my honor depend on God; he is my mighty rock, my refuge' (v. 7).

## David

*Find rest, O my soul, in God alone; my hope comes
 from him.*
*He alone is my rock and my salvation; he is my
 fortress, I will not be shaken.*
*My salvation and my honor depend on God; he is my
 mighty rock, my refuge.*
*Trust in him at all times, O people; pour out your
 hearts to him, for God is our refuge.*
*One thing God has spoken, two things have I heard: that
 you, O God, are strong,*
*and that you, O Lord, are loving. Surely you will
 reward each person according to what he has done.*
(Psalm 62:5–8, 11, 12)

*The One enthroned in heaven laughs.*　　　(Psalm 2:4)

## Sister Chen

The kings of the world who oppose the Lord plot in vain (Psalm 2:1). The Lord laughs at them (Psalm 2:4).

When Jesus was born in Bethlehem, King Herod wanted to kill Him, but in vain. The priests also tried to kill Him. It seemed as though they succeeded, when Christ was crucified and buried. But Christ rose from the dead.

During the time of the apostles, the Church in Jerusalem experienced tremendous persecution in Jerusalem. The believers were scattered all over the place. The enemy thought he had immobilized the Church. On the contrary. 'Those who had been scattered preached the word wherever they went' (Acts 8:4). That's how the Gospel was spread to the Gentiles.

People are still plotting against God. They want to get rid of the Church. They persecute believers, burn their Bibles, arrest their pastors, close their churches. All – in vain.

The Lord is building (and keeping) His Church and the gates of hell shall not prevail against it.

He who sits in heaven laughs. Let's join our great, almighty God in holy laughter. In full confidence that He who began a good work in you will carry it on to completion, in your life today, despite all circumstances.

*When you are brought before synagogues, rulers and authorities, do not worry about how you will defend yourselves or what you will say, for the Holy Spirit will teach you at that time what you should say.* (Luke 12:11–12)

## Sister Chen

Some years ago Brother Yuen was arrested. He was put in prison and then brought to the town square to be questioned openly. All believers were asked to join the accusation. The aim was to scare others by killing him. I was one who was forced to join the accusation.

This is what I saw: Brother Yuen stood in front of the government officials. No sad face, no frustration. Just a peaceful face which smiled. It was as if I saw a life overflowing with peace and love. I saw Yuen very clearly. How in the world could he be so peaceful? I saw a light shine in his eyes that I had never seen there before. O yes, Brother Yuen had always been a faithful Christian. I remembered him as a quiet man, who lived with God without wanting to stand in the limelight. But now ... the light of life was shining from God's throne onto this imprisoned Christian. Then he spoke, as he never had before:

'I love Christ, I spread Christ, I trust in Christ, I follow Christ and I remain faithful to Christ. I am willing to accept what will come to me. I seek nothing else except Him. I hope that more people will come to accept Christ.'

We came with sorrow, weakness and pain, yet we went back with comfort, strength and joy. We realized that this was not Brother Yuen, this was God, standing by, holding up, giving words to speak.

That God is ours today, His strength is ours.

Will Yuen's testimony be ours too?

# November 10

*The Lord watches over you – the Lord is your shade at your right hand.* (Psalm 121:5)

## Sister Chen

Difficulties, as high as mountains, come rushing towards me. Strong waves dash against my heel. When the power of darkness focuses on me to attack my faith, I lift my eyes to the hills and ask the Lord for help. He speaks to me: 'My strength is made perfect in the weakness of men.' This is always a wonderful paradox. I therefore worship His way, with tears.

The greatest joy in my life is to be under the protection of the Holy Spirit, freely walking in and out between the gap of the lion's teeth. I am in the shelter of the right hand of the Almighty, so that the devil cannot touch me. With His grace I can have victory over strong winds and high waves, defeating the attacking enemy.

The Lord is our shade at our right hand. You see the shade when you walk in the light. When there are clouds you may not be able to see that shade clearly ... but it is still there. Because He watches over our lives. He will watch over our coming and going, both now and for ever more.

# November 11

*He settles the barren woman in her home as a happy mother of children. Praise the Lord.* (Psalm 113:9)

## Sister Chen

I remember an old lady, 90 years old, serving the Lord in a very spiritual way. She has been ordained by the Lord to be celibate. To worldly people, she is a barren woman. And yet she is bearing more fruit, spiritual fruit, than everybody else. To this very day, at the age of 90, she lives a life of intercession. She gives birth to many spiritual children. She feeds many spiritual infants with milk, making them grow in the love of Christ.

Is this woman barren? No, she has more spiritual children than any other mother has natural children. The Church in China respects and loves this old, happy mother of many children, very much.

'The righteous will flourish like a palm tree, they will grow like a cedar of Lebanon; planted in the house of the Lord, they will flourish in the courts of our God. They will bear fruit in old age, they will stay fresh and green' (Psalm 92:12–14).

*They overcame him by the blood of the lamb and by the word of their testimony; they did not love their lives so much as to shrink from death'* (Revelation 12:11)

## Sister Chen

Are we willing to die for the Lord? That is a difficult question. A question that can be answered however is, are we willing to live for Him?

Sister Suk Wan was such a believer. She lived for the Lord, faithfully and courageously. She was arrested for her faith and thrown into prisons were she was beaten and tortured. She became seriously ill and requested to be brought to the town square to speak to the people. (People were often brought there to be shown to the public in order to deny the faith or to undergo self-criticism trials.) The organizers were convinced she wanted to deny her faith before she would die. Two policemen helped her onto the stage. She could hardly stand. She had bruises all over her face. She gathered her last strength and cried: 'To God be the glory. Jesus is my Lord.' Then she collapsed and died. She could die for the Lord because she had lived for Him.

'I have fought the good fight, I have finished the race. I have kept the faith. Now there is in store for me the crown of righteousness, which the Lord, the righteous Judge, will award to me, but also to all who have longed for his appearing' (2 Timothy 4:7–8).

*'I tell you the truth,'* Jesus replied, *'no-one who has left home or brothers or sisters or mother or father or children or fields for me and the gospel will fail to receive a hundred times as much in this present age (homes, brothers, sisters, mothers, children and fields-and with them, persecutions) and in the age to come, eternal life.'*

(Mark 10:29–30)

## Sister Chen

The parents of Sister Suk Wan were already in their eighties when their only daughter died. When the news of her death reached the body of Christ in their town, the Christians were deeply touched and decided to take care of these old people. After some time they said: 'We lost our only daughter, but God has given us back so many new spiritual sons and daughters.' Their brotherly love for each other touched many unbelievers.

Suffering is never in vain. The blood of martyr Suk Wan became a seed of the Church – growing stronger, in depth and number.

'A new command I give you: Love one another. As I have loved you, so you must love one another. All men will know that you are my disciples if you love one another' (John 13:34–35).

# November 14

David feels desperate. He is in deadly danger, like somebody who is drowning in a swamp. He can just about keep his head above the water. In this desperate situation he cries out to God. But it seems like God is turning a deaf ear to him. David thinks his end is near. He continues to pray and cry out to God. He is afraid that if he dies, other believers may stumble and lose their faith in the God of David. God's name is at stake.

## David

*Save me, O God, for the waters have come up to my*
*    neck.*
*I sink in the miry depths, where there is no foothold. I*
*    have come into the deep waters; the floods engulf me.*
*I am worn out calling for help; my throat is parched.*
*    My eyes fail, looking for my God.*
*Those who hate me without reason outnumber the hairs*
*    of my head; many are my enemies without cause,*
*    those who seek to destroy me. I am forced to restore*
*    what I did not steal.*
*I will praise God's name in song and glorify him with*
*    thanksgiving.*
*This will please the Lord more than an ox, more than a*
*    bull with its horns and hoofs.*
*The poor will see and be glad – you who seek God, may*
*    your hearts live!*
*The Lord hears the needy and does not despise his*
*    captive people.*                    (Psalm 69:1–4, 30–33)

*Again I tell you, that if two of you on earth agree about anything you ask for, it will be done for you by my father in heaven.* (Matthew 18:19)

## Pastor Zhu's wife

Praying according to God's will and in agreement with another Christian has great power. Both, however, are very difficult.

First, we need to pray according to God's will. How do I know God's will? We can have long discussions about this. So long, that in the end we only discuss, talk and argue instead of praying. Second, to find another Christian who will agree is also difficult. As individuals, we like to have our own opinions and views. The basis for any prayer according to His will is: to His glory. Does my request glorify God?

I experienced this spiritual battle in a very realistic way. I had been separated from my daughter for three years. We both encountered great problems, persecutions and hardships. One day we agreed to claim the promise of Matthew 18:19. We prayed very earnestly – believing it would bring glory to God to bring us together again. All the circumstances were against us. God would have to perform a miracle to unite us again. The people around us would know and acknowledge that only God could bring it about. For Him nothing is impossible.

Moreover, God delights to give good gifts to his children.

What seemed impossible became possible: we were united 'The king's heart is in the hand of the Lord' (Proverbs 21:1). He directed the authorities to grant us permission to be united. Let us have faith in a great God.

'For no matter how many promises God has made, they are "yes" in Christ. And so through Him the "amen" is spoken by us to the glory of God' (2 Corinthians 1:20).

*Your attitude should be the same as that of Christ Jesus.*
(Philippians 2:5)

## Pastor Zhu's wife

It is quite common that Christians have different opinions about certain matters. That is nothing to worry about. The important aspect is how we deal with differences.

Once two Chinese brothers had different opinions. They talked about it, but soon their discussion ended in a heated argument. They both thought that their way of solving the problem was the best. The Holy Spirit spoke to their hearts, so instead of arguing about their differences they started to thank God – in prayer – for the things they agreed about: God's love, His creation, His forgiveness and grace etc. As they were praying and praising God they humbled themselves.

Their discussions ended in arguments – their prayers in union and unity. Their attitude became Christ's attitude – that of a servant.

Maybe we should talk less and pray more, and see God at work.

*But when they arrest you, do not worry about what to say or how to say it. At that time you will be given what to say.* (Matthew 10:19)

## Pastor Zhu's wife

During the Cultural Revolution I was detained and isolated from the outside world because I refused to compromise with the enemies of God.

My husband was also detained. We were not allowed to communicate with each other. They tried to break our spirit by interrogating us individually.

One day they came and looked triumphantly at me. 'Your husband is a good man. You should love him dearly. He loves you too and does not want you to suffer any longer. He has finally given us the names of those who have visited your house last year. Thanks to his co-operation he will be sentenced less severely. And so will you. But before we release you we want to check with you if the names your husband has given are correct!'

Afterwards, one realises how simple and dirty this trick was. But at the time it was not simple – it was clever. Your body and spirit are weak – you want to get out of that dirty prison. Any offer sounds like an opportunity to be set free. How wonderful is God's grace and protection. When we are weak – He is strong. He will give us words to speak – and power to remain quiet where needed. How He does it? Through the Holy Spirit who lives in us.

If God's word exhorts us not to worry when we get arrested, how much less should we worry about small, petty daily matters.

'Do not worry – for He cares for you' (1 Peter 5:7).

# November 18

*The greatest amongst you will be your servant.*

(Matthew 23:11)

## Pastor Zhu's wife

This is not an easy command. Normally, people like to be served instead of serving others.

Jesus Himself set the example 'Just as the Son of Man did not come to be served, but to serve' (Matthew 20:28). The disciples of Christ should follow in His footsteps.

During the 1950s I was studying at Beijing University. I loved to attend the meetings of the Christian Students' Association. This association did not have full time staff members – no, those who served the Christian students were fellow Christians. Not because they wanted to be great or important, but because they **were** important, because they served other people. When the government clamped down on the Church they arrested many of our 'brothers and sisters'. We could not meet openly anymore. We had to meet secretly – in homes. But we had learned an important lesson from our 'brothers and sisters' – how to serve others. That's how we continued: serving one another. You want to be a blessing to other people? Then serve them maybe in a small way, a smile, a letter, a visit . . .

'Let your light shine before men, that they may see your good deeds and praise your Father in heaven' (Matthew 5:16).

*The very fact that you have lawsuits among you means you have been completely defeated already. Why not rather be wronged? Why not rather be cheated?*

(1 Corinthians 6:7)

## Pastor Zhu's wife

Quarrels among believers are never good. Lawsuits among believers are even worse. When there is a conflict among believers, they should talk it over in the love of the Lord – with a humble and forgiving heart.

Do not wait and grumble against each other. It only gives the devil a chance to intervene. 'Completely defeated' means: failure.

Jesus teaches us that victory is not the emphasis of personal innocence and fairness, but peace and humility among the Body of Christ (Matthew 5:39, 40).

We Christians in China often find ourselves in a situation where we have to appear in court. We are ill-treated, put in prison without cause; nobody defends our rights.

We have every 'right' to complain. But it will not be to our advantage. We will only suffer more and lose our peace in the Lord.

If we are learning not to react in a worldly way against unbelievers, how much more should the mind of Christ dwell in us when we disagree with fellow Christians? 'Make my joy complete by being like-minded, having the same love, being one in spirit and purpose ... in humility consider others better than yourselves ... your attitude should be the same as that of Christ Jesus' (Philippians 2:2–5).

'Therefore, if you are offering your gift at the altar and then remember that your brother has something against you, leave your gift there in front of the altar. First go and be reconciled to your brother, then come and offer your gift' (Matthew 5:23, 24).

*Like newborn babies, crave pure spiritual milk, so that by it you may grow up in your salvation.* (1 Peter 2:2)

## Li An

The Word of God nourishes us and meets the needs of our spiritual life. It generates in our hearts, causing us to grow gradually. Modern man prefers to listen to new and trendy teaching. It works temporarily as it is new and soothing to the ears. But it does not last.

'All men are like grass and all their glory is like the flowers of the field; the grass withers and the flowers fall, but the word of the Lord stands for ever' (1 Peter 1:24, 25).

This is the pure spiritual milk which causes us to grow up in our salvation.

'I rejoice in following your statutes as one rejoices in great riches. I meditate on your precepts and consider your ways. I delight in your decrees; I will not neglect your word' (Psalm 119:14–16).

'The unfolding of your words gives light; it gives understanding to the simple' (Psalm 119:130).

'How sweet are your words to my taste, sweeter that honey to my mouth. I gain understanding from your precepts; therefore I hate every wrong path. Your word is a lamp to my feet and a light for my path' (Psalm 119:103–105).

David is very, very sad. His best friends have left him, or even worse, they have turned against him. David is suffering from this, spiritually, emotionally and physically. He can deal with the fact that his real enemies are against him, but to be considered an enemy by his friends hurts deeply, very deeply.

### David

*O God, whom I praise, do not remain silent,*
*for wicked and deceitful men have opened their mouths*
*    against me; they have spoken against me with lying*
*    tongues.*
*With words of hatred they surround me; they attack me*
*    without cause.*
*In return for my friendship they accuse me, but I am a*
*    man of prayer.*
*They repay me evil for good, and hatred for my*
*    friendship.*
*With my mouth I will greatly extol the* LORD; *in the*
*    great throng I will praise him.*
*For he stands at the right hand of the needy one, to save*
*    his life from those who condemn him.*
(Psalm 109:1–5, 30–31)

*If you should suffer for what is right, you are blessed ...
in your hearts set apart Christ as your Lord. Always be
prepared to give an answer to everyone who asks you to
give the reason for the hope that you have. But do this
with gentleness and respect, keeping a clear conscience.*

(1 Peter 3:14–16)

## Oswaldo Magdangal

Every testimony of struggle and victory contains a danger.
After all, the person in question can be made the centre of
attention so much so that not Christ, but a man or woman is
glorified. When you read about victories in the coming week,
you must not think: how strong this man's faith was!

When you read about his pain, you must not think: how
he suffered!

Brother Wally himself said the following: 'My testimony
is not even my testimony, really, but the story of the Lord
Jesus Christ in my life. Every Christian has a story to tell
and it is always the story of Jesus. That is the most wonderful thing about being a Christian: we have a common story to
tell, the story of what Jesus Christ did in our lives. I thank
God that a Christian's life is the best life conceivable. Everything else pales into insignificance beside the privilege of being
called a child of God.'

So let our life and suffering, our struggle and our victory,
our words and silence always glorify His holy Name. 'Not to
us, O Lord, not to us, but to your name be glory' (Psalm
115:1).

*For your sake we face death all day long; we are consid-*
*ered as sheep to be slaughtered . . . I am convinced that*
*neither death nor life will be able to separate us from the*
*love of God that is in Christ Jesus our Lord.*

(Romans 8:36–39)

## Oswaldo Magdangal

Saudi Arabia is the cradle of Islam. Every Saudi who becomes
a Christian can be sentenced to death for it. Christians can
only meet in total secrecy, and building Christian churches is
strictly forbidden.

As the Saudi Arabian Minister of Information, Ali Ben
Hassan ash-Shair said in an interview with the French paper
*Le Figaro* in August 1992: 'The Saudi government cannot
allow any churches on its territory because it is Allah's
command.'

Brother Wally comes from the Philippines and he had
been working in Saudi Arabia for more than ten years, when
he was imprisoned and sentenced to death.

In Saudi Arabia, the death penalty can be executed in
two ways: decapitation or hanging. Decapitation is for crim-
inals, murderers, drug dealers etc. Hanging is reserved for
blasphemy and subversive activities. Brother Wally was
sentenced to death by hanging – because of his testimony
that Jesus Christ is the Son of God. Islam considers this blasphemy, which deserves the most dreadful way to die –
hanging. Brother Wally wrote: 'Although we had prepared
ourselves for suffering and the Lord had also prepared us
spiritually, it is quite different when it happens to you personally. In the middle of my struggle in a dirty little death cell,
the Lord encouraged me with the following words: "My son, I
have seen everything. I assure you that I will not leave you or
forsake you." The Lord is close to the brokenhearted. In the
deepest darkness, He is the light. God gives strength in suffering – always, everywhere.'

*This poor man called and the Lord heard him, and saved him out of all his troubles. The angel of the Lord encamps around those who fear him and he delivers them.*

(Psalm 34:6–7)

## Oswaldo Magdangal

The religious police in Saudi Arabia, the so-called 'Mutawa', interrogated and mistreated Brother Wally for many days. He was beaten in the face, punched and kicked. The flogging, on the back, palms of the hands and soles of the feet, were the worst.

'In the midst of the flogging, the Lord stood beside me,' Brother Wally testified. The torture lasted for two hundred and ten minutes – without interruption.

Later, Brother Wally said the following about it: 'Boxers fight for twelve rounds at the most. Every round lasts three minutes, after which they get one minute of rest. They are massaged, they get something to drink, the wounds are tended to and everything else is done to get them to box for another three minutes. So they are in action for thirty-six minutes at most and they have about twelve minutes of rest. I was beaten and flogged for two hundred and ten minutes on end. But glory to God, after two hundred and ten minutes they came to an end because – they themselves were tired. I was still standing straight. No knock-out. God had supported me all the time. It was a miracle. The Lord was very close to me.'

This is no theory, but practice. These are not pretty words about how God can help, but a testimony of strength in spite of suffering. The Lord allows suffering – sometimes even death – but: 'I will be with him in trouble' (Psalm 91:15).

*For he will command his angels concerning you to guard
you in all your ways; they will lift you up in their hands,
so that you will not strike your foot against a stone.*

(Psalm 91:11–12)

## Oswaldo Magdangal

In Saudi Arabia, when they flog you, the most painful lashes
are those given under the feet. After the flogging, they force
you to stand up, but because of the pain in the feet it is
impossible to do so. When Brother Wally had undergone this
torture, the pain was unbearable. He said: 'I began to feel
sorry for myself and begged the police not to make me stand
up. I was down on my knees before them, for I could not
stand up.' But the police forced him, although it was impossible.

Brother Wally: 'Suddenly I recalled Psalm 91 verses 11
and 12, just like that, in the midst of all this pain. It was the
Holy Spirit who reminded me of these words. 'For he will
command his angels concerning you ... they will lift you up
in their hands ...' And that was exactly what the Lord did
for me. I was able to stand up, hands and feet chained – but I
didn't feel any pain. The police were flabbergasted. How
could someone who just begged them to let him lie down be
able to stand up all of a sudden? Angels had lifted me up in
their hands. They could not see them, but I felt they were
there. They were carrying me.

'Praise be to the Lord, to God our Savior, who daily bears
our burdens' (Psalm 68:19).

# November 26

*If we live, we live to the Lord; and if we die, we die to the Lord. So, whether we live or die, we belong to the Lord.*

(Romans 14:8)

## Oswaldo Magdangal

It was the seventieth day of his captivity. The next day, he would be hanged. Brother Wally wrote a farewell letter to his wife and after that he prayed together with a fellow-prisoner. They recalled Paul and Silas, who praised the Lord in prison, after which the Lord made the walls of the prison shake.

They started to pray, too, from ten o'clock in the evening until eleven, but there was no shaking. Brother Wally looked at the bars and said: 'Lord, if we are hanged, we will be with You. It is always the story of Jesus Christ. If we are set free, You will still be with us – it's still the story of Jesus. So there is no room for Satan, no room for a defeat. Whether we are hanged or released, it is Your victory, Lord. If we are hanged, another chapter will be added to Acts – two more martyrs like Stephen. If we are released, it will be Acts 29, for then the Gospel will be spread even further.'

At a quarter past eleven, a high ranking police officer came in. Half an hour later we were released and I was put on a plane to Manila. I was free! On 25 December, Christmas Day, at eleven o'clock in the morning, we arrived in Manila.'

'If we live, we live to the Lord; and if we die, we die to the Lord. So, whether we live or die, we belong to the Lord.'

*We are therefore Christ's ambassadors, as though God were making his appeal through us ... Be reconciled to God.* (2 Corinthians 5:20)

## Oswaldo Magdangal

Every Christian is an ambassador. We represent God by presenting Jesus Christ as Savior of the world. Every Christian has a story to tell. The greatest story that this world has ever heard is the story of the coming of Jesus Christ, to save a dying world. We are Christ's ambassadors in proclaiming that great story. The second greatest story this world can ever hear is still the story of Jesus – in the lives of Christians like you and me.

Let us not hold back that story – the Jesus story, but tell the world. Proclaim the greatest news – in words and deeds, without counting the cost.

'They overcame him by the power of the Lamb, and by the word of His testimony; they did not love their lives so much as to shrink from death' (Revelation 12:16).

What a challenge.

What a responsibility.

What a privilege.

# November 28

*The Lord is my light and my salvation,*
*whom shall I fear?*
*The Lord is the stronghold of my life –*
*of whom shall I be afraid?* (Psalm 27:1)

*For in the day of trouble,*
*He will keep me safe in His dwelling;*
*He will hide me in the shelter of His tabernacle . . .*
(Psalm 27:5)

## Open Doors Contact Person

Comments of a Chinese pastor who has spent 22 years in prison for his faith –

'If there's no struggle, there will be no strength.
If there's no cross, there will be no crown.
There is no way we can follow Christ without a cross. Let us cherish it and cling to it.'

If a man in the free world would have spoken these words, one could have laughed at such theatrical statements. But now that a Chinese brother speaks from experience – 22 long years of imprisonment, torture, hard labour – we should listen carefully.

When asked what sustained him in prison he replied: Psalm 27 and the song 'The Old Rugged Cross'. 'Let us cherish it and cling to it.' Today and every day.

A song of praise to the Lord, the God of Israel.

In the midst of all his suffering and persecution, David knows he is safe under God's protection. The darker the night, the brighter the light. God gives us strength to bear our cross.

**David**

*May all the kings of the earth praise you, O Lord,
when they hear the words of your mouth.
May they sing of the ways of the Lord, for the glory of
the Lord is great.
Though the Lord is on high, he looks upon the lowly,
but the proud he knows from afar.
Though I walk in the midst of trouble, you preserve my
life; you stretch out your hand against the anger of
my foes, with your right hand you save me.
The Lord will fulfill his purpose for me; your love, O
Lord, endures forever – do not abandon the works of
your hands.* (Psalm 138:4–8)

## Remarkable Remarks
### Reaching Out

---

*Augustine; Church Father 354–430 AD:*

'Without God – we cannot
Without us – God will not.'

*Accad – Lebanon:*

'All efforts to evangelize the Arabs have failed, simply because we failed to love them.'

*Somebody:*

'God never gives a task without the ability to accomplish it; When He calls, He enables; When He appoints, He anoints.'

*Brother Andrew:* commenting on Acts 17:6 (RSV)

'As long as there is one Christian in prison for his faith in Jesus Christ, I am not free.'

*William Temple:*

'The Church is the only organisation in the world that exists only for the benefit of non-members.'

*For Christ's love compels us, because we are convinced that one died for all ... And he died for all, that those who live, should no longer live for themselves but for him ...'*                    (2 Corinthians 5:14–15)

# December

## Writers for the month

*Joseph Ton* from Romania. Joseph Ton describes a number of spiritual principles of God's faithfulness despite suffering. Edited with permission from the Dutch booklet entitled *Lessen in Lijden.*

*Ali Sougou* from the Comoros. This first Christian convert on this Muslim island came to know Jesus Christ in a special way. He writes about that experience. Edited with permission from the book *In the Shade of the Moon* published by Baruk, 1990.

*Horacio Herrera* from Cuba. Because of his leading role in the Cuban Church he uses a pseudonym.

*'Saul, Saul, why do you persecute me?' 'Who are you Lord?' Saul asked. 'I am Jesus, whom you are persecuting' he replied.* (Acts 9:4–5)

## Paul

The first time that we meet Paul is at the execution of Stephen, who was the first Christian martyr. Paul looked after the coats of the men who stoned Stephen. He hated Stephen as well as the rest of the Christians. He intended to do God a service by persecuting them. He had, therefore, discovered in which houses the Christians met and his henchmen would unexpectedly force their way in and drag the Christians off to prison.

Paul was filled with hate against anything that had to do with Christ – until he met Christ for himself and had a radical conversion. Would the Christians from the house-churches – when they prayed for their leaders in prison – have also prayed for the persecutor, Paul? Perhaps Paul met Jesus as an answer to their prayers. We do not know – not yet.

God intervened and changed the persecutor into a preacher.

Someone once said, 'If such a gifted man is converted, it is amazing what such a man can do for God.'

But an even greater thing is this: it is not what such a man can do for God is important but what God can do for him. Forgiveness of sins and a new life with and for the Lord. That is what God did for Paul.

There is hope for the persecutors of God's Church. Will you pray for them? Is anything impossible for God?

# December 2

*It has always been my ambition to preach the Gospel where Christ was not known, so that I would not be building on someone else's foundation. Rather it is written: Those who were not told about him will see, and those who have not heard will understand.*

(Romans 15:20–21)

## Paul

Paul had world vision. All nations must hear the Gospel of Jesus Christ.

He preferred to go to places as yet unreached. He visited strategic centres out of which the whole world could be reached in the quickest and best way.

He worked from that well known principle – *Urbi et Orbi* – the town and the world. It is surprising what such a man was able to achieve in such a short time and with so little material. For that he paid a price. He sacrificed everything, even friendship.

Turkey, Greece, Italy and Spain can be reached by us in just a few days but for Paul in his circumstances, it was an almost impossible task. But he did it. He was able to say at a given moment, 'But now that there is no more place for me to work in these regions . . .' (Romans 15:23).

Today the Lord gives us all the materials, all the technical know-how and all the possibilities to reach the whole world with the Gospel. The harvest remains plentiful, especially in lands which for many decades were closed to missionary work. The workers are few – people of vision and faith; people who are prepared to pay the price; those who dare to give up security for an unsure future; those who have a vision for the world; who dare to say 'the world is my church' instead of 'the church is my world'.

Pray, therefore, that the Lord of the harvest will send forth workers and be prepared to be the answer to your own prayers.

*About midnight Paul and Silas were praying and sing-
ing hymns to God, and the other prisoners were listening
to them.* (Acts 16:25)

## Paul

Paul and his co-workers had just entered into Europe and
they had landed in prison. They had released a poor woman
from evil spirits – to the great annoyance of her masters who
had made a lot of money through her as a fortune-teller. In
place of thankfulness (she could lead a normal life again) there
was opposition. Paul and Silas were thrown into prison after
being stripped, beaten and severely flogged. There they sat
with their bleeding backs and their feet firmly secured in the
stocks.

However, with every reason to complain, Paul and Silas
turned the prison into a church. They preached the Gospel to
the other prisoners who had to listen for it was impossible
to walk out of 'that church'. Paul had a captive audience.
They preached, prayed and sang songs to the glory of
God. They turned a bad situation into good account.

It is remarkable that this happens, even today. Christian
prisoners witness to their faith. This takes courage and faith
which comes from the Lord, just like the experience of Paul
and Silas.

Prisoners came to faith. When the earthquake came, the
walls shook and the doors flew open, but not one prisoner took
advantage of the freedom.

They stayed listening to Paul whose message of true freedom hit them like a bolt from the blue.

It is possible to remain faithful to God in all circumstances because He gives strength to go through.

Pray, with thanksgiving, for Christian prisoners you
know. God can also use them – in answer to your prayers.

# December 4

*Therefore I will boast all the more gladly about my weaknesses, so that Christ's power may rest on me.*

(2 Corinthians 12:9b)

## Paul

With these verses, Paul concludes a very impressive list of all the hardships he endured. In it he states the following:

'Five times I received from the Jews the forty lashes minus one;

Three times I was beaten with rods;

Once I was stoned;

Three times I was shipwrecked;

I spent a night and a day in the open sea;

I have been constantly on the move.

I have been in danger from rivers,

in danger from bandits, in danger from my own countrymen,

in danger from Gentiles, in danger in the city,

in danger in the country, in danger at sea, and in danger from false brothers.

I have laboured and toiled and have often gone without sleep;

I have known hunger and thirst and have often gone without food;

I have been cold and naked...

Who is weak, and I do not feel weak?'

(2 Corinthians 11:24–29)

He ends his enumeration by stating: 'That is why, for Christ's sake, I delight in weaknesses, in insults, in hardships, in persecutions, in difficulties. For when I am weak, then I am strong' (2 Corinthians 12:10).

What was his secret? The Word of the Lord – 'My grace is sufficient for you, for my power is made perfect in weakness' (2 Corinthians 12:9a).

Is there any reason why *we* should complain?

No, because God's power is still made perfect in weakness. Also today.

*God, whom I serve with my whole heart in preaching the gospel of his Son, is my witness how constantly I remember you in my prayers at all times.* (Romans 1:9)

## Paul

Prayer was not an incidental activity in Paul's life. It was fundamental to his ministry. He prayed for his fellow believers, constantly and at all times. Nowhere do we read that Paul had problems keeping his quiet time. He never needed to confess that he should pray more. Prayer was the source of his strength, his intimate fellowship with God. Even in prison, with his feet chained and his back beaten, he prayed and praised God.

His whole ministry was based on his prayer life.

Somebody once said: 'What you are on your knees, is what you really are and no more!' That's what made Paul so strong. Almost all of his letters start with: 'I pray for you . . . ' And he does not hesitate to ask for prayer for himself: 'Pray also for me.' Paul's hands were strong because they were folded. Prayer is not only the breath of the soul, but also the means to move the hand of God. Through prayer God revealed mysteries to him and he attained insight in the spiritual warfare in the heavenlies and his walk continued from strength to strength. Paul knew his priorities well and acted accordingly. And not in vain.

God hears and keeps your prayers.

Eternity will reveal how they were answered.

'Pray continually, give thanks in all circumstances, for this is God's will for you in Christ Jesus' (1 Thessalonians 5:17–18).

# December 6

*I am ready not only to be bound, but also to die in Jerusalem for the name of the Lord Jesus.* (Acts 21:13)

## Paul

One of the most touching speeches of Paul is his farewell speech in Acts chapter 20. In many ways the Holy Spirit revealed to Paul how much he must suffer for the Lord. The brethren tried to persuade him not to go to Jerusalem. They feared lest Paul would find himself in prison. In their eyes he was more serviceable to them out of prison.

Paul was not looking for problems. He was seeking God. The Lord had prepared Paul for what was ahead and his reaction was clear.

'However, I consider my life worth nothing to me, if only I may finish the race and complete the task the Lord Jesus has given me – the task of testifying to the Gospel of God's grace.' Then Paul followed with 'Keep watch over yourselves and all the flock of which the Holy Spirit has made you overseers.'

'Be shepherds of the Church of God, which He bought with his own blood.'

'Now I commit you to God and the Word of His grace, which can build you up and give you an inheritance among all those who are sanctified.'

When he had said this he knelt down with all of them and prayed. They all wept as they embraced and kissed him.

God must have placed great trust in Paul to convey to him what awaited him. Equally Paul trusted God enough to follow Him to the end.

May God also find in us that preparedness, whatever the future may hold. For our times are in God's hands.

In this beautiful psalm David confesses that God is the Omnipotent and the Omniscient One. David realizes that God knew him before he was born. This God will guide him until the day he will stand before His throne. That could be a long, difficult path. That is why David asks the Lord to guide him; to protect him from offensive ways; to lead him in the way everlasting.

### David

*O LORD, you have searched me and you know me.*
*You know when I sit and when I rise; you perceive my*
*thoughts from afar.*
*You discern my going out and my lying down; you are*
*familiar with all my ways.*
*Before a word is on my tongue you know it completely,*
*O LORD.*
*You hem me in – behind and before; you have laid your*
*hand upon me.*
*Such knowledge is too wonderful for me, too lofty for me*
*to attain.*
*Where can I go from your Spirit? Where can I flee*
*from your presence?*
*If I go up to the heavens, you are there; if I make my*
*bed in the depths, you are there.*
*If I rise on the wings of the dawn, if I settle on the far*
*side of the sea,*
*even there your hand will guide me, your right hand will*
*hold me fast.*
*Search me, O God, and know my heart; test me and*
*know my anxious thoughts.*
*See if there is any offensive way in me, and lead me in*
*the way everlasting.*          (Psalm 139:1–10, 23, 24)

# December 8

*. . . and free those who all their lives were held in slavery by their fear of death.* (Hebrews 2:15)

## Joseph Ton

Fear is an invention of the devil and a consequence of sin. The devil has countless kinds of fears: fear of failure, fear of disease and death, fear of unemployment, fear of the future, fear of suffering, fear of . . .

Through all these fears man is doomed to slavery. Through fear, Satan makes us passive, not only in countries where Christians are persecuted, but also in the so-called 'free countries'. Remarkably, there is often much fear in these free countries. It is the devil's instrument to enslave people. But the Lord sets us free from fear. There is no fear in love (1 John 4:18). The Lord sets us free, so that we no longer fear our enemies, but even love them.

This freedom is not related to living in a free country, for there are millions of slaves in the 'free' world. It is a deep spiritual freedom which turns fear into courage, unrest into peace, uncertainty into certainty, doubt into hope and death into life.

'And the peace of God, which transcends all understanding will guard your hearts and your minds . . . in Christ Jesus' (Philippians 4:7).

*Whoever lives and believes in Me will never die.*

(John 11:25)

## Joseph Ton

The Lord Jesus Christ delivers us from fear. Apparently, He does so in different ways. Hebrews 2:14 says: 'Through His death.' The Son of God loves me. He saw me with my sins, my failures, and my treason and even so He still loved me. He came to earth to take my sins upon Him. He died my death, went to hell – my hell – and He rose again. That is why Christ can say: 'I was dead, and behold I am alive for ever and ever! And I hold the keys of death and Hades' (Revelation 1:18). Christ died my death and now He says: 'death is My messenger' to invite you to heavenly glory.

A friend of Joseph Ton was once arrested by the police in Bucharest. One of the officers threatened to kill him, but Joseph smiled and said: 'If you shoot me, I will enter eternal life. You cannot frighten me with that prospect!' He was not afraid to die, for a Christian will never die.

'Where, O death, is your victory? Where, O death, is your sting?' (1 Corinthians 15:55).

'For I am convinced, that neither death, nor life ... will be able to separate us from the love of God...' (Romans 8:38, 39).

# December 10

*The eye is the lamp of the body. If your eyes are good, your whole body will be full of light.* (Matthew 6:22)

## Joseph Ton

The second way in which Christ delivers us from fear, Joseph Ton likes to call 'the mending or renewal of our eyes'. In Matthew 6, the Lord speaks about worrying (which is the same as fear of the future). Again and again He says: 'Do not worry.' Before this, He spoke about two kinds of eyes, good and bad ones. He says that if our eyes are bad, our whole body will be full of darkness. But if our eyes are good, our whole body will be full of light.

The bad eye sees enemies, problems, threats and dangers. Those were the eyes of ten out of twelve spies who returned from a mission to Canaan (Numbers 13). They saw the giants and said: 'We are grasshoppers compared to them. It's hopeless.'

The good eye also sees the danger and the enemies, for they are part of reality. But the good eye sees more than that: it sees the Almighty God. And this Almighty God is our Father through Jesus Christ.

'Let us fix our eyes on Jesus', Hebrews 12:2 says. The frightened heart cries: 'O, my Lord, what shall we do?' Victorious Elisha answers: 'Don't be afraid. Those who are with us are more than those who are with them.' And Elisha prayed: 'O Lord, open his eyes so that he may see' (2 Kings 6:15–17).

'O our God ... we have no power to face this vast army that is attacking us. We do not know what to do, but our eyes are upon you' (2 Chronicles 20:12).

Lord, our God, please give us these spiritual eyes!

*There is no fear in love. But perfect love drives out fear.*
(1 John 4:18)

## Joseph Ton

Years ago on a Sunday morning, Joseph Ton was arrested.
The following day, the interrogations began. Around midday,
a general came in who ordered the other two officers to leave
the room. When they were gone, he started to hit Joseph. On
the face, on the head – until he was exhausted.

A few days later, the same thing happened again. The
officers had to leave the room and Joseph expected another
beating. But the general sat down and said he wanted to talk
to him. Joseph said: 'I would like to offer my apologies first.'
The general looked at him in amazement. After all, he had hit
Joseph and not the other way round. Joseph said he had done
some thinking about the beating. 'I realized that this week,
we commemorate the Passion,' he said, 'I am sorry I cried
out when you hit me, for there is nothing more wonderful for
a Christian than to suffer like his Lord suffered. Actually, you
gave me the most precious gift I have ever received. Thank
you very much!' Joseph also told the general that he had
started praying for him and his family.

The general was so impressed that he promptly apolo-
gized. Later he would play an important role in Joseph's
release. He had seen what he had never seen before: someone
who told him he prayed for him and his family. There is no
fear in love. The Lord sets us free and gives us love in our
hearts for our enemies. We ourselves are blessed by it – and
others are as well. And God is given the glory.

# December 12

*For it has been granted to you on behalf of Christ not only to believe on him, but also to suffer for him.*

(Philippians 1:29)

## Joseph Ton

Suffering is not something strange. Actually, it is not even a tragedy, but a favor. 'To this you were called, because Christ suffered for you, leaving you an example, that you should follow in his steps' (1 Peter 2:21).

According to Peter, suffering is our calling. It is even a favor. Peter and John were flogged, which is a terrible punishment. But when they were sent away with bloody backs, they rejoiced 'because they had been counted worthy of suffering disgrace for the Name' (Acts 5:41).

Peter and John considered it a special honor to be flogged, as if they realized that they had received something which was not granted to everyone.

A Christian must be found worthy to suffer for the Lord. Such suffering is a calling, a favor and an honor.

*You also, like living stones, are being built into a spiritual house.* (1 Peter 2:5)

## Joseph Ton

Suffering is not without a purpose. Peter writes that we are living stones which are joined together to build up a spiritual temple.

Peter must have had King Solomon's temple in mind when he wrote this. Solomon had stone-cutters working for him who hacked out the stones one by one from the mountains and polished them. Then, all the stones were transported to the building site, where they only needed to be put together. The Bible says that there was no sound of a hammer or a chisel on the construction-site; the polishing had already been done in the quarry (1 Kings 6:7).

Peter writes that we are living stones used to build up a spiritual temple. One day, the last stone will complete the building and what a wonderful temple it will be! God will reside there. But it also implies that we are now in God's quarry, a place of cutting and polishing, and that hurts.

Moses regarded disgrace for the sake of Christ (the pain) as of greater value than the treasures of Egypt, because he was looking ahead to his reward. He persevered because he saw him who is invisible (Hebrews 11:26, 27).

That way God can use us – a living stone to build a spiritual house.

# December 14

The righteous suffer at the hands of the wicked. The wicked do not shrink back from anything. They do not fear God nor His commandments. The righteous clash with these wicked men. Their faith is tested. Will they join the wicked or will they continue to trust in the Lord and follow Him?

They have made their choice.

## David

> Rescue me, O LORD, from evil men; protect me from
> men of violence,
> who devise evil plans in their hearts and stir up war
> every day.
> They make their tongues as sharp as a serpent's; the
> poison of vipers is on their lips.
> Keep me, O LORD, from the hands of the wicked; protect
> me from men of violence who plan to trip my feet.
> Proud men have hidden a snare for me; they have
> spread out the cords of their net and have set traps for
> me along my path.
> O LORD, I say to you, 'You are my God.' Hear, O
> LORD, my cry for mercy.
> O Sovereign LORD, my strong deliverer, who shields my
> head in the day of battle –                 (Psalm 140:1–7)

*If we are distressed, it is for your comfort and salvation.*
(2 Corinthians 1:6)

## Joseph Ton

What Paul wants to say is: I am suffering for your salvation.

To illustrate this, we must go back to the time when Romania was still suffering under Communism. In Joseph Ton's church, one Christian was a manager in a big factory. As a consequence of his conversion, all employees of the factory were called together by the Communist Party to witness his degradation from manager to the lowest job in the factory. 'How should I defend myself?' he asked Joseph. 'Don't defend yourself at all,' Joseph advised him, 'you'd use the time they give you to defend yourself better, by telling them who Jesus is and what He means to you.'

It was really impressive how he bore witness of his Savior in front of all those people. Afterwards, he was degraded and his salary lowered accordingly. But his faith was rewarded. His suffering brought salvation to other people, for later on, he told Joseph, 'everywhere in the factory, people take my hand and ask me to tell them about Jesus. Many of them ask me to get them a Bible.'

Because this brother was prepared to suffer for his Lord, other people were saved. Those who are prepared to pay the price (status, salary, defamation) will be a blessing to others and will also receive God's prize: eternal life.

# December 16

*Shall we accept good from God and not trouble?*

(Job 2:10)

## Joseph Ton

Job had to suffer for God's honor. Satan contended that Job only served God out of self-interest. Then God allowed Satan to take everything away from Job: his whole fortune, all his children and his health. His own wife said: 'Curse God and die.' And his 'friends' said, 'you're done for. God has become your enemy.' But Job answered, 'I don't know what He has against me, but even if he slay me, I will hope in Him.'

At that moment, there must have been a burst of applause in heaven. God really had people on earth who possessed nothing and still remained faithful to Him. Job did not worship God because He was so good to him, but because God is **God**.

Such people give God glory. They live and suffer for the glory of God. God is looking for people like that.

*Does Job fear God for nothing?* (Job 1:9)

## Joseph Ton

In Romania, there was a Christian poet named Traian Dorz. He spent more than sixteen years in prison because of his faith in Jesus Christ. One day, he was sentenced to another two years in prison because of a book he had written, a collection of Christian poems for children. He was seventy years old at the time! In prison, he wrote another poem, in which he says:

'Lord, help me to love You,
even if none of my prayers are heard.
Help me to trust You,
even if there will be
no reward in eternity.'

Of course there will be a reward for this saint in heaven, but what he wanted to make clear, was that he loved God not because He answered all his prayers, not even because he was hoping for a reward, but because God is worthy to be served. He served God for Who He is, not for what He does.

God's answer to Satan's question: 'Does Job fear God for nothing?' is 'Yes!'

God was faithful to Job and Job was faithful to God, in spite of all the 'why's'.

# December 18

*Remember those in prison as if you were their fellow pris-
oners, and those who are ill-treated as if you yourself were
suffering.* (Hebrews 13:3)

## Joseph Ton

Suffering is a favor that is to be shared with the whole of
Christ's Church.

If my hand hurts, I say: 'I don't feel well.'

If one part of the Body suffers, the Bible says
(1 Corinthians 12) the whole Body suffers.

Millions of Christians in other countries are suffering. Do
you feel the pain too? If they suffer, I, who am part of the
same Body, should also feel pain. If we do something for
persecuted Christians, we suffer with them.

For example, persecuted Christians always pray for a
Bible of their own. Printing Bibles in the free world is very
expensive. Those who are prepared to make a financial sacrifice for the printing of these Bibles suffer with those who have
none. They work hard to send spiritual food to the people who
suffer. When they receive their long-awaited Bible, they shed
tears of joy.

Jesus said: 'Whatever you do for one of the least of these
brothers of mine, you did for me' (Matthew 25:40).

If a Christian is beaten, Christ suffers.

If a Christian is helped, Christ is helped.

If we pray for those who suffer, they will be comforted.

That is the way God works, and we are God's fellow-
workers.

*You will know the truth and the truth will set you free.*

(John 8:32)

## Joseph Ton

Hardly anyone in Eastern Europe believes in Marxism. The real Marxists live in the West. A friend of Joseph Ton in Moscow once told him: 'Marxism was pure deception, but what is the alternative?' Many people know what they don't believe, but they don't know what they do believe. What they are really saying is this: 'We tried Satan's lies and we got hell. We now know that we were deceived, but what is truth?'

Lies enslave people, but the truth always sets you free. The world tells our young people: 'Why shouldn't you be free to do anything you like? Why shouldn't you live it up?' And young people say: 'Yes, I want to be free.' But soon they discover they are not free at all. They have become slaves to all kinds of bad habits. Satan promises freedom, but enslaves people. His sole aim is to destroy our personality.

God's truth really sets us free. 'So if the Son sets you free, you will be free indeed' (John 8:36). It is a freedom that is real and lasting. Forever. Through the Son – Jesus Christ – the Savior.

## December 20

*We have escaped with our lives as a bird from a hunter's snare. The snare is broken and we are free!*

(Psalm 124:7 LB)

### Joseph Ton

When Joseph Ton was forced to leave his native country Romania because of his faith in Jesus Christ, the Lord encouraged him with this beautiful psalm.

*If the Lord had not been on our side (let all Israel admit it), if the Lord had not been on our side, we would have been swallowed alive by our enemies, destroyed by their anger. We would have drowned beneath the flood of these men's fury and pride.*

*Blessed be Jehovah who has not let them devour us. We have escaped with our lives as a bird from a hunter's snare. The snare is broken and we are free!*

*Our help is from the Lord who made heaven and earth.*

(Psalm 124 LB)

Let us pray that the truth of this psalm may be experienced by all who suffer for His Name.

God will help them out, and you.

David pours out his heart in a moving prayer. He feels deserted by everybody and everything. 'No-one is concerned for me' (v. 4).

Only God can deliver him from prison.

'Set me free from my prison that I may praise your name. Then the righteous will gather about me because of your goodness to me' (v. 7).

---

### David

*I cry aloud to the LORD; I lift up my voice to the LORD for mercy.*

*I pour out my complaint before him; before him I tell my trouble.*

*When my spirit grows faint within me, it is you who know my way. In the path where I walk men have hidden a snare for me.*

*Look to my right and see; no one is concerned for me. I have no refuge; no one cares for my life.*

*I cry to you, O LORD; I say, 'You are my refuge, my portion in the land of the living.'*

*Listen to my cry, for I am in desperate need; rescue me from those who pursue me, for they are too strong for me.*

*Set me free from my prison, that I may praise your name. Then the righteous will gather about me because of your goodness to me.* (Psalm 142)

---

# December 22

*Is anything too hard for the Lord?*      (Genesis 18:14)

*From the lips of children and infants you have ordained praise.*      (Psalm 8:2)

## Open Doors Contact Person

Although the Russian government no longer persecutes Christians for their faith, some believers still suffer for confessing Jesus Christ.

In April 1992 a twelve-year old boy, Volodya, experienced the following:

> 'I heard about the church meetings on Karl Marx Street and went there because I wanted to know more about God. When I was told that Jesus loves children as well I asked him to love me too. When I told my mother, she was very upset and angry. She told me that God does not exist. I was beaten every time I went to church. But I still went. Then one day my mother decided to join me so she could talk to the pastor and tell him not to let me go to church any more. But I took her to the pastor on a Sunday so she would have to listen to his preaching first. As she sat there, something happened, she started to cry almost uncontrollably. She realised her need for God ... and asked the pastor to pray for her. Now we go to church together.'

May you be encouraged today, as you pray for members of your own family. If a twelve-year old boy dares to take such a stand for Christ why not you today? God will honor such a commitment. 'Is anything too hard for the Lord?'

*Then it was said amongst the nations: 'The Lord has done great things for them.' The Lord has done great things for us and we are filled with joy.* (Psalm 126:2, 3)

## Open Doors Contact Person

Some time ago, while travelling in central Cuba, we wanted to visit a pastor we had never met before. We only had his name and address. We had no idea how old the pastor was or to which church he belonged. We had just brought his address along in case we would come near his home. Today was the day. When we arrived at the house the door was opened by an elderly woman. We mentioned the name of the pastor, after which she invited us into her home. She showed us a picture on the wall. 'That is the man you are looking for' she said. 'He was my husband, but he died many years ago.'

We felt ashamed, very ashamed. We did not know what to say. Before we left we gave the woman what we had brought for her husband, a Study Bible. When she saw it she exclaimed, 'I have never been visited by a foreign missionary, but I have prayed for a Study Bible for twenty years. Today God has answered my prayer and released me from my prison of loneliness. He sent you and you gave me the greatest gift I had prayed for. Thank you for coming.'

We left a woman filled with joy. We were there too late, and yet on time.

Take a moment today to give thanks to the Lord for what He has done for you.

*The true light that gives light to every man was coming into the world.* (John 1:9)

## Horacio Herrera

Our century is often called the century of light. So many new discoveries, so many new insights – indeed a century of light. Yet, we see more darkness around us than ever before.

Why? Because people do not see **The Light**, but follow other, destructive lights – horoscopes, fortune tellers and the zodiac. They think that these are trustworthy stars: 'It is written in the stars.'

Remember that Satan himself masquerades as an angel of light (2 Corinthians 11:14).

Jesus is the light of the world – leading to salvation. Satan appears as an angel of light – leading to bondage and destruction. Which star do we follow?

Psalm 36:9 says: 'For with you is the fountain of life. In your light we see light.'

He has revealed that light to us through his word, which is a light for my path (Psalm 119:5).

In my country of Cuba Christmas is not officially celebrated. Only the Christians celebrate Christmas, and although we don't have commercial Christmas lights, we have **the** light, Jesus, who enlightens us daily.

The star of Bethlehem still brings everlasting light and joy to those who seek **Him**.

As a bumper sticker reads: **Wise Men Still Seek Jesus**.

*. . . and they will call him Immanuel, which means, 'God with us'.* (Matthew 1:23)

## Jan Pit

If you want to know who God is take a good look at Christ. 'The Word became flesh and made his dwelling among us. We have seen his glory, the glory of the One and Only, who came from the Father, full of grace and truth' (John 1:14).

Philip said, 'Lord, show us the Father and that will be enough for us. Jesus answered, 'Don't you know me, Philip, even after I have been among you such a long time? Anyone who has seen me has seen the Father. How can you say, "Show us the Father?" Don't you believe that I am in the Father, and that the Father is in me?' (John 14:8–10).

God came to dwell among us. He became man in Christ. He, the Almighty Creator became man. That is why He can identify with us in good and bad days; in storm or shine; in times of happiness and in times of deep sorrow and loneliness.

That is why he is called 'Immanuel: God with us'.

Not an abstract God above us, but a man of flesh and blood alongside us, giving us a model on how we should live.

We can entrust ourselves to such a Savior and through Him we can call God 'Abba-Father'.

What a privilege.

What a God.

What a Savior.

Whose birth you can celebrate each blessed Christmas season.

Kneeling at the manger, because you have knelt at the Cross.

Have you never done that before? Why not do so today?

# December 26

*When I saw him, I fell at his feet as though dead. Then he placed his right hand on me and said: 'Do not be afraid, I am the First and the Last. I am the Living One; I was dead and behold I am alive for ever and ever.'*

(Revelation 1:17, 18)

## Ali Sougou

Ali Sougou was the first ever indigenous Christian of the Comoros Islands, a beautiful group of islands in the Indian Ocean, east of the continent of Africa. Born and raised in a Muslim family, Ali met Christ in a supernatural way.

His first contact with Christ came through a Christian who visited his island. Ali was confused about what he had heard from the man. 'Jesus loves me and died for my sins? Who is this Jesus?' He dare not ask the Christian. He could not anyway, as the Christian had already left the island. And there was no other Christian to ask.

Ali went home – disturbed and confused. All he wanted now was a quiet rest and a good sleep. That night something happened. Ali realised he was not alone in the room anymore. Facing him across the room stood a man. The beauty of His countenance was beyond description. His white robe lit up the room. His eyes were as blue as sapphires. 'He held out his hands and placed them on my forehead.' Ali said later 'I know now that I was in the presence of the Lord Jesus Christ.'

It was Ali's first introduction to Christianity, or rather, to Christ Himself. 'I rose from my bed and searched the room; the windows were closed.' Jesus appeared to him – a night to remember. That night became Ali's new day.

A supernatural meeting with the unknown Savior. There was nobody to tell Ali about Christ – so Christ revealed Himself to him.

If God could meet Ali in such a wondrous way, can He not meet you – today?

*I consider my life worth nothing to me, if only I may finish the race and complete the task the Lord Jesus has given me – the task of testifying to the Gospel of God's grace.* (Acts 20:24)

## Ali Sougou

Ali Sougou grew in his Christian faith, especially after he had received a Bible. But then another crisis came: Ali was arrested by the police and thrown into prison. Three months later he appeared before a special court. Those presiding were Muslim leaders, army officers, village leaders and other authorities. The trial took place in the open air with a huge crowd of spectators present.

The verdict was unusual, Ali could choose his own punishment from three alternatives:

1  Life imprisonment.

2  Death by firing-squad.

3  Deportation from the country.

As he stood there, wondering what to say, Ali knelt down and started to pray. He prayed loudly so that the crowd could hear his prayer also. 'Lord Jesus, here I am and I know you are with me. Help me to choose what you want to me choose.' The judges were astonished. They had expected Ali to choose deportation, but he seemed to be willing to be shot. The crowd shouted: 'He is a fool – he is mad, he is crazy. You cannot sentence a crazy man – let him go home.'

He never had to choose – the crowd chose for him, which was accepted by the judges – fearing the crowd. Ali could go home! He learned the secret of spiritual victory: if we are willing to lay down our lives on the altar and leave the verdict to God, He will choose the best for us – to His glory.

*Faith by itself, if it is not accomplished by action, is dead.* (James 2:17)

## Ali Sougou

One of the people who witnessed Ali's trial was a police inspector, whose duty it had been to watch all of Ali's movements: Whom did Ali visit, who visited Ali, what did they talk about?

When Ali was set free the Muslim leaders of the judges called the Commissioner of Police and told him to provide Ali with a truck and driver and send him home. The police officer was to escort Ali. Upon their arrival at Ali's house, the truck driver left – but the police inspector stayed. 'Can I talk to you in private?' he asked Ali. They went into another room. 'I was surprised to see you did not choose your own punishment. You prayed to Jesus Christ, I would like to know more about Him. Your God worked very hard on your behalf.' Some days later – after many hours of discussions – the police officer received the Lord Jesus Christ as his personal Savior and Lord.

Now there was not one but two Christians on the island. Ali's steadfastness spoke to the crowd. Ali's willingness to die led to the policeman's salvation.

The world will judge us by our deeds – not our words. 'In the same way, let your light shine before men, that they may see your good deeds and praise your father in heaven' (Matthew 5:16). Your good deeds are no guarantee for your salvation, but they may become the way to salvation for someone else.

*In all your ways acknowledge him, and he will make your paths straight.* (Proverbs 3:6)

## Ali Sougou

More people became interested in the Gospel of Jesus Christ and accepted the Lord. They not only experienced many trials and hardships, but also the provision of the Lord in great and small matters. One such provision was experienced by an elderly Christian couple, travelling home one day when their car started to sway dangerously. It wobbled to a standstill and Brother A discovered that they had a puncture. They had no spare tyre in their car – hardly anybody has on those islands – so what could they do? They found themselves on a deserted road in the middle of nowhere.

'Let's pray about it' Sister B said, 'Our Father in heaven knows our problem. Let us ask Him for help.'

Yes, their help came from the Lord (Psalm 121). Another Christian came along the same way and had a spare tyre! (first miracle). But ... nobody had a jack. 'Lord, we thank you for the tyre, please send someone with a jack.' After some time a lorry-load of men stopped next to them. 'Can we help?' they asked. 'We've got a puncture, there is a spare tyre, but we don't have a jack.' 'No problem,' the men said, 'we'll fix it for you.' More than ten men jumped out of the lorry, hoisted the little car in the air with their bare hands while another man changed the tyre (second miracle). A few minutes later the happy bunch of Comorean workers jumped back onto the lorry, waved and were gone.

Were they Comoreans ... or were they angels? Sent by God?

*On him we have set our hope that he will continue to deliver us, as you help us by your prayers.*

(2 Corinthians 1:10)

## Jan Pit

From our hotel on the Comoros Islands we had a magnificent view of the Indian Ocean, while behind us there were charming hill-tops to be seen. On the slopes we discerned small villages, tucked away behind palm trees and banana plantations. In one of those villages there is a Christian, the only one among thousands of Muslims. Visiting him was impossible, for it would endanger his life. He was so close ... and yet so far away. We prayed for him and pleaded his case with the Lord whom he followed. The Lord knows his whereabouts, his situation and He is acquainted with his loneliness.

We would so much have liked to hold his hands for a moment and to have encouraged him. To have told him that we remembered him. But we could not. It goes without saying that you start praying for someone like that, knowing that your prayer will be experienced by him as God's strength.

In prayer we can bring him before the Throne of God, so that he will know that though he may be lonely, he is not alone. The Lord is with him and we can visit him in spirit and encourage him that way.

That afternoon, I learned from another Christian that although he is having a hard time, he is standing firm. Yes, we ourselves will receive many blessings when we read of God's faithfulness in their lives. We can also encourage them by praying for them. A blessing and a responsibility.

Have you already 'visited' someone today?

*More than conquerors.* (Romans 8:37)

## More than conquerors

On the last day of the year and on the last page of this devotional book we can sum up everything with the wonderful words of Paul:

'What, then, shall we say in response to this? If God be for us, who can be against us? He who did not spare his own Son, but gave him up for us all – how will he not also, along with him, graciously give us all things? Who will bring any charge against those whom God has chosen? It is God who justifies. Who is it then who condemns? Christ Jesus, who died – more than that, who was raised to life – is at the right hand of God and is also interceding for us. Who shall separate us from the love of Christ? Shall trouble or hardship or persecution or famine or nakedness or danger or sword? ... Now in all these things we are more than conquerors through him who loved us. For I am convinced that neither death nor life, neither angels nor demons, neither the present nor the future, nor any powers, neither height nor depth, nor anything else in all creation, will be able to separate us from the love of God that is in Christ Jesus our Lord.'

That is the comfort for the Suffering Church. It is also her testimony.

May this also be your comfort and testimony – now and always.

## Jan Pit

Jan Pit worked as a missionary in Laos for eight years, together with his wife, Lies. On three occasions they had to flee from the Communists. Lies and their son Peter narrowly escaped death during one attack in which a Communist tried his best to kill them.

Jan has worked with Open Doors to support and encourage the Suffering Church around the world since 1975.

# Open Doors Page

If you would like to receive further information about 'Open Doors with Brother Andrew' and its ministry to the Suffering Church worldwide, please write to one of the addresses given below.

Upon request we will gladly send you – free of charge – our monthly magazine, which gives up-to-date news and information about persecuted Christians around the world.

Open Doors
PO Box 6
Witney
Oxon
OX8 7SP
United Kingdom

Open Doors
PO Box 53
Seaforth
New South Wales 2092
Australia

Open Doors International
PO Box 47
3840 AA Harderwijk
Netherlands

Open Doors
PO Box 27001
Santa Ana
CA 92799
USA

Open Doors
PO Box 990099
Kibler Park 2053
Johannesburg
South Africa

Open Doors
PO Box 597
Streetsville
Ontario L5M 2C1
Canada